MICHAEL

'Michael was a blessing to this planet, his friends and his family. He had what so few possess; talent, looks, charisma, drive, charm. His story is told by the one who knew him best, who watched him grow up from being a shy boy to becoming a worldwide star—his sister. If you love music, mysteries and most of all, Michael, you won't be able to put this book down.'

—Richard Blade, popular Los Angeles radio, television, film personality, DJ

'An effusive man with a seductive puppy-dog grin and a disarmingly direct gaze got up and loped towards me, and held out his hand. He said his name was Michael . . . A sense of well-being and relief washed over me. We were gonna do great things together and I didn't have to be a rock-star anymore . . . Michael would do it for me.'

—Richard Lowenstein, writer, director, producer

'Lost boy Michael, who was my dear friend, and who is very much missed. All respect and thanks to Tina for sharing these stories and keeping the memory alive.'

—Simon Le Bon, singer/songwriter, Duran Duran

Other books by the authors

Tina Hutchence

Just a Man: The real Michael Hutchence
(with Patricia Glassop), Sidgwick & Jackson (2000)
Just a Man: The real Michael Hutchence
(with Patricia Glassop, updated edition), Pan Books (2001)

Jen Jewel Brown

As author:

Great Southern, Rare Objects poetry series, Vagabond Press (2010)

Gutter vs Stars, poetry illustrated by photographers including
Carol Jerrems and Clara Law, Flat Chat Press (2006)

Alleycat, poetry and prose illustrated by Michael Leunig,
Feral Books (1988)

Skyhooks' Million Dollar Riff, photos by Carol Jerrems,
Dingo Books (1975)

As editor:

Co-edited (with Gig Ryan) *Nebuchadnezzar* by Shelton Lea,
Black Pepper (2005)

Edited *Aboriginal Country* by Lisa Bellear, The University
of Western Australia Publishing (2018)

MICHAEL

MY BROTHER, LOST BOY OF INXS

TINA HUTCHENCE

WITH JEN JEWEL BROWN

ALLEN&UNWIN
SYDNEY • MELBOURNE • AUCKLAND • LONDON

Allen & Unwin
83 Alexander Street
Crows Nest NSW 2065
Australia
Phone: (61 2) 8425 0100
Email: info@allenandunwin.com
Web: www.allenandunwin.com

A catalogue record for this
book is available from the
National Library of Australia

ISBN 978 1 76087 696 8

Set in Minion Pro by Midland Typesetters, Australia
Printed in Australia by The SOS Print + Media Group

10 9 8 7 6 5

To Michael, a beautiful, gentle soul,
and to all the children in the family

SERGE THOMANN

Michael in December 1986,
in Hobart, at the beginning
of the Australian Made tour

'I don't think one thin page of words can change the world, but it can push things around.'

—Michael Hutchence

contents

0

intro

MY BROTHER roamed the world with a book in his hand and one in his suitcase. Like the beat poet Lawrence Ferlinghetti, whose work inspired him, Michael started writing poems when he was twelve. And he was a great, precocious reader. As Sydney schoolboys, hyper and pubescent, he and Andrew Farriss would whirl in from Davidson High mid-afternoon and hole up in Michael's room to discuss not only music, including jazz, but books like Charles Bukowski's *Diary of a Dirty Old Man*.

Michael always loved being read to, ever since he was a tiny child.

In 1984 he played his first UK show, with INXS, at the Astoria on 26 May. Troubled by chronic post-gig insomnia in his hotel room, he called his live-in girlfriend Michele Bennett, who was back in Sydney.

That night he asked her to read to him, as he had so often before. And she would reach for the book beside her bed, as she would throughout his life, and read Michael to sleep. He and Michele spent six years together.

In January 1986, he was himself reading *A Very Easy Death* by Simone de Beauvoir.

I bet you're thinking, how does she know these things—right?

My brother wrote about them in his diaries. A diary was just another piece of flotsam to him, I guess. Part of an astounding, ongoing cascade of paperwork including cards, scrawled lyrics and legal documents he'd leave with me—in the wake of yet another departure, for yet another tour.

When we asked his great friend, Chris Bailey, of the Saints, about what writers he liked best, he recalled that 'Mick' once gave him a book of letters by the Welsh poet Dylan Thomas, who wrote 'Do not go gentle into that good night'. I threw my mind back to Michael's bookshelves; the titles and authors he talked and wrote about. I turned the pages of some he loved the most, looking for what might have sent wings for his own *poetry*, as he thought of it: his lyrics. And so from time to time these books that Michael read connect me to the story of his life again. They brush across these pages too, leaving a trail of hints about their reader, lost too soon.

There have been at least nine biographies written about Michael so far. This book is different because I was one of the closest people on the planet to him.

Twelve really is a special age, poised on the brink of life. That's how old I was when I first held him, the day he was born. I spoke to him five days before he died.

I became his pre-teen, stand-in mother when ours was working, and he became the five-year-old DJ for my go-go dance rehearsals in Hong Kong. We were kids roaming the planet, eager for experience. We shared crazy, terrific and trying years of growing up, with or without each other, our brother, Rhett, and each of our parents at different times. We went our separate ways and faxed and phoned to bare our worries and share our wins, comparing notes and planning distant meet-ups.

As adults, Michael and I rendezvoused all over Europe and America. We had hilarious dinners in myriad cities. Our shared, nomadic, spreading family spent Christmas after Christmas hanging out.

Sure, there was frustration and tragedy in Michael's life, but one thing I can say for certain—he didn't die wondering. He lived a series of grand adventures.

Nevertheless, in his last months on earth, there were signs that he had begun to realise what a naive leap of faith he had made in delegating his business affairs. For Mother and me, compounding the profound, ongoing trauma caused by his sudden death, a legal battle loomed. It was impossible to ignore the opaque and secretive twists of the shape-shifting business empire set up by others with Michael's money. The defendants to later proceedings included Michael's financial adviser and named executor of his estate, Colin Diamond, Hong Kong accountant and co-executor Andrew Paul, and a labyrinth of corporate trustees that held various assets including many real estate properties, which we alleged were held beneficially for Michael. Patricia Glassop—our mother—and I were two of those named in his will, and we especially felt compelled to fight on behalf of Michael's only child, Mother's granddaughter, my niece. Heavenly Hiraani Tiger Lily Hutchence was, still is, the nominated heiress of 50 per cent of her father's estate.

But Patricia and her husband, Ross, were ageing. Due to the stress of legal matters dragging on, making them sick, combined with our less than bottomless pockets, we agreed to settle the case at a mediation in May 2000. I can't say what it was settled for, but I can say that the payout by the defendants to us didn't fully cover our legal costs. Mother and I returned this to Ross to repay his kind loan for the lawsuit. I am indebted to her for having the strength and courage to co-author *Just A Man: The real Michael Hutchence* with me.

Our patriarch Kell Hutchence passed away in 2002, Ross in 2009 and Mother in 2010, sadly.

As the twentieth anniversary of Michael's death approached, Diamond sought investors for a two-part telemovie about Michael, containing some new original music. Called *Michael Hutchence: The Last Rockstar*, it aired on Channel Seven in Melbourne. Just after it aired, in November 2017, the Paradise Papers opened the floodgates of information on the Hutchence estate with actual legal documents exposed in the media.

The Paradise Papers became the biggest leak of documents ever published. In these the International Consortium of Investigative Journalists (ICIJ), including ABC Television's *Four Corners* in Australia and *The Guardian*, helped expose a great many high-profile financial controversies. There had been a massive leak of client records from the law firm Appleby, in the tax haven of Bermuda, that represented many people and bodies of elite wealth in their efforts to minimise or negate tax. They included the Queen of England, Bono and Michael.

The leaked financial dealings of Michael's financial adviser Colin Diamond with Appleby showed that Diamond had control of rights to Michael's music and copyrights after his client's death, through Chardonnay, the 'Vocals Trust' set up to channel Michael's royalties through tax havens when he was alive.

Appleby had initially assessed dealings over Michael's music as 'high risk' in 2005, since two lawsuits—ours and another involving INXS—had already headed Diamond's way.

Investigations into the Paradise Papers just keep evolving as the Australian Tax Office (ATO) looks into the history of arrangements such as Michael's affairs. These investigations have the scope to change laws, and many people's lives.

Above and beyond all of this, for his legions of fans, Michael Hutchence left the world a better place by his passing through it. This genuinely mattered: to leave a lasting musical legacy was what he wanted and hoped for as an artist. And as I write, love for Michael's singing, his songs, his music and his performances around so many countries seems evergreen. So now I'm going to do my best to conjure up the adventurous Lost Boy, the sensitive, playful man I miss every day, but remember with laughter, by sharing my stories with you.

guns in the sky

BEFORE HIM, an endless sea of people swayed towards the horizon, rising and falling in a multitude of waves. The dying summer sun warmed his shoulders. The rhythm of the song the band was playing was like a Bo Diddley strut.

'Guns In The Sky': a gospel shouter's invitation to raise your hands then bring them down 'like a clock at two'—the peace sign. This rallying cry that Michael wrote alone often opened INXS's shows. Inspired by the arms race, President Reagan's proposed Star Wars missile shield and materialism, he hollered out loud about how he wanted to stop the world, shake its war-makers free.

Guns in the sky! As he half danced, half ran towards the crowd, 74,000 souls roared.

The night was just beginning. You could see Michael drink in the moment, the deep rush of pleasure on his face. An hour and a half of musical courtship to go. He wanted them to swoon. He wanted them to *know* he wanted them to swoon. Throwing his arms wide, he took them in his embrace.

Now that quirky music his band had lived for, sweated since they were schoolboys to build, had become lithe, hard-edged, subtle and stadium-ready. Now INXS could take them on a ride they'd never come down from.

That tiny, happy baby boy who used to beam at me in the morning when I ran to pick him up had turned into a shining star.

• • •

Wembley Stadium, founded in 1923, is soccer's hallowed grass cathedral. The charismatic stadium is also famous as the site of the British leg of Live Aid in 1985. Queen played two shows of their Magic tour there in July 1986, supported by Status Quo and some antipodean upstarts called INXS—who were pelted with bread and tomatoes for their trouble.

So five years later, and after being serially savaged by some English reviewers, it was a real test of pulling power for INXS to be able to headline at Wembley Stadium.

The word that comes to mind for their show there on 13 July 1991 is exultant. Musically elite and fighting fit, with each song in the set honed to kill, INXS played the show of their lives that night.

I am so grateful it was being filmed and recorded, no expense spared, for posterity. Prominent British director David Mallet, who'd been responsible for David Bowie's inspired 'Ashes To Ashes' and 'Let's Dance' clips, was in charge. He used 35-millimetre film running through seventeen cameras, even from a helicopter, to catch an experience that just takes you there. Just as good as that extraordinarily intimate framing of INXS's kinetic performance was the sound quality. Mark Opitz, who'd produced INXS's third album *Shabooh Shoobah*, was backstage in the BBC recording van. He was in charge of recording and mixing the show live-to-air for BBC radio—and for later use in the DVD *Live Baby Live* (it rhymes with Sieve Baby Scythe).

Capturing that Wembley show cost half-a-million Australian dollars. The result, one seamless, hedonistic concert of INXS at the top of their game from start to finish, is quite an experience.

Chris Murphy, the band's manager, and INXS went right out on a limb to risk that kind of money when they could have walked away with fat pockets and the applause ringing in their ears. It is such a dynamic, completely confident, physical show: staging, lights, the amazing mix, the band's ardent attack and their ability to float from hard funk back to a moody, shadowy dream of a song like 'Mediate' part of the intrigue. Michael wooing the deliriously happy crowd. Michael the master frontman, modern dancer, R&B/soul/pop/rock/ singer/poet/crooner, whisper to scream. Stager, charmer, shaman, sex symbol, revelling in every second. A beautiful repertoire. All of it adds to the musical theatre of INXS performing live at their absolute peak, and the *Live Baby Live* DVD is still selling today to prove it.

INXS's best concerts—and I was fortunate enough to see so many shows—often looked so full of crazy energy, they gave the impression everything had kind of spontaneously sprung into place on the night. How much deduction, trial, error and rehearsal lay behind that spon-taneous effect! And so many people worked to make them shine; so many interesting elements were involved, really, behind the scenes, that it's worth going into a little detail about some of the Wembley show minutiae that night, from the point of view of a working insider.

Mark Opitz was and is an in-demand producer, engineer and mixer, a quiet achiever behind the desk on some of Australia's greatest pop and rock records ever, including for AC/DC, Cold Chisel, INXS (starting with 'Don't Change'), Divinyls, The Angels, Australian Crawl, Jimmy Barnes and Models. He's also worked with Kiss and Lenny Kravitz.

Softly spoken, slim, savvy and good-looking, Mark spent a year touring the world with INXS in 1991 as their production adviser.

Earlier on the day of the Wembley show, INXS and their guests had been collected from the Carlton Grand Hotel and loaded into a flash tour bus.

'We had a police escort,' Mark remembered, in his low, clear murmur, 'all the way from Hammersmith up to Wembley Stadium. Which was really weird, because we were all high as kites.'

Inside the venue there was a very big backstage area leading to massive dressing-rooms. 'The girls had the wardrobe cases out in one room; make-up was in another room. We knew everyone on tour, 'cause we'd been doing it for a year. The difference, of course, that night, was all the guests. There was like Rolling Stones, there was Deborah Harry, Helena Christensen; Naomi Campbell, I think, and other super-models. Kylie Minogue. Michele Bennett; everyone was backstage including various English people. Lots and lots of people.'

As show time approached, Mark had already been on and off stage several times; checking the battalions of microphones in place and making sure all the recording gear was ready to go, both onstage and in the BBC live recording studio van he would soon be operating.

'Colin [Ellis, INXS's regular sound mixer] had gone and put all his mikes out first,' Mark recalled, 'and then I'd just gone to see if they were suitable for me. Sometimes adjusting things, so it worked a bit better for me without affecting him.'

Michael Long was INXS's long-term tour manager—a tall, quiet man with serious eyes, who practised meditation. He'd previously done this critically important job for the band's friends Cold Chisel. Ten minutes before show time, he cleared the main dressing-room of guests, leaving only the band, their powerhouse of a manager Chris Murphy, his assistant Sam Evans, Paul Craig (a long-time INXS management connection in London) and Jeff Pope, who had taken time off from the

New South Wales police SWAT team to run INXS's security. Even the supermodels had gone to their special seats.

A hush fell while INXS went through their last-minute changes. Michael did a few vocal warm-ups. Then he started listening to something on his Walkman. Taking off his headphones, he put them on Mark instead.

'He was playing me "Unfinished Sympathy"'—from Massive Attack's *Blue Lines* album—'saying, "How good is this, how good is this?" And I became a Massive Attack fan from that moment, by the way,' Mark said.

Jon Farriss would be the first member of INXS to take the stage, crawling through a secret door behind the drums. He settled into his sleek black-and-silver kit up on a riser behind where Kirk Pengilly would soon be plying his sax and guitars. Jon had the song list and could control various things electronically from back there. He'd really just emerged to check everything was working, but when he saw that flood of animated, sensation-hungry young faces, he gave them the peace sign with a gloved hand and heard their roar. Nonplussed, he waited briefly, but suddenly decided he couldn't bear to keep them waiting a moment longer. No one expected it when spontaneously he just started playing, jamming on the big loop of his own drums he had down, sitting back and kicking up a storm.

'We're all in the change room,' recalled Mark, 'and Michael was speaking to Kylie just outside it and you could hear *BHOO-BHOO-BHOOH!* It's this *thunder*, coming from somewhere. Drum thunder. And everyone's going, "What the fuck?" And starts running, 'cause it's a long way—you have to go down the stairs and along this huge backstage area and up the runways to get to the backstage pod, under the stage area. Then run along up front to get around all the gear and get onstage.'

The band had been touring internationally for fourteen months already, featuring the *X* album, with minor breaks here and there.

On their *Summer XS* leg, they were riding an updraught as hit followed hit around the world. So much was working for them now, and mostly they were enjoying playing together. Here's the set list from the show: 'Guns In The Sky', 'New Sensation', 'I Send A Message', 'The Stairs', 'Know The Difference', 'Disappear', 'By My Side', 'Hear That Sound', 'Original Sin', 'The Loved One', 'Wild Life', 'Mystify', 'Bitter Tears', 'Suicide Blonde', 'What You Need', 'Kick', 'Need You Tonight', 'Mediate' and 'Never Tear Us Apart'. For the encore, they played 'Who Pays The Price' and finished with 'Devil Inside'.

After 'I Send A Message', with its snarling, wailing sax towards the end, Michael addressed the crowd for the first time.

'Yeah . . . G'day! We'd like to play some new songs . . . From *X*. This is called "The Stairs".'

Cameras zoomed out and lingered in long shots as the stage lights went down. Michael disappeared from sight as the moody chords and subtle, shifting harmonics of the instrumentation brought the pace down. It was as though night had just fallen.

Richard Lowenstein, who shot so many clips for the band over the years, reckoned that's when Michael dropped ecstasy that night. 'Being as he was into the sensual arts, it was his drug of choice there for a while.'

Michael had handed pills round to 'his gang' (as Richard put it) that night before he took the stage, telling them to take it when 'The Stairs' began. That's when Michael dropped his E too, so they'd all 'peak' together, when the drug reached its zenith in the middle of the show.

Mark Opitz backed this up. When Michael took his Walkman headphones back off Mark in the dressing-room before the show started, Mark said, 'he opened my hand and put an E into it, and closed my hand and said "The Stairs—during The Stairs". And that's what happened, four songs in. Michael would have made sure the show started alright. Then he dropped an E, I dropped my E as instructed, and I'm not sure whether Kirk, Jonny or Tim did. They might have.'

By the end of the concert, after everyone else had run offstage, Michael grabbed Kirk's guitar and began grinding it slowly against the amplifier with his hips, Jimi Hendrix–style. It was wailing and moaning feedback.

From just offstage came a squeak of protest.

'*Hey!*'

After the show they went up to the Hyatt Carlton Grand Ballroom next to Sloane Street near Harrods, at the very top floor, right in the middle of Sloane Ranger territory. The G7 conference was to commence in London two days later.

'We all had suites,' Mark Opitz remembered, 'that we had to vacate—mine to the German Chancellor—the very next day. We had a big party.'

Well, most of INXS and their entourage did. In fact, bass player Garry Beers had been spirited away by the police right after coming offstage at Wembley and taken to a private area. There, alarmingly, his heavily pregnant partner Jodie Crampton was under medical supervision, after apparently going into early labour. Garry found Jodie selflessly doing her level best in the medical area to talk down a large group of kids who'd taken what he would later describe as 'the brown acid—the bad acid'. Luckily, down the track, she and the baby were okay.

In the morning, quite the worse for wear, Mark and INXS—or some of them—headed to a studio in Chiswick to try to record a new song they'd been working on in sound checks.

'Those were the days,' sighed Mark. 'On Sunday morning—whose idea was that? Like, oh *yeah*, we'll go over there, it'll be over by ten o'clock in the morning.

'And so,' said Mark, 'we began recording "Shining Star". Of course they didn't have the time or energy to finish the track that morning, so they followed the session up by watching the first edit of the filmed

Wembley performance, which would become the INXS DVD, *Live Baby Live*.

The DVD is one, long, seamless concert with no time edits; nothing but the show, start to end. That's one of the most amazing things about it, that I *love*. It's just like being there—like being on the stage.

'There's no overdubs in that show, there's *nothin'*. You know, that's just the best vocal that I've ever heard Michael do,' said Mark. 'Relaxed *as*, all the way through. And it's the most fabulous show that was ever caught on film.'

Honestly, *Live Baby Live* is truly a sensational record of what happened as the London sun lit an enraptured crowd on its way below the horizon. Mark mixed the soundtrack over three days at Air Studio.

'We had so many things go right,' he continued with a hint of a smile. 'INXS just played the best they'd ever done. The sound was just phenomenal because they played so well, it was so easy, and I'd been working with them so much.

'I had the BBC Wembley Stadium live SSL [Solid State Logic] truck mixing live to BBC radio, broadcasting live to London and round the country. I was recording the show flat [with no sound effects] as well, and then I took those tapes to Air, at Oxford Circus. Then there was just me and Michael mixing this fucking thing, three days and nights, flat out. No band members would come in. To the point where I had a car waiting downstairs to spirit me off to QF2, back to Australia. But yeah, that was good. It was a really *fantastic* experience.'

Years into the future, someone else would be witnessing this extraordinary video in disbelief. First came astonished recognition. Then tears of joy and pride. What he discovered next about the singer lost to him since boyhood, would shock him to the core.

2

caravanserai

BY THE TIME he was twenty, Michael had lived in Sydney, Perth, Brisbane, Hong Kong and Los Angeles, in at least seventeen different homes. He'd learned you could come, go and return to a place without a second thought. One of our most fun places, when he was five and I was seventeen, Rhett two, and Kell and Mother were still together, was the Hong Kong Hilton—for three months.

We were always on the move. From one caravanserai to the next. Michael, the lover of words, would have rolled this ancient Persian term around his mouth, delighting in its syllables. *Caravan*, a company of travellers, and *sarāi*, an inn or palace: a nice place for a nomadic family to crash.

He certainly developed a taste for many caravanserais. It came naturally.

Let me tell you how it all began. Once there was a beautiful, dark-haired young model with soft curls called Patricia Kennedy: mother to me, Michael and Rhett. Back in the 1800s, one of our ancestors, a Kennedy man, had married a Jamaican woman called Josephine. Now my grandson Benjamin has inherited those dark Kennedy eyes like Michael and crazy, curly hair that makes heads turn in admiration. Yes, Michael's family has a touch of Jamaican blood.

The women in our family can be shy yet quite adventurous. They have style, and a lot of backbone. Patricia was certainly like that. Like many of us, she grew up fast. Her father, Michael's grandfather Stephen Kennedy, was killed, sadly, crossing the road. The same year she left home, at seventeen, to marry. Her mother and grandmother had been child brides too. I was born just over a year later.

My father was a quiet man who himself had been orphaned young. The marriage didn't last—Mother was no doubt too young and perhaps had married for the wrong reasons—but she had me and, as a single mum, had to pay the bills.

While I was still a toddler, she worked as a cigarette girl at the Copacabana nightclub in Melbourne. She wore this tiny, black lace outfit, like a strapless leotard with fishnet stockings. The cigarette tray had a soft strap that you put behind your neck to hold it at waist level. She also worked as a cinema usherette before her modelling career took off.

She was only 23 when she opened her own modelling academy in Melbourne. That was very radical for a woman in 1952. I was four then. Catwalk rehearsals were my playground. I followed the sound of her high heels and loved—as Michael and Rhett would too—watching our mother transform herself beyond recognition for photoshoots. Later on she morphed herself into a make-up artist—the profession she would end up specialising in and handing down to me—venturing into television and motion-picture work. Sometimes I was thrown a line or two of dialogue and spontaneously cast in some production or other.

Michael seemed blessed by the best traits of both his parents.

It's about time I told you how they met.

Kelland Hutchence—my stepfather, Michael and Rhett's father—was an adventurous charmer who took pleasure in lacing the storytelling of his life with humour, much to the delight of his dinner-table audiences. He was confident, enterprising and happy to strike out in a new business venture or corporate role in any country of the world.

In 1958, one of Mother's friends was the reigning Miss Australia, Leah McCartney. She joined Leah and her boyfriend for pre-Christmas drinks one night and the silver-tongued Kell happened to be there too.

At 34, Australian-born Kell was the handsome, well-educated son of UK migrants. Five years older than Patricia, he was a popular bachelor around Sydney. Despite this, he was still living at home with his mother. Kell's father, Frank, a sea captain, had died young, in his fifties; his mother, Mabs, would have appreciated Kell's company (when her son was not off travelling, of course).

His moustache was trimmed as sharp and straight across his upper lip as that of another dashing trader, Rhett Butler—played of course by Clark Gable in the film *Gone with the Wind*. And there was a resemblance between Kell and Clarke, there was.

'One of these days I'm going to marry you,' he told Patricia the night they met. After two months of phone calls, dancing, dining, roses and proposals, she agreed—on one condition: that he adopt me, since we came as a two-for-one deal. Kell agreed and he and Patricia married on 31 January 1959. Three months later she was pregnant with Michael.

Our mother was softly spoken and well-read. Despite a rocky start in life and a marriage to Kell that jolted us from place to place at regular intervals, she was determined to forge her own career outside the house. She could have remained defined by the roles of homemaker, wife, mother and, as the family's fortunes progressed, socialite, but that narrowing of possibilities bored her. Patricia really was ahead of her time; she was a strong, independent woman who believed she could conquer anything she tried her hand at, and she did.

At the start of married life for Patricia and Kell in Sydney, I was living in Melbourne with my maternal grandmother, Agnes 'Kate' Kennedy Martin, known to us as 'Nanny'. That might seem strange, so let me explain.

Mother and I were both born in Melbourne and our family lived there. My parents divorced by the time I was two. Not long after this, Mother's brother Johnny—Michael's uncle—was accidentally shot and killed at his 21st by his best friend. Nanny stepped in to help raise me, transferring the love and care she would have showered on her lost Johnny onto me. She cared for her own ageing parents in our home too, and took in clothing alterations to earn money. We formed a loving, bonded family in Melbourne, and I remember those days with fondness.

Then Mother sent for me to come to Sydney to live with her and my new stepfather, Kell Hutchence, in Neutral Bay on the north side of the Sydney Harbour Bridge. Kell gave me a gold heart-shaped locket with a red rose painted on the front. On the back was inscribed my new name: *Christina Elaine Hutchence*. The three of us were happy together, despite having a lot new to adjust to, and very jazzed about the coming addition to the family.

Mother was still a catwalk model, now showing off maternity wear in various shows. She would put her feet up in the afternoon though, to some big, beautiful, soothing sounds from André Kostelanetz and the New York Philharmonic Orchestra. The record had been given to her by our family friend Bob Rogers, who was then presenting Australia's first Top Forty radio show on 2UE and would soon tour Australasia with The Beatles.

Michael Kelland John (after his Uncle Johnny) Hutchence had an easy birth at the Mater Misericordia Hospital in North Sydney on 22 January 1960. I'm not into numerology, but I'm told 22 is a 'master' number. (It would be the same day he would die: 22 November 1997.) He was an Aquarius, and if you believe in star signs that meant he was likely to be curious, a gifted writer, to believe in an altruistic future for humanity, and sometimes be scattered and hard to pin down. He certainly grew into all of that.

As a baby he was relaxed and easy to be around. He was soon smiling and giggling a lot, and, in Mother's words, 'loved being on this earth'.

We were living in Lane Cove by then, north-west of Sydney. We had a national park nearby and the Lane Cove River threading through the suburb, down to the Parramatta River and the sea. Despite Kell's thrilled pride in his little son—his firstborn child—he wasn't a changed man. He still took off on overseas business trips, disappearing for large chunks of the year. He was highly sociable and loved to entertain, something he would hand down to both his sons. Mother wasn't ecstatic about Kell's keen relationship with the liquor cabinet. He could drink his way through various cocktails and a bottle of wine over dinner with ease.

I was a schoolgirl, only twelve when Michael was born, but I'd rush right home on the bell to see my baby brother after school. About a week after he came home I was allowed to babysit him for a couple of hours to start with. Despite being inexperienced, I was good at it. I took to it like a newborn dolphin to the waves. My caring for Michael soon became my regular joy and my parents' escape hatch. I protected the soft fontanelle of his head with my palm when I picked him up and carefully changed him, sliding the outsize safety pins in and out of the cotton folds I'd layered snugly on each side with great care.

Kell switched jobs constantly, it seemed. I admired him for being so brave and bold. The thought of changing cities, even states, did not deter him in the least. In contrast, I was tongue-tied at becoming the 'new girl' in the wrong uniform in a succession of schools. From the time I arrived in Sydney at eleven years old to when I turned fifteen,

I went to six schools in three different states over four years. We even moved three times before Michael's first birthday.

So caring for Michael, then Rhett as well, gave me the continuity I longed for. I rose to the challenge. Thinking back on Michael's first three years I can still hear his first, experimental words wandering out, feel his tiny, warm hand reach out to grip mine to help him balance those first, wobbly steps. I even gave him his first teaspoonful of Farex. Mouthing the unfamiliar mealy consistency produced a torturous look on his little face. He fixed his big dark eyes on me as if to say, 'I trusted you, what's *this*?' Then, as he spat the mess right back at me, he let out a high-pitched giggle.

Michael was always laughing, actually. Right through his childhood he was a very happy, easygoing and affectionate boy, always ready with a smile and a hug.

It must have hurt Mother to miss some of his baby milestones, but she enjoyed the make-up work she was now specialising in, and was good at it. And as we came to recognise Kell's propensity for frequent career changes, we often relied on her income too.

Sometimes, when a cast and crew got together to shoot exterior scenes, a production raced against time and failing natural light. They just had to keep going until the light died. And then again the schedule might be so pressing that even after sundown they would go to a studio to continue shooting interior scenes. So Mother was often on location for long, stretching hours, arriving home well after I had put Michael down in his cot.

When the house was adult-free I'd crank up the radio and groove to the latest Hit Parade spun by Bob Rogers. At first Michael just sat on the floor and watched me dance, but when he began walking he tried to imitate my moves. I wouldn't get much homework done but I had a good excuse. If I danced around with Michael in my arms and he threw up a little because I'd just fed him, he would just laugh even more.

Then, in 1963, after we had made a move to Brisbane, our baby brother, Rhett, was born. He was so different from his brother. Rhett, apparently, slept three hours maximum. Now, with Kell overseas so often, I began to help Mother get up to attend to him at night, taking turns. Michael was such a sound sleeper then! It seemed he was the only one Rhett *didn't* disturb.

Our parents began taking weekend excursions to Surfers Paradise where many of their friends lived. I was given more responsibility, babysitting overnight. I didn't mind because I was allowed to call a friend to keep me company. But my brothers were quite a handful.

At the time we were living in a split-level home in Kenmore with stairs everywhere. Kell had bought it on a whim—as usual without consulting Mother. As three-year-old Michael took off one way, Rhett, who was the Usain Bolt of the crawling set, would take off in the other. So I trained both boys to respond to 'Babe'. It was a matter of mutually assured survival, really, to be able to yell *'Babe!'* and have both those daredevils stop in their tracks.

We returned to Sydney later that year where our parents bought a three-bedroom home on a corner block on Bantry Bay Road, Frenchs Forest. It was a relatively new neighbourhood back then. Across the street a small opening beckoned us seductively into thick forest. There, a narrow bush track led to Wakehurst Parkway where you could stand seemingly in the middle of nowhere and catch a bus to civilisation: the city or the beach.

The house was surrounded by eucalypts and waving, long grass that didn't get mowed very often. I constantly imagined snakes slithering through. They would have been there somewhere but they went about their business quietly enough.

Truly, it was an excellent place to raise children.

Once I'd built Michael his first 'fort' out of crisp white sheets stolen from the clothes line, he had a great time cajoling me into building him more and more. Afterwards we'd both get into trouble, of course, although I was the one who 'should have known better'. Michael would put on his little cowboy boots and hat and pretend he was in the Wild West, or maybe Africa. The next-door cat became his prey—to pet. We didn't have pets of our own; we moved around too often.

Rhett was still a baby then so I did almost everything with him on my hip as he couldn't keep up or walk through the tall grass. When Michael wanted me to help him with his scooter or to climb a tree or toss him a ball, he would pull at Rhett, saying, 'Put him down, put him down'. But even if I wanted to, Rhett was strong and his little legs would wrap tighter around my waist as he smiled down at Michael.

With its deadly funnel web and redback spiders, eastern brown, red-bellied black and tiger snakes, copperheads and death adders, and less last-rites-inducing but still venomous and possibly damn painful brown tree snakes, golden crown snakes and black-bellied swamp snakes, wolf spiders, white-tailed spiders, mouse spiders, bull ants, wasps, bees, scorpions, centipedes, millipedes and other unpredictable wildlife that shared the area with us, Mother was always a bit nervous in that house. Of course, if we splashed into the salty water of the surrounding shores, we'd also have to watch out for bull, tiger and great white sharks, blue-ringed octopus, stonefish, poisonous jellyfish like bluebottles, and various stingrays as well.

After a persistent magpie began swooping down at Michael when spring came he became afraid to be out in the yard alone. I thought perhaps it was attracted to his silvery hair—he was very blond at the time.

'She's probably just looking for the right materials to build her nest,' I said, but as the black-and-white missile plummeted towards us again, Michael ran screaming for the back door.

I hadn't had the chance to finish high school before we left Queensland and came to Frenchs Forest, and couldn't face being the new kid again, so Kell gave me the choice of secretarial school or hairdressing. I found a job as a junior apprentice at a rather exclusive beauty salon in Spit Junction. This meant Mother had to leave her job as a make-up artist. Otherwise, who was going to care for the boys? They had not begun their schooldays yet. I longed to be as unaffected as Michael and Rhett seemed to be despite this constant upheaval.

Our mother occasionally worked as a make-up artist on commercials at the time, but for the most part she was at home with Michael and Rhett.

Returning from a business trip early in November 1964, Kell announced that he had accepted yet another new job, quite a prestigious one. He had been appointed managing director of a British import-export company supplying top-flight spirits, champagne and wine to restaurants and hotels in Hong Kong. He departed immediately. As usual, he had accepted the job without discussing the ramifications with his wife. It seemed that was the way in which their relationship had operated for six years. He rarely consulted her on anything, despite the fact that she was a real financial contributor to the family. Of course every ad hoc decision he made about moving would throw our lives into confusion again as Mother and I faced the loss of whatever social ties or work arrangements we had just managed to make and once again began packing everything into boxes.

Anyway, we got ready to leave Sydney and follow Kell to live in Hong Kong. The plan was for Mother, Michael, Rhett and me to spend Christmas in Australia and join Kell in January having packed the house and rented it out. Despite the prospect of leaving our pleasant neighbourhood, we were all glad to be moving. Perhaps we had become so accustomed to change that it seemed normal after two years.

Before we departed Australia, Mother wanted me to meet my biological father. This was puzzling to me as I didn't remember him and didn't see the point. Nevertheless, I stood near the entrance of the coffee shop I was dropped at until a man with eyes like mine came over to me. He led me to a table where his other two children, from his second marriage, Faye and John, were sitting. It was terribly awkward for all of us until finally John told me that I looked different from the only photo he had seen of me. I was three in it so no surprise there. I guess he just didn't know what to say. None of us did. I felt so sorry for my father at that moment, knowing that we had missed all of those years, and this memory still really, really hurts. Sadly I never saw him again and I regret that, but he was not one to keep contact and, at that point in my life, after having to leave so many friends and family behind, neither was I.

It's so much easier these days with social media. My half-sister Faye found me again in 2009. I found out from her that our father was a very shy man with a sad upbringing. The youngest of four children, he lost both parents—my paternal grandparents—at the age of six. He was shuffled between relatives, never seeing his older siblings again until much later in life. Of course I never knew any of that back then.

But when he passed, among his effects was found a 1966 *China Mail* newspaper clipping about a teenager's life in Hong Kong—featuring me.

3

Hong Kong and beyond

THE HUTCHENCE BOYS, Michael and Rhett, were maniacal. It was understandable. We'd been talking about this trip for two months. Now finally they were 'sitting', if you could call it that, in a huge aircraft on their way to Hong Kong.

Christmas 1964 had just finished. Mother, the boys and I had somehow survived the woozy fallout of our combined cholera, typhoid and smallpox inoculations through the packing, celebrating and vacating-the-premises process. Now the tinsel and pine needles were history for another year, and Mother and I had to somehow keep the boys quiet for nine hours en route to Hong Kong and Kell.

I sat with four-year-old Michael, his colouring books and his Dr Seuss collection. It was a night flight and he soon fell asleep. Mother and amped-up two-year-old Rhett were sitting in the pair of seats right in front of us. In those days there were no movies on seat-backs and even though we'd kept Rhett up through his usual afternoon nap time he was a livewire. Mother and I switched seats and took turns looking after the two of them, sleeping when we could. Finally, after a 4.00 a.m. stopover in steamy Manila, we approached Hong Kong's airport with bleary eyes.

Landing a jet at the notorious old Kai Tak airport was challenging for a pilot but unforgettable for the passengers. Rather than slow down, our plane seemed to accelerate as it hurtled lower and lower towards the island's exotic-looking mountains swathed in mist. The whole thing looked like something out of the old *King Kong* or *Godzilla* movies. Michael sat next to the window. I had trouble keeping him in his seat, and the look on his face was magic. Eruptions of cloud kept ripping past, blinding us as we sank. Just before a crash seemed inevitable, the plane banked so hard you could see everyone leaning to one side as it swooped bravely into the belly of the harbour. We flew so low we could see strange rows of washing flapping between buildings while the sea streamed past close by. We hit the runway, the pilot braking like crazy as the ocean loomed dead ahead, before swinging hard left and idling to our disembarkation.

Heart-stopping to say the least.

Michael let out a '*Whooooop!*' and turned to me.

'Did you see, Tina, did you?'

Kell was waiting with his chauffeur and newly acquired white Mark X Jaguar which came with his position. It was one of those times when you wanted to sit next to the window and give the 'royal wave'. The only way you could get from the airport on the Kowloon side (on mainland China) to Hong Kong Island with a vehicle was by car ferry. That would drop you in the red-light district of Wan Chai—then full of American sailors, most of whom would visit Wan Chai at least once during their measly five-day R&R from the horrors of the Vietnam War. We found out right away that even though Hong Kong literally means 'fragrant harbour', it is anything but.

Kell was already living the high life in a suite at the Hong Kong Hilton in Central District when we arrived. He—somewhat regally, it seemed to me—took a second suite, next door, for the boys and me. It was all terribly exciting as we invaded the luxurious adjoining rooms. Michael and Rhett immediately started jumping on the Hilton's beds to trampoline-test them before we all collapsed, exhausted, under the covers.

The next day I took Michael for a walk. He was so thrilled to see this new city of ours. Although Hong Kong was a British colony then, the local people and customs were unique. There were very British-looking places cheek by jowl with local buildings being extended via bamboo scaffolding.

The noisy, crazy traffic was controlled by policemen, who stood on round concrete risers in the middle of the street. These contraptions had a flimsy railing and a cover on top to keep the sun from beating down too fiercely on the occupant as all eyes watched for his hand signals. With so many people walking the streets, he would stop all traffic—including rickshaws—and let the pedestrians walk wherever they wished at intervals. Michael's golden Beatles mop-top was quite a novelty. He drew a crowd talking animatedly among themselves. I noticed he was quite unbothered by it all and just smiled at them.

On that first outing Michael and I took a rickshaw ride around the block and sampled some of the local ice-cream, which tasted like it had been in the freezer too long. With some urging we bought a bag of lychees in the street. We had never seen anything like the strange, succulent, red-shelled globes before. The vendor, eager to sell his daily haul from Guangdong province, opened one up and halved it for Michael and me to try. The rough outer shell disguised a fleshy, sweet-perfumed fruit that seemed to burst in our mouths. We took them back to the hotel to share with the family.

'Never eat food from a street vendor, you might get sick!' Kell warned, but I never worried about such things. And Michael was always eager to try any strange-looking or odd-smelling concoction from a vendor's box.

Back at the Hilton, the boys and I took full advantage of room service while our parents threw themselves headlong into business-related parties and dinners. Occasionally I was invited along. My wardrobe changed from casual-Sydney-teenager to budding-uptown-socialite within weeks.

The 26-storey Hong Kong Hilton had been built in 1963. It was the only five-star hotel on the island at that time. The top floor was a restaurant called The Eagle's Nest (very glamorous too). In the basement was a popular nightclub called The Den where an Italian band with a handsome, lascivious singer thrilled the tourists.

Realising that my job prospects were limited since I spoke neither Mandarin nor Cantonese, I jumped at an offer from the Hilton's resident photographer to take some head-shots and full-length poses of me. Mother oversaw the session, of course. Most of the models at the time were Asian and there were few teenagers, so I did get quite a bit of runway work.

The boys found the Hilton lifts alluring. If left to their own devices they would ride them up and down ad infinitum. Mother and I often found ourselves in a panic, pushing elevator buttons frantically and subduing kidnap fantasies as we chased the little devils from floor to floor to floor. Fortunately, they would normally stay together, Rhett holding Michael's hand.

The lads arrived at The Eagle's Nest one night, perhaps planning to put a three-course meal on Kell's tab. Luckily the staff knew the drill by then and they were suavely shown the lift and sent back 'home'.

As you might imagine, it was a great relief to finally move into our own place.

It was a handsome, sweeping apartment halfway up Victoria Peak in an area known as the Mid-Levels. It had three bedrooms, a big living and dining area and a huge patio with a magnificent, unobstructed view of the harbour.

Along with the apartment came our first 'amah'—home help. People in Hong Kong were, and still are, expected to create jobs by employing locals as household servants. A general amah is a housekeeper who also cooks, while a baby amah is a nanny. We eventually settled on Ah Chang, who preferred to work alone and told Kell so. Our beloved Ah Chang was a stout woman with the most gorgeous shiny black braid that reached down past her waist. She proved to be a 'take charge' person who had gone through hardships in her lifetime that most people would never have to face. When she arrived in the colony looking for work, she had had to leave her own children and husband back home in mainland China—perhaps hoping to bring them over later. The boys gave her a rough time until she got a handle on how the household ran, then she made her own rules. We Hutchences were all living a fast-paced lifestyle. Kell, Mother and I all had work that took us outside of the home and we socialised for fun and business reasons as well. Ah Chang would stay with the family and be highly valued for the rest of our time in Hong Kong.

Mother quickly got bored with mahjong and afternoon teas and lunches. One morning, after reading about an American film company arriving in town, she dressed, showed up at the production office and was hired for the make-up department. The first assistant director was a young Peter MacGregor-Scott who would weave in and out of our lives over the next 50 years. He went on to co-produce several megahits including *The Fugitive* (1993). While producing *Batman Forever* in 1995, he would get Michael to record the Iggy Pop song, 'The Passenger', for the soundtrack.

23

Life was very different for Michael now he was attending Glenealy Primary. He was picking up Cantonese phrases both at school and from Ah Chang. When he couldn't get his point across, like the rest of us he resorted to mime. Perhaps these skills contributed to his remarkable body language as a stage performer later.

Nevertheless, this 'dreamer' who needed to get serious about his education (a familiar refrain) was for the most part academically lacking. Indeed, in subsequent years his younger brother, Rhett, would get much better results. Teachers would lament that Michael wasn't paying attention. Luckily he scored high for his manners, his mingling, his eager class participation and willingness. He just couldn't seem to get more than average grades. In fact, in *some* subjects he was close to failing.

What would he, could he, become? It wasn't clear.

I don't remember when he developed his lisp. Maybe it was always there; so much a part of him that I never thought about it.

In 1884 several bored Hong Kong wives had written to the acting Colonial Secretary and requested a club of their own. Thank heavens— the legendary Ladies Recreation Club was born and it was still flourishing in the 1960s. We often took Michael and Rhett there after school for a swim, and there was a family clubhouse and tennis courts as well as the pool. Michael certainly took to water. Fortunately Kell was a strong swimmer and taught the boys, along with professional help, because Mother never learned how to swim and neither did I. We wondered if Michael's asthma, which he would struggle with to some degree for his whole life, would prevent him from doing his best. But it didn't, and in fact Michael was pretty healthy as a child. Nothing affected his swimming or other sporting activities, not even the occasional bout of bronchitis, although a broken arm achieved by falling backwards while awkwardly trying to kiss a girl didn't quite set right; it stopped him competing in swimming and diving tournaments at higher levels.

During those years in Hong Kong, Michael took on so many extra-curricular activities when I look back. He studied music, violin and classical guitar for a time. There were lessons in kickboxing, judo, fencing, archery and chess. He built a million model aeroplanes and cars. That takes a steady hand and so much patience. I can't tell you how many times I walked into his room and almost stepped on a delicate balsawood model. But none of these pursuits were expected to earn him a living one day.

Meanwhile, I worked out some go-go routines with three teenage girlfriends and we scored a gig as the resident go-go dancers on the Hong Kong version of the popular American music TV show, *Shindig*. Dubbed The Telstar Dancers by a local disc jockey, we were soon swamped with bookings. We were also modelling, and suddenly The Telstar Dancers were looked upon as the authorities in teen fashion.

When we rehearsed routines in the Hutchence living room, Michael would sit on the floor with a small record player, carefully moving the needle back to the beginning of the track as we'd declare, 'From the beginning, one more time!'

Within a year or two Kell changed jobs again. This time he joined an American company, Mandarin Textiles, which, among other things, made couture for Lanvin. They also had the Dynasty label, which was sold in up-market hotels. We lost the chauffeur and the gorgeous apartment but stayed in Hong Kong.

Now, we were told, we were moving to a fantastic house owned by *Time* magazine that sat on a cliff face in Stanley, about 30 minutes south of town, on the coast.

From the front, the two-storey house looked like one you might see on any Main Street, USA—except for the bars on the windows, which were commonplace in Hong Kong. But as we walked into the spacious living area, with stairs on our right, we passed a literally enormous floor-to-ceiling library before arriving on a patio with a windswept view across the South China Sea. Kell let out a whistle and the boys copied him in their own, high-pitched way. Several small islands were dotted in the blue-green expanse. It was magnificent.

But then we looked *down*. Originating from the side of the house, wooden stairs hugged a sheer, spray-bathed cliff plunging down, down to a private beach with a natural rock pool and crashing waves.

'Perfection!' said Kell with satisfaction.

Mother was agog. She was clearly impressed by the view, as was I, yet as she looked from the perilous, weather-beaten stairs back to little Michael and Rhett, now wrestling and tumbling into a coffee table, you could see the whites of her eyes.

'There are so many open steps down to that beach,' she said quietly, with a noticeable quiver. 'What if I get the children down there and I've forgotten something?'

The Stanley house came with its own amazing cook—although that term would be an insult for Ah Lee, our chef from Shanghai. I can still see him perched on a stool in the kitchen, carving carrots and parsnips into hollowed-out pagodas. These would arrive at the dinner table standing upright, lit from inside by small candles. Ah Lee was also a first-rate cocktail maker and drinks waiter. As he walked in balancing trays of martinis, margaritas and daiquiris, never forgetting who had ordered what, our parents' friends were so impressed that several tried to lure him away.

That summer I met a boy who gave me a copy of Walt Whitman's *Leaves of Grass*, published in 1892. I was caught up in the romanticism of the gesture and carried that book everywhere. It seemed most appropriate that I read it on the beach. Seven-year-old Michael became my audience when he wasn't in the waves.

'The atmosphere is not perfume', I read, '. . . it has no sense of dis-tillation . . . it is odourless, it is for my mouth forever . . . I am in love with it . . .'

Michael shrugged his shoulders, looking at me with curiosity. 'What does it mean?'

'It doesn't matter, as long as the words made you feel good.'

It was a wild, beautiful summer but with the typhoon season came the realisation that ours was not the safest house. I experienced some of the most frightening weather I have ever witnessed—mostly because home was often too far away for me to get to before the warning went up to Level 8 ('Danger: stay where you are'). And it was maybe even *more* frightening to be *in* that Stanley house with no protection except for the boarded-up windows shuddering and banging away. Michael often came to my room during the storms and we would sit under the covers with a torch reading stories until it passed over. After six months at the beach we moved back to a small home on Old Peak Road.

In March 1967, the Chinese Revolution began to have repercussions in Hong Kong. There were widespread strikes, rioting and arrests. A couple of months later communist sympathisers began planting bombs around the city. Students and strikers demonstrating against the British colonial rule were locked up by riot police. The clashes became so violent that a curfew was set. When socialising, we had to be sure to reach our destination by 7.00 p.m.—after which time, of course, you couldn't go home. Honestly, it was a fabulous excuse for a teenager like me to stay out partying till morning. I admit it: I was more inter-ested in having fun than in 'boring' politics. Mind you, as time went on, and certainly with Michael's influence as well, all that would change.

By June, mainland China decided to show the British authorities in Honkers who was *really* boss. In solidarity with the leftist protestors, they shut off our water supply. Hong Kong completely relied on water from Beijing. Although it was calculated we'd have enough till October, people were talking about the troubles lasting for more than a year. The British requested extra supplies. No dice.

Now the situation was so desperate that the water supply needed to be rationed. The city was split into four sections. Each was allotted four hours of water, every fourth day. We stored supplies in huge tubs and used it sparingly. *Playboy* magazine joked that Hong Kong might be the only city where you could ask a girl to come home to shower on a first date and she would take you up on it.

I felt sorry for Ah Chang; she had to heat the water for the boys' baths, shuffling back and forth between the bath and the kitchen with large, steaming hot pots. When Mother or I tried to help she saw it as a personal affront to her job security. I remember Michael and Rhett once had a shoving match in the bathroom where the water was stored and they knocked over a huge barrel. We heard quite a few obscenities screamed in Cantonese punctuated with the odd '*Lett!*' and '*Michael!*' as Ah Chang ran for towels while the precious water flowed down the hall into the living room. Rather than go thirsty, we checked back into the Hilton for three days. We recognised we were lucky that we could.

I speak of this lightly today, but, in fact, many people—students, protesters, innocent bystanders, police and several journalists speaking out against the violence—lost their lives.

In fact it was then, at just seven, that Michael felt the power of a political coming-of-age, a 'first realisation of the physicality of politics—that it can go beyond a distant figure of England and the local pushover government and the Governor walking around in a silly hat', as he told the *South China Morning Post* in a 1994 interview.

He told the newspaper that at the time of the unrest, ou
home had been painted with slogans. Bombs were left in the scho
playground in what he described as 'a paid campaign of subversion'.
A friend of his was blown up. He saw a man running down Garden
Road in the middle of quiet streets in the curfew, with a horde of
rioters, 'so-called Communist sympathisers', after him, and his father
run from the Hilton Hotel bar past security guards to help pull the
fleeing man through the hotel's doors to safety.

Michael would never forget the look of fear on that man's face.

With bombings and bomb threats becoming common, even in our
favourite hotel, people were stressed out over what was to come next.
The police presence was formidable but, in turn, the sheer numbers of
demonstrators were overwhelming. Hong Kong is a very busy city that
survives on tourism and foreign trade, so I do think the enormity of
the strikes and unrest—the *gravity* of it all—really resonated at home.
But the international print media at the time didn't seem to have a real
sense of the size of the problem.

In his last year on earth, 1997, Michael would shoot a series of three
documentary-style videos for MTV called *Rough Guide to Hong Kong*.
The interviews he would do with residents then would show he personally empathised with the strong sense of the influence and power of
the incoming Chinese rule they were feeling, when the handover
from the British occurred on 1 July 1997.

Anyway, back in 1967 in Hong Kong, the danger and uncertainty
continued right through the year. In December it was decided that
Kell would stay on in Hong Kong for work while Mother, Michael,
Rhett and I took a ship to the relative quiet of Sydney to ride out the
political storm.

4

Kowloon Tong

THE WIDE STREETS OF KOWLOON TONG, situated on mainland China, closely flanked the island of Hong Kong. The district housed predominately well-to-do locals, CEOs and movie stars. Since Kell was working in Hong Kong on a contract back then, and Caucasians like him (yes, that distinction was regularly made) often lived in Kowloon Tong, in Kowloon City West, that is where he rented the next house Michael would live in.

By March 1968, Hong Kong politics had settled down considerably so Mother brought the boys back from their brief sojourn of relative security in Sydney. I actually stayed on in Sydney independently and worked as a buyer for the Sportsgirl boutique chain till November, when I rejoined the family's Asian adventures. Then we were all briefly under the one roof again; although, as I was almost 21, I was itching to live my own life and wouldn't stay long. The Kowloon Tong house was nothing fancy: a typical single-storey, three-bedroom house.

Nevertheless, the generous servants' quarters off the kitchen were very much appreciated by Ah Chang.

On her Tuesday afternoons off she'd visit the local market, never failing to return with fresh white sea bream, Chinese mackerel and grey mullet for Tinkerbell, the scraggly little tortoiseshell cat that had followed Michael home one day. This little waif reminded us of delightful Bashō's seventeenth-century haiku: *Why so scrawny, cat? / starving for fat fish / or mice . . . / Or backyard love?*

Ah Chang spurned the idea of anything less than fresh fish for Master Michael's 'mao', as they call a cat in Cantonese. And in fact Michael's rescued stray would become famous! She posed with him for a photograph to go with an article in the local newspaper, *The China Mail*. He'd entered her in a pet competition and lo and behold, they won.

And there—there is *another* character name that Michael chose for his beloved ones that was lifted from the pages of J.M. Barrie's Peter Pan and Wendy tales. His pretty tabby Tinkerbell was named after Peter Pan's hyperactive, mischievous fairy protector, and his baby would be called Tiger Lily, as the Native American princess in Neverland was called.

Master Michael and Master Rhett, as Ah Chang called them, had always shared a room. Now they had their separate domains. Top priority for Michael's was a bookshelf spilling over with titles he loved to read including *The Egypt Game* by Californian Zilpha Keatley Snyder and Roald Dahl's *James and the Giant Peach*. I also recall reading him Ursula K. Le Guin's fantasy classic *A Wizard of Earthsea* out loud, as it was a little harder. We loved that book. His chess set was nearby; his favourite model aircraft of the moment carefully set up on a top shelf. A boomerang on the wall hinted at his Australian background. Tinkerbell shared Michael's bed, later joined by her kitten Tabitha. From this vantage point, the terrible furred twosome took delight in lunging at

Ah Chang's braid as it swung from side to side while she firmly tucked in the sheets. None of us had *dared* try to make our own bed since an earlier amah, who didn't stay long, had summoned the chauffeur, who agreed with her 100 per cent: for us to make our own beds would be a dire insult to her housekeeping skills.

Then it came time for Michael to enrol at the newly opened Beacon Hill School, an international primary one. Being friendly and confident, he immediately began making friends. Once again he was not exactly top of his class, but he got by. His teachers enjoyed having him there. But that didn't stop him from getting up to mischief.

One of the other boys at Beacon Hill Primary was Tim Stewart, an American. One lunch time Tim walked out of a stall in the upstairs boys' restroom to wash his hands and found Michael staring intently out the window. The two of them were about nine years old.

'What's so interesting out there?'

'See those girls playing jump rope?' asked Michael.

'Yes . . .'

'Do you think if we soak rolls of toilet paper and throw them down at them, we could get them wet?'

They looked at each other with intent. The best way to solve a physics problem like this was to give it a go, really. You would never know if you didn't. So they took all the extra supplies of toilet paper and began soaking them in the sink. Michael threw the first. It landed short. The girls didn't even notice. Tim was up next and fared better, coming closer to target. Michael realised he needed to aim a little more to the left. His next shot was *much* better as it landed—*sploosh!*—right next to the rope, spraying the girls. The boys congratulated and high-fived one another. They grabbed their next sog-balls with joy. They weren't bad marksmen, they found, and could actually connect with individual girls who at this point were hopping and running in different directions.

Just as Michael ducked into a stall to retrieve more ammunition, a teacher marched in, catching Tim with a dripping toilet roll in his hand. In one swift movement he had Tim by the back of his collar and was dragging him towards the door when he noticed Michael.

'Are you involved in this villainous behaviour too?' he asked. Caught off guard, Michael started to give an explanation but the look on his friend's face said, 'Just say no.'

Tim never 'ratted' on Michael and their childhood bond was cemented that day in a close friendship, the depth of which few people understood at the time.

At first Mother stayed home, concentrating on being the dutiful wife and hands-on parent until once again, with the family in need of extra funds, she returned to make-up artistry. Independent movie producers would call when they came to town to shoot as Patricia Hutchence had by now built a reputation for being talented, professional and reliable. The boys regularly visited her on set. They were well-versed in set protocol. They stayed in one place unless asked to move and understood all the commands called out by the assistant director.

'Final touches'—make-up artist, hairstylist and wardrobe must do their final check. 'Okay, ladies and gentlemen, this is a take, quiet on the set.'

And depending on the size of the set, or if it was exterior, several assistants would repeat, 'Quiet.'

'Roll sound, roll camera,' the assistant director would say, and get the reply: 'speed', then 'marker' as what used to be a clapperboard was clamped down in front of the camera or the actor's face. 'Scene 23, take three.'

And finally the director would get to call out, 'Action!'

Bless their hearts, Michael and Rhett would be stationary, barely breathing; what a feat for two little boys who normally couldn't stand still if you promised them the first ride on *Apollo 11*. Of course they were always forewarned: 'One sound or trip over a cable and you are banned from the set.'

Mother's large make-up case intrigued them, particularly the special-effects products. Michael taught himself how to extract the 'blood' to use on his GI Joes and tiny soldiers when he was very young. He and Rhett would send their friends home with scorched bullet holes and gore-dripping gashes for maximum parental effect. But for our mother, their surreptitious raids on her kit were no joke. Authentic-looking 'blood' was not easy to come by in Hong Kong and more than once we had to scrounge around and find some of the local stuff they used at the big local film production house, Shaw Brothers, which was not nearly as convincing. We eventually figured out how to make it with gelatine.

When I returned to Hong Kong from my time living independently in Sydney, I found that Mother and Kell had separated—although it was clear that Michael and Rhett did not grasp this. While Kell was hard at work between an office in Kowloon and a factory in the New Territories, our mother would be at the house waiting for the boys to arrive home from school. When Kell was at home, we ate dinner together as a family. They even attended business functions together. She went to school events and planned meals, took Michael and Rhett to their swim meets and shopped for their clothing. She always put the boys to bed and stayed over occasionally but in fact she was sharing an apartment on the island with a friend from the Gold Coast who was appearing as a showgirl in one of the popular nightclubs in town. It was a very central place and I moved in with them. It wasn't that she wanted to move out of the family home; it was that when they decided to separate, Kell, like a lot of men, decided *he* was not going to be the one to move out.

When he was eleven, in grade six, Michael made his first recording. It came about because one night at a party, Mother found herself chatting with a director of the global ad agency network Ling-McCann-Erickson. In passing she mentioned her two sons.

This grabbed the advertising man's attention. 'Can either of them sing?' he asked.

She mused for a long moment. 'Well, Michael has recently begun guitar lessons. He isn't tone deaf.'

Obviously desperate to fix a client's crisis at this point, the director asked her to bring Michael to a recording studio directly the following day.

Michael was excited though a bit apprehensive. There had been no preparation and he wasn't sure what they were going to ask him to sing.

Our mother was nervous for him too. He was given a list of Christmas carols including 'Jingle Bells' and 'Silent Night', directed to an isolation booth and given headphones. It was a bit touch-and-go at first. They played the backing tracks but he forgot the words. He needed prompting from the control booth, but in no time at all, it seemed to Mother, Michael was singing out loud and clear. It was obvious that he enjoyed it too, and not just because he was handed a cheque for HK$300 (US$50). He was much more excited about actually getting his hands on a copy of his first record when it came out. As Christmas approached, we were sent to an address where we were told his recording was on sale. We were baffled to find it was the toy department. And astonished to purchase our copy, because Michael's first record turned out to be a little orange disc you slotted into the gut of a plastic Santa. Still, we were amazed and delighted to hear those carols jingling away with Michael's clear voice, before it broke, piping out in the foreground.

Soon it was time for him to uniform up to attend King George V School in Ho Man Tin. (Michael's third school in Hong Kong is now known simply as 'K-G-Five'.) He looked so handsome in his long navy-blue trousers, white short-sleeved shirt with the school badge on the pocket, navy-blue V-neck pullover and polished black shoes.

Although Hong Kong drew a whirlpool of immigrants from around the globe, KGV was predominantly British. Just to be understood, Michael had to learn to anglicise his vowels and sharpen up his consonants. He also discovered he had a knack for mimicking the foreign brogues and language variants spoken there and quietly worked up some spot-on imitations of the principal and various teachers. He had us all in fits.

I'd like to tell you a bit more about the history of that school, actually, because it really illustrates the turbulent background of Hong Kong, which in turn helped make Michael Hutchence.

KGV is the oldest English-speaking school in Hong Kong. When it first opened in 1894 as Kowloon College, it only let in the children of British subjects. Two years later it was laid waste by a typhoon. Upon reopening, it was renamed Kowloon British School and it thrived until 1937, when China was invaded by Japan.

The majority of European women and children then in Shanghai were evacuated to Hong Kong, where Michael's old school was designated a refugee camp to cope with their influx.

A few hours after the attack on Pearl Harbor in early December 1941, Japanese forces began a brutal ambush of the tiny British Crown Colony. For the seventeen days before the Fall of Hong Kong was complete, the heavily outnumbered British and allied local forces commandeered the school to use as an impromptu hospital for the many casualties. After that, the Japanese used it as a hospital for their prisoners-of-war. From 1946, it reopened as a school, and a year later welcomed students of all nationalities, including, in the autumn of 1971, Michael.

However, his stay was to be short-lived. By the following year, Kell had plans to be on the move again. The school provided a letter, dated 22 September 1972, with a report on Michael's progress.

'Michael Hutchence was admitted to KGV in September 1971,' it stated, 'and completed Form One. His attainment during the year was slightly below average for his form.' On the plus side, 'Michael has taken part in a number of extra-curricular activities including Swimming and Athletics for his House, and is a keen member of the Model Club and Sailing Club. Out of school he is a Scout and member of a Christian Youth Fellowship, with Judo and fencing and guitar playing as hobbies. He has a pleasant, affable personality and should adapt easily to his new school. I have pleasure in recommending him for a place in high school in Australia.'

This is the letter Michael would take with him on his first day at Killarney Heights High School, a day of jagged downs—and one big up.

5

you'll never make
a living as a poet

IN LATE 1972 Kell and Patricia bought a house in leafy Belrose near the Northern Beaches of Sydney, where cicadas screamed in an attractive mass drone with many intonations from the gum trees, and mirages shone like water on the streets.

There was such a sense of place there for Michael; a return to at least part of what his 'homing' instinct recognised. Yet he had been so remoulded by the urbanity of Hong Kong for nearly eight of his twelve years on earth that he was not prepared for what he found.

Australia is a very old continent with a comparatively small population. Aboriginal people arrived at least 65,000 years ago, the first European settlers in 1788. And despite wave after wave of various immigrants, some Australians can be quite intolerant. At that time, they also liked to make fun of the upper-crust British accent more than any other. To them it sounded snobbish and stuck-up, while Australians traditionally prided themselves on being unpretentious.

And since many of their ancestors were transported to the colony as convicts by the English ruling class—often for petty theft—a powerful history of home-grown rebellion against 'rule Britannia' and, specifically, its upper class, was ingrained in Australia.

And sure enough, having been schooled among British subjects and their offspring all his educational life, by then twelve-year-old Michael sounded more like a well-to-do English lad than a flat-drawling Aussie.

Risky.

Anyway, he stepped off the school bus at Killarney Heights High incongruously wearing the uniform of his previous school. (It was always happening to me too, perennially wearing the wrong uniform. Oh, how I remember that ghastly first contact at each new school.)

Some kids ganged up, threw tennis balls at him, teased, harassed and heckled.

'It was such a shock to come back [to Sydney],' Michael would tell the *South China Morning Post* in 1994. (I can't help being impressed by how he would always seem a whole different man in Hong Kong. He was visiting the city with INXS then, to play. The local papers treated— and still treat—him as a respected prodigal son; one of their own. The city celebrates his intelligence and successes as a matter of course. Perhaps they never really saw him like some Australians did, as a tall poppy that needed scything down to size.)

'It was a sea of freckly red-haired kids and blonde kids . . . there was a certain amount of roughness shown to me. Australia is a very young rough place, and I've grown to love that, but for me, I went from a very sophisticated, modern society to cowboys. And that's hard. Suddenly I had to learn to fight . . .'

Standing up to their attack at Killarney Heights High that day was easier said than done, especially when your every word sounded 'la de dah' to a mob of jeering Aussies. For a shy kid who'd just been forced to leave his childhood friends overseas, this was calamitous.

Fortunately for Michael, another new kid called Andrew Farriss had arrived not long before and had swiftly become mates with Paul, a useful ally.

'He was getting bullied and was about to get into a huge fight when I stepped in with my six-foot mate to rescue him,' said Andrew. 'I've always hated bullies.'

Andrew and Michael did not become instant friends then, but they gradually developed a respect for one another that grew into not only a lifelong friendship, but the song-writing backbone of INXS.

I'd have to say the atmosphere at our Belrose home was not the best. Our parents had decided to stay together for—what else—'the boys'. Honestly, watching your parents live separate lives in the same household is torture for a child. If you think you can smile as you interact with your children while giving your spouse the silent treatment, and they won't notice, think again. Message received loud and clear. The obvious fraudulence of an estranged couple, our parents, being 'together' just amplified the awkwardness. Resentment built. Michael was just four months shy of becoming a teenager and Rhett was growing fast. Mother and Kell were not fooling them anymore.

Then, only a short time after they bought the house, Kell took out a second mortgage on it so he could set up business at a factory in the city of Maitland—once again without discussing it with Mother. As it was a two-hour drive north he'd leave early Monday morning and be back in Belrose on Friday evening. With this new, demanding business and a heavily mortgaged home, a second income was imperative. Mother picked up work as a make-up artist in television.

Michael was struggling a little at this stage. Not only socially, but also as he tried to settle into the New South Wales high school curriculum.

I could relate to this too. With every move our family made, I'd fallen further behind in my studies as well. It's one thing to move across town, but when you switch states, or in my brothers' case, relocate overseas, there's a lot of adjusting to do. Grade seven in Sydney is different from grade seven in Brisbane is different from grade seven in Hong Kong. Our parents never investigated the differences in educational approach or thought it necessary to wait until the end of the school year before they relocated.

Further to that, Michael was a boy who'd just been forced to abandon his friends overseas. The bedevilling tensions in his household were confusing and he was affected.

As a distraction our parents bought the boys motocross bikes. Michael was immediately, ferociously hooked. It was obvious that he would own a Harley someday. If Kell couldn't make it back for the weekend, Mother would get the boys to hitch the trailer and bikes to her white Holden Monaro instead. She'd drive them to some small country town with winding, looping hills of track that two young dirt-bike fiends could burn around together all weekend. They'd arrive back at the motel covered from head to toe in mud, take a shower and fall into bed after dinner. Michael would curl up with a book—something like S.E. Hinton's coming-of-age book *The Outsiders*, which he devoured around this time—and fall asleep by the second page.

After two years back in Sydney and many years of a failed (and somewhat emotionally and financially abusive) marriage, Mother couldn't bear to keep up the facade a moment longer.

She wanted a divorce.

She asked Kell to move out. He was gone five days a week, every week, anyway, she pointed out. He wouldn't hear of it and read her the riot act. He swore that if *she* wanted to leave the marriage, *she* could leave both the *house and the boys* too. Options were thin on the ground. Their family home was mortgaged to capacity and savings were nil. There was nothing to divide.

If Mother tried to take Michael and Rhett, *he would come and get them*, he said. Everything Kell promised her was a tug of war.

Of course he had a lot of pride. He loved the boys and believed the man should rule the roost. There would be no compromise.

Mother felt cut off at the knees. There was no love left in the marriage but she adored the boys too.

Australian law was also rather harsh in 1974 when it came to divorce. No-fault divorce was not enacted until a year later. You had to choose between a range of blameful accusations you'd have to prove in court and having a two-year separation, which Kell refused to consider.

Through her film contacts, Mother had been offered work in the USA in paramedical make-up, a new field. If she took it up, she would be working alongside physicians and plastic surgeons to improve the lives of burn survivors and others with traumatic injuries. Fleeing to America for at least a couple of years to take up this new challenge seemed like the most reasonable, sensible thing to do. She could work, live frugally and return with some savings and perhaps a new skill to start over later.

She felt confident that she could manage with easygoing Michael and, after setting up a home and routine, send for Rhett. Of her two boys, Rhett never took the easy route. He questioned authority and tended to listen to his father more. But Kell was away so much. Rhett was in with a bad mob, getting into deep troubles and defying her authority so much that she didn't know how to handle it. In fact, she didn't think she could.

Rhett needed more male input in his life, she was sure of it. Kell had been away so often. He needed more of his father's attention. She knew it.

Mother took Michael for a walk one afternoon and told him her plan. She invited him to give his view. She explained that she would not go through with it if he objected. After a short discussion on the possibilities, it became their secret.

Our mother worked every job that came her way over the next three months and saved until the day came to leave.

'When are we going, Mum?' Michael would ask, every now and then. One day she just booked the flights. As the day grew near, Mother suffered great anxiety over the dreadful secret she and Michael were keeping. There was so much uncertainty facing her and Michael in just running. She truly thought that Rhett would be better off—that he was the lucky one. In her mind she imagined Rhett and Kell bonding. He always seemed to be craving Kell's attention. This way he would have it all.

Nevertheless, she dreaded the day she had to sit her youngest child down and explain. She was wracked with guilt. For the rest of her life she carried a deep, unseen scar from that decision. She felt she could never make it up to him. Even when Rhett wrote to her many years later and told her he had forgiven her, she still couldn't get over it.

The day came in late 1974. I think it was September. Michael was fourteen. After the boys went off to school, some movers came to help Mother pack extra clothing, special keepsakes such as Michael's dog-eared copies of Theodore Taylor's *The Cay* and Walt Morey's *Gentle Ben*, and small pieces of furniture that she and Michael didn't want to leave behind. They were going into storage.

She had no illusions that Kell would still be at our Belrose home, with Rhett, when she and Michael returned. After all, they'd moved a dozen times in the last sixteen years.

When Rhett arrived home from school she sat him down and calmly told him her plan. Of course he erupted into tears and begged her to take him too. She promised she would send for him shortly and asked him to be good for his father. She assured him she loved him and would miss him and it wouldn't be long before she could send for him.

Michael arrived home and calmly changed, put the last of his toiletries in his bag and laid his uniform out on his bed. By this stage he had changed schools to Davidson High. Our Aunt Maureen, Mother's sister, arrived to drive them to the airport. It was a quiet ride. Rhett was naturally distressed.

When it came time to depart through customs, Michael said his goodbyes and told his brother he would see him soon.

'I promise I'll be good if you take me,' Rhett cried out to Mother.

'Be good for Dad, and it will only be a couple of months before I send for you.' She looked at her youngest son's face and wanted to turn back but it was too late. Her heart was breaking as she realised what she was about to do.

Michael was the only one not crying now. He hugged Maureen, then Rhett again, telling his brother he'd see him in Los Angeles, and walked through the gates. He stopped and turned around.

'Come on, Mum,' he said, waving her on, 'if we're going, let's go.' Mother gave her sister and Rhett one last, tearful hug each and followed Michael out of sight.

I'd taken a great gamble going to California in December 1970 to pursue a career in make-up artistry. I'd married and had a son, Brent.

I was fast asleep when I was jarred awake by the phone ringing so loudly on my nightstand it jumped and so did I. Before I could say hello I heard an extremely emotional, inebriated Kell sobbing loudly in my ear.

'She's left me and taken my Michael, is he there?'

I tried to calm him down. Surely he was confused. I could hear a glass clink in the background.

'Dad? What? What are you talking about? Why would Mother and Michael be with me? Dad, I'm in California.'

I guess it was understandable for Kell to feel convinced Mother would have confided to me such a major plan as leaving him and taking Michael overseas, especially if she were coming to California. She told me later that she wanted to spare me from the worry. I'm glad she did. But I don't think Kell believed me at first when I said I didn't know a thing.

Though incoherent through much of the conversation, he was able to give me the basics of what had gone down. I asked about Rhett, urging Kell to take care of him. I would let him know the moment I heard from Michael and Mother, I assured him.

I will never forget Kell's words. Not just 'Michael', but 'my Michael'. Perhaps my stepfather might, I meditated sadly, now trade some of that angst for a long overdue, more intimate relationship with our younger brother.

Personally, I was still smarting myself from discovering Kell hadn't really adopted me, when he'd told me he had, and after promising Mother he would. He'd understood it was a condition of their marriage. He'd only 'changed' my name in that inscription on the locket he gave me when I was eleven. Nowhere else. He hadn't even changed it via deed poll. When the boys and I were about to move with our mother to Hong Kong for the first time, after Kell had moved there first and sent for us, the surname anomaly caused absolute havoc with my identity for passports and visas until Mother gave a teary performance worthy of Bette Davis and someone just buckled, looked the other way and applied the required rubber stamps to certify me as a Hutchence.

I was devastated by that. My trust in my stepfather's word and his authenticity, my sure sense of being *worth* the 'bother' of adoption—they all took a terrible beating.

As I put the phone down on this sobbing man, having done what I could to comfort him, I realised that it had been over six months since I'd seen any of my family.

The previous May, I'd returned to Australia. I'd brought my two-year-old son Brent to stay at the family home in Belrose, keen to introduce him to the Australian wing of his family.

Mid-afternoon Michael had burst through the front door, hurling his backpack across the floor. I ran over and threw my arms around his neck. He'd grown considerably. Gone was the controlled short-back-and-sides; his curls fell over one eye. Waiting at the open door was a very shy Andrew Farriss.

'What're you doing standing there? Come in, she won't bite. Andy, this is my sister Tina from America.' I stepped over to Andrew, who was about a head shorter than Michael, and he greeted me politely. Brent came running up behind me and wrapped himself around my legs. Michael knelt down and smiled at him.

'You must be Brent—hi mate.' He held out his hand to his young nephew. Brent continued to bury his face into my legs.

'He's a bit overwhelmed,' I told Michael, 'but once he gets going, you'll be sorry!'

Big smile from 'Uncle' Michael then.

'Ahh that's all right, mate, we've got plenty of time to make friends.'

Andrew and Michael grabbed a snack and disappeared into Michael's room. When I checked on them later they had their heads in a book and were deep in conversation with Miles Davis's *Bitches Brew* playing in the background.

It was obvious at the time that there was tension between our parents. It seems that they were really working each other's nerves. They always had. One source of friction was symptomatic. Our mother had worked on and off her whole life; there were many times when we would not have survived without the money she brought in.

46

Despite this, Kell would trivialise her work effort and professiona...
by saying she was working on sets 'for fun'.

I felt sad for them all, especially my two young brothers. I couldn't
help thinking that it didn't have to be this way. Clearly there should have
been a way to compromise, but for a traditionalist like Kell, who had
come of age in an era that believed men made the decisions in a household, that was not going to happen.

After Kell's disturbing distress call I could not get back to sleep.
This couldn't have come at a worse time for me. My own marriage was
breaking down. So far, I had kept it from my family.

Within a few hours I heard from Mother, who had landed in Los
Angeles with Michael. I don't think she had really thought through the
logistics of her plan too much. She just knew she had to get out of her
marriage to Kell. But she had thought it through enough to book their
flights to San Francisco, just north of where I was living in San Jose.
Soon we would be reunited.

As he came towards me for a hug at the airport, I noticed Michael
hadn't changed much since I last saw him. His teenage skin was
flaring up though, and he was self-conscious about it, hiding behind
his tumbling forelock as he grinned. The first thing we did was find a
rental apartment for Mother and Michael nearby. He was enrolled in
a local high school, Leigh High, where I remember him being relaxed
and happy. Mother bought him a yellow dirt bike which he spent many
hours maintaining. He was a pretty good rider too, coming second in a
local motocross competition.

But that was still to come. Late one night, soon after they had
arrived, just as things were 'normalising', I received a frantic call from
Michael. No doubt brought on by all the complexities and stresses of
leaving her husband and youngest son and fleeing with the other to a
foreign country, Mother was having what we would now recognise as
a panic attack. The doctor I called had advised she should breathe into

ounter hyperventilation, and that's what she was doing
. She'd calmed down somewhat by then but Michael
fright. He was so relieved to see me. It was only then
egan to understand all of the pain and the fearful, covert
worrying that had been going on for the past three months.

Soon Mother departed for Los Angeles to see about the job offer
and find some housing, leaving Michael in my care. She needed to stick
to her plan. She could be steely when it came to getting something
accomplished; she was never one to go off track. It didn't take her long
before she was settled and sent for Michael.

We decided to join forces to support each other through these
testing changes, so a month later I followed with my little son, Brent,
joining her and Michael in a small, 1940s California Ranch-style house
in Studio City. I found it comforting to have family so close after living
on a separate continent for almost five years. And when Mother was
offered make-up work for a movie, she didn't have to worry about who'd
look after Michael: I'd be there. Certainly neither of us was dating back
then and it was an opportunity for us to connect and make up for lost
time. Michael had his little nephew to bond with too, and vice versa.

Studio City is in Los Angeles, in the San Fernando Valley. CBS
Studio Centre is situated there. When we rented there in the mid-
1970s, it was a nice neighbourhood with many pockets of wealth. A lot
of actors, writers and technicians in the motion-picture and television
industry lived in the area, but luckily it wasn't out of our range.

The house we rented was small: only two bedrooms, a decent-sized
living area and a separate dining room with French doors at both
ends. The bonus was one set of these led directly to the pool. Michael
was thrilled to make this dining room his bedroom. If he rose early
enough he could swim before breakfast—a great incentive to get a
teenager out of bed. From Michael's door it was no more than a metre
to the edge of the pool, so I was understandably nervous about Brent,

who stuck to Michael like a tiny shadow. I'm not a strong swimmer at all, so dear Michael took it upon himself to teach his toddler nephew the basics. He really was great with kids. Soon Brent could at least dog paddle to the side if he fell in.

As for furnishings, we didn't even have a couch. We started with mattresses in the bedrooms and settled on throw pillows and a television set for the living room. Since we no longer had a dining room, we didn't need a table. The boys were happy, there was plenty of food, we had job prospects and things were looking up.

With Brent at preschool and Michael now at North Hollywood High, both Mother and I could work. Mother, daughter, son and grandson. Like so many others before us, we went to southern California and formed a new family constellation.

We bought a ten-speed bicycle for Michael to get to school. If I was going to be late collecting Brent from his preschool, my brother would swing by and collect him instead on his way home.

Compared to the straitlaced, English style of education and the perfectly turned-out uniforms he'd been expected to wear before, the laidback approach of North Hollywood High was a breeze for Michael. Getting to wear whatever he liked to school was fun and he was fitting in well. It was strange at first, he thought, how when the teacher asked a question, the kids wouldn't put their hands up. They'd just call out the answer or casually raise a pencil. The difference was the accent on individuality and the high value put on free thinking, I guess.

Michael often watched the African-American kids dancing and working out routines in the quad at lunch time. He was fascinated and often bought the steps home to show us. Toddler Brent would be right there trying to copy his teenage uncle.

By now Michael was listening to music constantly. Elton John, Iggy Pop, AC/DC, War, David Bowie and the Eagles were his favourites back then. He was also hit by the unpredictable winds of inspiration, absent-mindedly jotting down lines here and there. As Percy Bysshe Shelley (Michael would later play him in the movie *Frankenstein Unbound*) wrote in *A Defence of Poetry*, in 1840, 'Poetry lifts the veil from the hidden beauty of the world, and makes familiar objects be as if they were not familiar.' It was this ability to cast a spell he was feeling for, experimentally, I suspected.

Despite Michael's enthusiasm for North Hollywood High, his grades were still lacklustre. One day some work arrived home marked by his English Lit teacher. One particular comment I will never forget. 'You'll never make a living as a poet.'

In early 1976, after eighteen months in California, Michael returned to Sydney with Mother and they were reunited with Rhett, moving into a house Kell had rented in Belrose. He himself was working overseas in Manila then, which was just as well considering our parents' past. Mother was hired by the Reg Grundy organisation to work on the TV soapie *The Young Doctors*. Rhett and Michael were pleased to be together again; and of course he and Mother had a lot to catch up on too. A kind of healing began.

Michael, who was just sixteen, began seeing a lot of Andrew Farriss once more. He was very excited because Andrew had put together a band called Doctor Dolphin he was fronting with a couple of Davidson High boys, Kent Kerny and Neil Sanders, and a Forest High boy, Garry Beers. Michael was allowed to stand on the sidelines and work a tambourine. Then one day when they were trying out a new drummer, Andrew in an offhand manner handed the microphone to Michael and asked him to sing while he concentrated on the musical side. It sounded pretty good, so Andrew decided he'd promote this loose wheel from tambourine player—a basically insecure role—to lead vocalist.

While Doctor Dolphin experimented in the Farriss family's garage with Michael practising his mike technique and Andrew mainly on keyboards, the elder Farriss brother, guitarist Tim, nineteen, was forging ahead with his singer/songwriter/guitarist/sax playing friend Kirk Pengilly in their own band, Guinness. Named after their bass player's dog, Guinness had been playing for around six years with different line-ups, even checking out Tim's little brother Jon Farriss on drums at an early stage. He was pretty good for a nine-year-old back then but not quite there yet. The young impresario Tim was showing a talent for booking by scoring some local wedding and party gigs. One day he checked out Doctor Dolphin (who would never get out of the garage) rehearsing. He was knocked out by Andrew's keyboard chops, Garry's funky grunt on bass and Michael's voice and developing grasp on becoming a frontman. At sixteen, Jon was finally old enough to join too. The fateful merger was on.

The Farriss Brothers first appeared in public at Tim's rip-roaring twentieth birthday, 16 August 1977, at his house party in Whale Beach, northern Sydney. Tim, Andrew, Michael, Jon, Kirk and Garry agreed this was it. There would be no plan B. No turning back.

6

burning in the sun

AUSTRALIA'S NULLARBOR PLAIN is the longest, spookiest stretch: 'so flat, could well have been ocean', as Perth band The Triffids' David McComb moaned in their rather gothic live favourite 'Lonely Stretch'. (Nullarbor in Latin means 'no trees'; ipso facto The Triffids, whose music Michael loved, called their debut album *Treeless Plain*.) As you drive from the east coast to the west of an epic continent that's bigger than Europe, you better watch out. You'll be taking on a notoriously dangerous, isolated three- to four-day drive across some of the most ancient country on the planet. If you break down or have an accident, it's easy to die of thirst or exposure or just disappear in the desert before anyone passes.

In late 1977 the Farriss Brothers crossed the Nullarbor in three separate vehicles. The Farriss Brothers' move from Sydney to Perth was in solidarity with their youngest member. Jon was based in the Farriss parents' HQ in Perth and had his whole final year of high school to go before he could abscond to play drums with the boys full-time (he hoped). They were all still teenagers except Garry and Tim, who had both turned twenty a few months earlier.

It's a huge sign of dedication for a whole band to move interstate, simply because they chose to stay with a single member. Cold Chisel spent most of 1975 in Armidale, New South Wales, because their song-writing keyboard player Don Walker was doing his honours year in physics at the University of New England there, and the Farriss Brothers went to Perth in late 1977 because their drummer Jon did. This demonstrated investment of being in it for the long haul, even when it meant moving to an area out of the limelight, meant both bands' membership fidelity was excellent and they became tough as nails professionally.

According to Michael, the day after he finished high school (in late December 1977) Kirk picked him up in a bright red 1967 Holden panel van and the two of them rattled westwards with their heads teeming with dreams. Although my brother was well travelled for a seventeen-year-old, this was his first flight out of the family nest. Kell was not happy. He blamed Mother for encouraging Michael towards 'showbiz' when he should be looking for *productive* employment. Our parents had a blazing argument over the phone about it. Had Kell been living in Australia at the time, it is doubtful his elder son would have been permitted to drive the inland road to Perth in some clattletrap chasing this sketchy band thing at all.

Anyway, the band all arrived safe and sound in the end. Jon stayed at the Farriss family's place in Nedlands and tried earnestly to pass his final year, while in nearby Subiaco, the band house was a hotbed of free love, joints, booze and rehearsals, I'm not sure in what order.

Terri-ann White was helping stage events with Paradise Promotions when they picked up the newly arrived Farriss Brothers.

'The energy onstage was fabulous,' she recalled. 'I remember meeting Michael for the first time. Had no idea he was that young (one year younger than me) until recently. He was deeply charming in a very understated fashion . . . a gorgeous boy. Very attentive and interested in the world.'

Her colleague Michael Lynch met the other Michael in late 1977 or very early 1978, when the singer 'was only seventeen, at his first Perth gig fronting the Farriss Brothers'. (Lynch had just turned 22.) 'My company Paradise Promotions (in partnership with Larry Marsden and Terri-ann White) got the band all their gigs in the year they were in Perth.' Lynch dealt mainly with 'band leader' Tim Farriss, creating the Farriss Brothers' posters, ads and other promo material.

Perth is a beautiful, hot city on the Swan River with great Indian Ocean beaches abounding. But to its east and north there is desert. It may be the capital city of Western Australia—physically the largest state, taking up around one-third of the Australian land mass—but Perth's population was small back then. True, small bars and clubs were proliferating and there were also some big beer barns, although not as many as in Melbourne or Sydney.

Tim booked a run of gigs himself in Western Australia's tough, dust-slathered mining towns like Port Hedland. The macho-mad, heavy-drinking atmosphere at many of these outpost gigs (in Michael's words, 'like a rocket to another planet') left the band with lasting memories, not all of them good. Some punters thought a guy who spoke and moved like Michael did must be 'a poofter', making him a major target in the often-homophobic outback of the 1970s. A New Year's Eve show in some wild outpost he called 'one of the most horrifying experiences of my life'.

Michael kept in touch. In early 1978, he wrote to our mother reporting that he was earning about $100 a week, and missing both her and Rhett. The fact that four pairs of his jeans had been stolen from their washing line and he and the band had all been 'roughed up' more than once—'I even got punched a few times'—may have accentuated his homesickness. But he was quick to reassure our mother that they now knew how to look after themselves.

The Farriss Brothers had residencies 'at the Broadway Tavern, the George, the Kewdale and sometimes [they played] at the Orient', Lynch remembered, 'often with me, Larry or Terri-Ann on the door collecting the cover charge. There was bugger-all money after expenses but lots of free drinks—luckily bar staff never twigged that [initially] both Michael [seventeen] and drummer Jon Farriss [sixteen] were under age—and it was a bloody great year partying with our other bands and particularly these guys who went on to become INXS.

'One pool party at a mansion in Nedlands I can never forget is when everyone jumped in naked after a day and night doing everything in excess! I recall vividly when I went around to the band house late one morning that Michael was still in bed with two hot girls. He was a major chick magnet.'

The nascent punk scene was big in the late 1970s in Perth with guitar-based garage rock played by The Victims, featuring Dave Faulkner and James Baker, who would become Hoodoo Gurus down the track. Alternative music was making its mark with The Triffids forming in May 1978, along with the raw, dirty sounds of the Scientists who evolved from the Invaders. Blues band The Elks, featuring singer/actor Terry Serio, was very accomplished—a well-established drawcard throughout the Farriss Brothers' time out west.

Notably the band appeared on a big, six-band bill promoted by Paradise, that included Dave Warner's From the Suburbs and The Manikins, drawing 600 people to Pagoda Exploda at the Pagoda Ballroom.

In Perth, Tim, Michael, Andrew, Kirk, Garry and Jon rehearsed five or six days a week. They steadfastly wrote new material, replacing their well-known Bob Marley and Stones covers with their own, unknown originals. As they did, the commercial pressure to play more covers grew intense, but still they wouldn't buckle, and in the end, they had to leave.

In late 1978, as Jon (barely) graduated high school and was finally deemed old enough to move out of home, the band members prepared their exodus. Tim and Andrew invited Michael Lynch back to their parents' place. There they asked him to come to Sydney with them and become their full-time manager.

'I said no, because although I was pretty good at promoting bands I would have been a crap manager,' Lynch admitted.

Partly because of these trials by fire, the band had grown up during their WA sojourn. The six energetic youngsters had forged a tentative path and presence as an independent band able to scratch out a living from music.

Nevertheless, they were very excited to drive right back across the continent to their hometown, Australia's biggest city. Their timing was perfect. Sydney's population was growing, spreading quickly far out to the west, north and south from the inner eastern beach suburbs and city. Dozens of 'Leagues' clubs originally set up for returned soldiers filled with hundreds, even thousands of young music fans after a drink and a rage to their favourite bands. Sydney was becoming *the* boom town for rock.

Around the northern suburbs pub gigs, Tim began his New South Wales offensive. While sticking flyers under car wiper-blades one time he stuck up a conversation with Gary Morris, then manager of Midnight Oil. 'The Oils' were then forging a stronghold in the northern beaches en route to immense national popularity and eventual international fame.

Gary offered Tim a support gig, then ended up taking over management briefly. He wasn't happy with the rather daggy 'Brothers' name of the band. Briefly they became The Vegetables (as per the B-side of INXS's May 1980 first single, 'Simple Simon'/'We Are the Vegetables').

But vegetable-like they weren't. And by then there were several exciting bands using numbers and letters in their names: U2, UB40 and XTC from Britain and MC5 and the B52s from North America.

Street posters said it all to the punters, so the go was to have a name as short as possible, because then you could be huge on the poster. Midnight Oil's sound and lighting guy Colin Lee Hong suggested INXS. The band liked it, although it was set out two different ways initially: first InXs, then IN X S, then INXS.

Their parties at their Newport Beach share house were legendary, and indeed Michael's unique approach to stage, his mix of grace and jerkiness as he flung his body round, gave the impression that this was a party in action. Well, often it was. They were six incredibly handsome, sexy young men wearing some pretty unusual gear at times. They loved having partners and were in touch with their feminine sides. Kirk was heading for a real preppie look while the others often jumped into black, red and white, as they would in the *Kick* era, knowing these colours for their knock-out appeal. Long-sleeved shirts on Michael, T-shirts and simple black pants evolved into different looks every month or so. In the coming times their androgynous (some thought effeminate) lead singer would seem strange too, on the blues-based pub circuit of the capital cities.

The five of them first appeared as INXS at the Oceanview Hotel, Toukley, New South Wales, on 1 September 1979. On the second anniversary of their first gig, as the Farriss Brothers, they still had their original line-up. That wouldn't change until Michael's death.

I was visiting Australia with my family—husband Jeff, Brent and baby Erin—and the band were working so constantly that Jeff and I practically had to trail around after them to their gigs just to *see* Michael.

I'll never forget the first time I ever saw him perform with INXS. It was a little gig in the heart of Sydney—maybe the Metropole Tavern, a weeknight, I think. They played there quite a bit around this time. Jeff and I went backstage before the show, and when their dressing-room door opened a virtual marijuana mushroom-cloud enveloped us.

The place was only half full. I was standing with Michael's girl-friend of the time, a great barracker for him and INXS, Vicky Kerridge. Lights went down and Michael stepped forward and grabbed the microphone, head down, hair covering his eyes. Right on cue he looked into the audience and his voice burst forth abruptly. He sang about someone who found himself through love—their forthcoming first single 'Simple Simon'—and his connection to that audience was instant and undeniable. I was mesmerised. This creature was still my brother Michael, but so intense. He threw himself into character for that song, and with barely a breath went directly into the next one, 'Jumping'.

The inebriated down front were shaking up their beer cans then ripping back the ring-tops when Michael prowled near, showering him with rainbows of cold lager. He repaid the favour. One particularly big bloke doused him every time.

'If you don't stop doing that, I'm going to get to *like* it!' Michael yelled to a chorus of catcalls, yowls, yips and yahoos from the crowd.

INXS were all so young and fresh back then. How can I forget the feeling of euphoria back in that tiny band room backstage after the gig? Not only Michael but Tim, Jon, Andrew, Kirk and Garry, dripping with sweat but so genuinely grateful for the support. They were warm and humble, jocular and fun to be around, sharing themselves without a second thought before turning, businesslike, to pack up their own equipment—all the while making jabs at Michael who was absorbed in yakking with us.

In those lean early years I kept my eyes open for potential stage clothes for Michael too. Like Mother, he was a great clothes horse and carried off all kinds of unusual looks, always understanding the power of the cut, fit and flow of a fine fabric, the impact of colour blocks and simple lines. I knew he'd spotted a pair of fantastic, military-style, lace-up boots in a shop window he'd been yearning to wear onstage. He just couldn't afford to buy them. As a reward for his hard work and his manifesting of brave stage magic, I handed him an envelope with $150 in it and with profuse thanks he immediately went out and bought them. They were a perfect fit.

• • •

INXS continued to support Midnight Oil and other local bands like Cold Chisel, The Angels and Flowers (soon to become Icehouse), gathering an enthusiastic following and experimenting with their image and sound. In the more individualistic climate on the east coast, they were free to express themselves in their own powerful way. They were tight, high energy and musically intense. Their frontman/singer was extraordinary and the songs were unique and well made, with a wide palette of instrumentation to colour them and a rhythm section evolving into something critically intense, immediately recognisable. Having scored the right support spots, they instantly grabbed attention.

They were not really into all of Gary Morris's management ideas though—such as being 'inaccessible' to the media. And since he was so busy managing the steady rise of Midnight Oil and their label

Powderworks on the local and international scene, he did not really have time for them. So he decided to help out both the band and a friend—Chris Murphy—by putting them together.

Wendy Murphy Moss and I have been friends since I began taking my family to Australia on a regular basis in early 1980. In late 1979, Wendy was eight months pregnant with Stevey, their first child, a little girl, but insisted on going with her husband to see INXS.

'We were immediately impressed,' she told me. 'Michael was shy, but he still had stage presence; the other five band members were excellent musicians.' Little did the Murphys know that night that this slightly awkward, eye-catching young man would within a few short weeks be so embraced by them that he'd become their baby's godfather.

Christopher Mark Murphy, now referred to as C.M. Murphy, had been working alongside his mother in the family's booking agency MMA—Mark Murphy and Associates—since the age of seventeen, after his father suffered a fatal heart attack in his thirties. Wendy met him when she herself began working for his mother at MMA too.

The couple were living in Windsor, around an hour's drive from Sydney (if the traffic was merciful) at this time. With Chris working day and night, Wendy was often coping alone with baby Stevey and fourteen spirited Arabian horses on a farm. Then when Chris fell asleep at the wheel one night on the way home from a gig and ran off the road, they knew things had to change. So they moved to Mosman, a modest business hub in suburban Sydney, where MMA was run from their home.

Murphy was good-looking, a little shorter than Michael (who was 5'10½", or 179 cm), and six years older, with an imposing, level stare. His thick hair was prematurely greying, which made him appear older than his 25 years. He was all about business and had a take-no-prisoners attitude when it came to protecting his interests. Chris would soon have INXS touring every little town in Australia. He proved himself to be a sharp, ambitious young manager, and in his first year in Mosman, whenever the band was in Sydney, Michael stayed with the Murphys.

This was a good time for young bands in Australia, as far as live music went. But while there was a healthy business in pubs and clubs, selling records was harder. The population for the whole of Australia in the early 1980s was about 15 million—a small market. Overseas artists were generally more valued, and the 'industry' had not yet produced the tough, experienced, daring and entrepreneurial music business managers essential for international success. 'Stranded' as the Saints called it, in those pre-internet days, cut off from the USA and Europe by sheer distance and opposing time zones, it was brutally hard for Australian recording artists to break out beyond local shores.

But Chris and the band shared an invincible ambition to succeed internationally. Chris made a plan. From 1980 to 1983, 'Murphy', as outsiders called him, spent nine of every twelve months either touring with or negotiating for the band around the globe. He had a healthy ego; he was tenacious, determined, ambitious and aggressive. There was no way he was going to take 'no' for an answer.

In early 1980 Chris played a rough demo tape of his charges to former AC/DC manager Michael Browning, who'd started up an independent label called Deluxe Records. Deluxe had signed Sydney's promising trio The Numbers and Perth's The Dugites. Chris took Michael down to check them out live in a small theatre in Wollongong, south of Sydney on the New South Wales coast. Without further ado the businessmen negotiated a five-album deal.

INXS's debut single 'Simple Simon' on Deluxe garnered some interest around the scene. Although it wasn't very well realised, the band had a fresh-sounding, punky, new-wave style personified by the fact that the A-side and its B-side 'We Are The Vegetables' came in at the very short, programmable times of 2 minutes 32 seconds and 1 minute 53 seconds.

'Simple Simon' was audaciously released in France, as well as Australia, in May 1980. The band made its television debut on *Simon Townsend's Wonder World!*, the long-running children's television show, designed to appeal to young adults as well, on the Ten Network. The show created a fabulous, raw, in-your-face little film clip for 'Simple Simon', playing up on the fact that the show's host was called Simon, of course. Andrew got into a long overcoat and wore a pork pie hat, of the kind Madness from England might do. And Michael was singing with a strange, mannered English accent then, a bit working-class like Paul Weller of The Jam, holding his knees knocking-close, his arms falling or flailing puppet-like by his sides, his long neck holding his head so high he looked like a wild horse about to shy.

'Simple Simon' made some good initial noise for the band but didn't chart anywhere. Nevertheless, INXS were happy to tour and tour and tour in their homeland (while they longed for overseas interest), mainly around the rock capitals of Melbourne and Sydney. They couldn't wait to get into the studio with an album budget to play with.

Michael also sent me some newspaper clippings, which I still have, long since yellowed. Jen Jewel Brown (then writing as Jenny Hunter Brown) was a very early fan who wrote about INXS in both *RAM* (*Rock Australia Magazine*) and *The Sunday Telegraph*, where she had a weekly rock and pop column for a year or so. In her *Sunday Tele* story she begins with this observation of Michael:

He stares quite fearlessly, slightly surly, out at the milling pub crowd. And for a moment Michael Hutchence echoes the late Jim Morrison. He clamps both palms just beneath the microphone and clenches them. He's 20, fit, a fine dancer. He swings side to side with the mike stand as axis in a mutant Austral skank. A great mat of damp curls flopping over one angry eye, he shoots out each rounded word like a rocket off a pad. Michael has reason to look fearless. He is fronting one of the brightest new bands on the horizon.

At this stage Michael used to drop into the *RAM* offices in Crown Street, Darlinghurst, unannounced and just sit slumped against the wall, kind of shyly trying to talk to its maverick editor, Anthony O'Grady, while the latter grappled with slinging another issue of his fortnightly, full-colour, national hit music paper together. Michael became a regular fixture for a while, showing a fascination with how the nation's then leading young adult rock and pop paper, which also ran articles from *New Musical Express* and *Melody Maker*, ticked.

In the July 1980 issue of the Australian rock rag *Roadrunner*, another young rock writer called Elly McDonald wrote a piece on INXS. She'd later write a cover story on them for *RAM*. In 2014 she wrote on her blog, in remembrance of Michael: 'a sweet, rather whimsical boy with cosmos-encompassing curiosity.' He reminded her of a character from the Moomin books by Tove Jansson. 'Snufkin was a wanderer,' she wrote, 'seeking spring and summer meadows . . . a provocateur, baiting authority and despising convention.' Michael, barely through his teens, was dressed 'like a fan of French new wave cinema, in a Breton fisherman's long-sleeved T-shirt with horizontal stripes. He told me he was fascinated by post-War bohemianism, especially the literary and artistic bohemianism of the '50s and early '60s.'

Since his father, Kell, had been a textiles trader in Hong Kong, 'Michael loved colour and texture and trends, so he loved textiles', Elly continued. 'And he loved Hong Kong. He loved noise and close-pressed flesh and variety and change.'

Deluxe gave INXS AU$10,000 to record their debut self-titled album in a good Sydney studio, Trafalgar, at Annandale in the inner west.

The band co-produced with renowned session bass player Duncan McGuire. Duncan was a wonderful musician, a bass player with Doug Parkinson in Focus (that band's beautiful rearrangement of The Beatles' 'Dear Prudence' went to #5 on the Go-Set national charts in 1969), Leo De Castro and Friends and also Ayers Rock.

The whole band co-produced the debut LP and, although Andrew had written the lyrics for 'Simple Simon', they also shared co-writing credits on the suggestion of Chris Murphy. Such an arrangement was unusual for the time, but it was a good incentive for band harmony. After playing gigs five or six nights a week, sometimes two gigs a night, they'd head into Trafalgar and work till dawn. They released their self-titled debut album *INXS* in October 1980. This was the point when Garry Beers, whose name had always been spelled 'Garry', added the extra 'Gary' in the middle of his name. He'd been given the double name as a nickname at school, and after it was misspelled 'Garry Gary' on the debut album, he took the eccentricity as his permanent stage name.

Looking back, Michael would shrug when asked about the first album, calling it 'naive' and 'cute'. He recognised the early struggling for a sound of their own, something youthful that would evolve.

The album *INXS* included 'Just Keep Walking', a second single that made a great impression with its originality. It was their first national Top 40 entry, just scraping into the Kent Report at #38.

The track had the stabbing, automaton feel of a super-modern, too-busy industrial city. Its cut-up-style lyric and Michael and Andrew's early love of the pogo punk moves lent it extremely well to a remix-revision called 'I'm So Crazy' in 2001, by Italian house duo Par-T-One Vs INXS (categorised as 'Punk-House'), which has an intense film clip featuring punks dancing.

In 1981, INXS played almost 300 shows, crisscrossing Australia on four separate tours. Chris Murphy spaced them out so that each had a special name and poster to keep the public, record company and press interest up. There was the Stay Young tour, the Campus tour, the Tour With No Name and the Fear And Loathing tour.

Road life was less than flash in those forging days, of course. Two vans to tote six band members, two crew members and all the gear. Of course there were plenty of pretty women, fans, parties, hilarity and a certain amount of free drugs—which basically meant an ongoing supply of powerful, earthy, organic marijuana grown by mates at the tops of rainforest mountain properties and freely shared. Accommodation was the cheapest motel, three to a room. They'd take turns sleeping in the van en route to the next motel and eat whenever they could. They shared their resolve to conquer the world along with soggy hamburgers, eggs and beans, and fish and chips awash in tomato sauce.

In March 1981, INXS released a third single: a cover of the wonderful Australian hit of 1966, 'The Loved One', by Melbourne cult band The Loved Ones. INXS's stylishly rearranged version was produced by Richard Clapton, himself a fine singer and songwriter who had also been managed by Chris Murphy. Cheered by 'The Loved One' becoming a Top 20 hit, Clapton would go on to produce INXS's second album.

Underneath The Colours was a moody, artistic second album; one a young band could be proud of. The title track seemed to speak of the dangers of nationalism and war and the universality of tribes. Released in October 1981, it reached #15 on Australia's album charts. The first single was 'Stay Young' and its charming video, directed by Jim Warpole, had a homemade look. Just friends and their children dancing around the band playing on the beach. INXS enlisted everybody's help, of course. They had a great big happy friendship group to call on. Mother did the make-up and held reflectors when the sun began to go down. It was shot in Clontarf, on the beach in front of a house belonging to our parents' friends Elizabeth and Oliver Campbell, who had a daughter called Hiraani. She'd grown up childhood friends with Michael, playing on the sand, splashing and thrashing around in the Pacific. He would never forget her beautiful Hawaiian name.

Working in the studio helped define the inner dynamics of the band. Each member brought creative excellence and special musical qualities to the test. Andrew took charge, becoming very specific about musical arrangements, while Michael's poetry was emerging into commentary on society and relationships.

Michael made a call to me in America to ask if Chris Murphy could stay with Jeff and me while he was in Los Angeles hunting for an American record deal for INXS. Success was of course a long road in the USA, and Chris came back more than once. He brought INXS T-shirts and posters that I handed out to my childrens' babysitters. I drove him to his appointments and often accompanied him to business dinners. There was a real feeling of teamwork. So many of us were dead keen to see the boys make it.

On those early visits, Chris kept us up on the latest news of the band. He would grill me about Michael, what made him 'tick'. He told me that women really loved Michael, that he had a strange, charismatic power source that he was only half aware of at this stage.

Nevertheless, Michael was evolving rapidly into a confident frontman, a guy who could find just the right thing to say to an audience. The best thing about it was that he did it just by letting his true self out of the box.

He was still reading enthusiastically and writing down streams of lyrics. Poetic fragments often ran through his consciousness. His confidence kept building and building, but it takes a lot to walk out in front of an audience. The person at the microphone carries the load. Michael just needed time and experience—and the ability to find his calm centre and bring it to each show.

It was difficult to find a quiet place on the road, but Michael began with breathing exercises: deep breathing in a quiet place, even if that meant sitting alone in the van. You can see from even early videos of the band that he seemed to exude a Zen-like confidence. Sure as hell he *owned* that camera. He seemed to know instinctively that he could contact people directly through that medium—that beating hearts and willing minds were waiting to play with his own on the other side of the glass.

He told me about the visualisation techniques he used, so he didn't get stressed out performing.

'The afternoon of a performance, I close my eyes and play it in my head—just as I want it to go,' he told me. 'I see the crowd and build them to a crescendo.' As far as I know he used this technique for many years. In the latter years, as his pressures increased, he came to depend on other, more dangerous crutches.

7

the one thing

SEVENTEEN-YEAR-OLD MICHELE BENNETT was in Bombay Rock in Melbourne one night in 1980, watching the up-and-coming Models shake the place up, when Michael spotted her.

Bombay Rock had a kind of grungy, understated atmosphere, great sound and the best live bands. The low-slung brick ex-warehouse in Sydney Road, Brunswick, had an affinity for brash, underground music and was rough at times. Some of its regulars would end up famous and dead for gangland-related reasons, like Alphonse 'the Black Prince' Gangitano.

Michele was in her final year of high school then, still living at home with her parents. She hadn't really bothered with boyfriends up till that point, hadn't found anyone who caught her interest. She was technically too young to drink, but not too young to soak up some inspirational alternative sounds. Michael was there with INXS's tour manager Gary Grant. As he surreptitiously watched this gorgeous brunette swaying to

68

the band, flashing a huge smile now and then at her friends, he knew he couldn't stay away. She felt watched, and vaguely recognised him. But then she was leaving; they barely spoke and that first, semi-felt connection was broken.

One night some months later, in 1981, with great serendipity (or powers of judgement) they found themselves both at the popular rock club Martinis on the corner of Rathdowne and Neill streets in Carlton. INXS was on the bill with a couple of other bands; when Michael jumped offstage after their set, he came over to say hi.

Now many young men have a habit of talking about themselves with a kind of forced confidence. Michael was not like that at all. He was genuinely interested in what a woman had to say. Within minutes he found out that Michele was studying Mandarin, which gave them common ground, although Michael only knew a few words in the language (the most common dialect in Hong Kong was Cantonese). He was based in Sydney, of course, at this time, with his first live-in girlfriend, Vicky.

Then on crossing crowded Toorak Road in South Yarra some time later he and Michele ran into each other yet again. She was at university now and working at a beauty salon nearby a couple of days a week. Michael might have been staying at Macy's (Her Majesty's Hotel) across the road from there. Perhaps it was when INXS played Macy's on 15 April 1981. As they talked, Michael felt an electric, spiritual connection. It went way beyond physical attraction, although there was plenty of that. He invited her to the INXS show that night.

It took some time before they got involved. In the meantime, she started dating Greg Perano, the percussionist from Hunters & Collectors.

Michael was reported as asking someone he knew who spoke the language, 'How do you say "I love you" in Cantonese?'

Many, many phone calls later, Michele moved to Sydney to be with him. And that was that. Still their phone calls would flood on, because even though they were now living together, INXS played and toured around so endlessly that they were often torn apart. Michael would call from different towns and cities, wanting to wind down and reconnect after a gig. One of the many things they shared was an abiding love of literature; so Michele would reach for whatever book she had on her bedside table and read to her restless man, often till he fell unconscious. Even when, after six years of living together, they eventually separated as partners, she showed him this lifelong kindness. They would always be close friends.

It's funny, but their relationship reminds me of that of the principal characters in J.M. Barrie's 1911 novel *Peter and Wendy*. In the following passage, Peter Pan, the boy who never grew up, has just flown in the Darling children's bedroom window in Bloomsbury. He is especially keen to hear Wendy, the eldest, read bedtime stories. She asks him where he 'mostly' lives now:

'With the lost boys.'

'Who are they?'

'They are the children who fall out of their perambulators when the nurse is looking the other way. If they are not claimed in seven days they are sent far away to the Neverland to defray expenses. I'm captain.'

'What fun it must be!'

'Yes,' said cunning Peter, 'but we are rather lonely. You see we have no female companionship.'

Peter manages to convince Wendy and her sleepy brothers to fly out the window with him to Neverland, mainly so she can read him and the straying lost boys the bedtime stories they crave so passionately to hear:

'Very well,' she said, 'I will do my best. Come inside at once, you naughty children; I am sure your feet are damp. And before I put you to bed I have just time to finish the story of Cinderella.'

Not long after Wendy and her brothers arrive in Neverland, they are swept up in a battle against Captain Hook and the pirates as Peter sets out to rescue a certain Native American princess—Tiger Lily.

* • * • *

Michael was beside himself with excitement when INXS scored their first overseas tour in late January 1982. It was just 'across the ditch' to neighbouring New Zealand, but they were supporting Cold Chisel, a truly great live rock'n'roll band then absolutely huge in Australia. Michael respected Chisel enormously, especially Jimmy Barnes who was not only your onstage wild man but also a very authentic, soulful singer-songwriter. And Michael also really looked up to the band's rather more serious main songwriter, Don Walker.

It was a great opportunity for INXS to win over some Kiwis in what would become a great market for them, and also to get to know the fascinating and very different members of Chisel. Their Circus Animals tour came after an eight-year, slow-burning then finally multi-platinum career. Jimmy's vodka-swilling ways, combined with some powerful chemistry between him and Chisel drummer, Steve Prestwich, led to some almighty blow-ups here and there. INXS had never had those kinds of explosive fights and they were pretty amazed.

Soon after the New Zealand tour, in early 1982 Don was set to produce a soundtrack to Scott Hicks' debut feature film, *Freedom*. He asked Michael to come in and put some lead vocals on a couple of tracks he'd written: 'Speed Kills', which would become the first-ever Michael Hutchence solo single, and 'Forest Theme'. Mark Opitz was engineer for the *Freedom* sessions (with Don producing) at Paradise Studios, a beautiful, cosy little studio in an old warehouse in a no-through-way in Woolloomooloo with everything a good band needs to make a smashing record. Paradise had been set up by singer-songwriter Billy Fields and a mate of his at 70 Judge Street, Woolloomooloo. It was a short stroll from Kings Cross, the naval docks and the famous Harry's Cafe de Wheels that sold pie floaters—meat pies in pea soup—very late at night.

'It was a very interesting session,' Mark Opitz remembered, 'because I was Michael's security blanket. He knew Don, but Don was from the famous Cold Chisel, and he was the famous Phantom, the Ghost Who Walks, as far as the public was concerned . . . this dark figure, this magic man, supposedly, behind the piano, who said nothing. Svengali up the back there, you know. So Michael came into that session nervous. I've only seen him that nervous a couple of times. Once, it was me, him and Ray Charles. And also with Don Walker.'

'Speed Kills' is a drag-racing-style rocker. Well, Michael Hutchence, have you ever wanted to sing with Cold Chisel? Now's your chance! Cold Chisel's Steve Prestwich on drums and Phil Small on bass throw down the gauntlet. '*Speed kiiiilllls!*' Michael opens in a chilling, full-throated cry. It's a wild romp with a scorching lead guitar from Chisel's Ian Moss.

Very low in the mix with Michael on 'Speed Kills' is a female vocalist trading lines with him. First listed as Quito Ray, then on the later reissue of *Freedom* as Jenny Hunter Brown, it's my co-writer Jen. She was helping to organise the sessions and ended up getting roped into singing on some tracks.

The second piece Michael was asked to tackle for *Freedom* was 'Forest Theme', a slow, slightly Spanish-sounding piece that he put a very gentle spoken-word vocal on.

'And Michael wasn't really confident about what to do,' remembered Mark Opitz. 'He just did what he was told, and didn't really understand the tracks, or how it was all going. Because Don wasn't the most effusive speaker, in the studio. Just "do this", or just "try that". And it's all in here'—Mark pointed at his temple—'rather than communicated. No one sat down and got into big creative confabs about, "oh, let's do this, do that"; it was always come in and do your job.

'And so it was a bit more up to me,' Mark said, 'to do more of the talking, talking, talking . . . That is the way it was done. Michael had no idea about the end sound of the whole thing. None of us did, I think. But yeah, that was his first single, I guess, in that aspect. So he was nervous.'

No big hits for Michael or Don came from it but *Freedom* remains a very widely respected rock soundtrack, and one of the most confidently realised Australian soundtracks of all time. It was remastered and reissued in 1996. The film's director, Scott Hicks, went on to direct topnotch movies like *Shine*, which won an Oscar for Best Actor for Geoffrey Rush in 1997, and *Snow Falling on Cedars* (1999).

The *Freedom* soundtrack experience would impact on Michael's career in more ways than one.

Now INXS followed some directions that had already been set in motion. By 1982, the well-liked and capable Gary Grant had gone from their tour manager to Chris Murphy's business partner. Chris with Michael Browning at Deluxe had been trying hard to break them in the USA, without any luck. Now the band felt so strongly about the hit potential for Michael and Andrew's new song 'The One Thing' that they decided to finance it themselves.

Michael had had good vibes from Mark Opitz in their *Freedom* soundtrack interactions at Paradise. He had a track record INXS respected, having produced *East*, *Swingshift* and *Circus Animals* for

Cold Chisel, engineered *Let There Be Rock* and *Powerage* for AC/DC alongside producers Vanda and Young, and been the primary producer-engineer behind The Angels' output. He had produced The Reels, and the Divinyls' mini-album *Music From Monkey Grip*, featuring their debut single 'Boys In Town', which had smashed up the charts like Godzilla in late 1981, as Divinyls were then doing live, and got to #8.

Mark was versatile and patient, efficient and hard-working. He was an engineer-producer from the ground up—a real sound hound. There was nowhere else on earth Mark would rather be than in a recording studio hunting sounds and he put in some crazy hours doing that behind those soundproof doors. His records reflected the live-sounding best of the acts he produced rather than his own style.

Interestingly, just as INXS had signed with Deluxe, WEA (Warner Electra and Atlantic) Records had appointed Mark Opitz as A&R manager and he'd turned up at a gig in Paddington in Sydney to sign the band his then girlfriend had raved about as 'Inks'—and been pipped at the post by Browning's label. So INXS knew Mark was already a fan when they went into Paradise Studios to record with him. They also knew he'd produced *East* in Paradise, and that album had great radio sounds and gone gangbusters for Chisel as well as doing them proud with its authentic approach.

'"The One Thing" worked out really, really, really well,' remembered Mark. 'They'd given me a choice of three songs to record: "Black And White", "Johnson's Aeroplane" or "The One Thing". I said they're all great, but "The One Thing" is going to get there first. It's going to be much more identifiable and accessible. And I rearranged "The One Thing". Between every verse and chorus there'd be this quirky bit which would come out of nowhere. So I just looked at the song, took all those bits out and put it all back together again, took it over to rehearsal and said, "Okay, now we're going to *build* this song. Not just do it flat out like you were doing it. This is going to come in here; this is going to come in here. The chorus is going to get stronger here and the next chorus is going to be stronger, until we get a really blown-out chorus.

"'And we're going to get rid of the quirky bits, because they're acting like sea anchors, holding the feel up." In "The One Thing", it was very much about build the thing up, you know, and use the saxophone as your weapon. So they trusted me to do that, and "The One Thing" worked.'

At a meeting with WEA Records Australia, Chris played 'The One Thing'. WEA was still chasing INXS, now with a new A&R manager, Gibson Kemp. They offered Chris a deal with the standard international rights sewn in. Holding his nerve like the major poker player he can be, Chris held out. He needed WEA to commit that their international head companies would either sign on to support and promote the band internationally or leave these territories free. To say this was not the standard Australian record deal in those days is an understatement.

Gibson, incidentally, was the Liverpudlian who replaced Ringo Starr on drums in Rory Storm and the Hurricanes in 1962, when Ringo joined The Beatles.

Anyway, Gibson was sold on INXS and their international potential. He came back with an offer to sign the band for the territories of Australia, New Zealand, Japan and South East Asia only to WEA Australia. Polygram, who was showing interest, could then sign them for Europe and the UK, while Atco Records (a subsidiary of Atlantic) would sign them for North America—theoretically.

But INXS sounded so unlike everything else selling at that time that the people who counted at Atco were hesitant. Chris invited Atco president Reen Nalli out to Australia. INXS did what INXS did live, and she and Chris had drawn up battle plans to overpower North America by morning.

In a stroke of good timing, MTV, the original 'Music Television' cable channel, launched on 1 August 1981. MTV and super-visual INXS were made for each other.

One night Chris Murphy called my husband, Jeff Bushelman, who was a renowned Hollywood editor, to discuss making a video for 'The One Thing'. The concept of INXS and some beautiful women hand-feeding each other was Jeff's. He put together a detailed treatment and storyboard, intercutting close-up performances from Michael, Tim, Kirk, Garry, Andrew and Jon. He even threw in a kitten—well, it was stalking on the table and stole some close-ups.

Jeff was co-owner of Burbank Editorial and Sound studios, a well-respected film and sound editing business in Hollywood. Working for director George Miller's company Kennedy Miller, he'd dubbed the first *Mad Max* (1979) movie with 'American-speak' for its release in the USA. The American ear at that time was not used to Australian slang or accents, so the distributors requested changes. Jeff worked hard to keep the US version as close as possible to the original—it would be a shocker if this adaption stood out. George Miller and his producer, the late Byron Kennedy (who I've since found out was a distant cousin), spent time at our studio, of course, and at the house, where they called ahead for my special chilli.

I couriered Jeff's concept and handwritten notes on 'The One Thing' clip to Australia and shortly afterwards INXS filmed it. 'The One Thing' had a more polished look than what had been done before for INXS, mainly because—thanks to Michael's family and their connections—professionals worked on it for free. Michael asked the assistant director from our mother's soap, *The Young Doctors*, to direct. (That happened to be Peter Clifton, who had written and co-directed the 1976 Led Zeppelin documentary, *The Song Remains the Same*.) He bought new clothes and set them off with a flat-brimmed black Spanish Cordobés hat he borrowed from Mother. She did the make-up and talked a couple of the actresses from her soap into working for nothing, including Karen Pini, *another* former Miss Australia who was a friend of our family. Michael's arrival, hand-in-hand with Michele, on the set, was Mother's first introduction to her (she was most favourably impressed).

When we arrived in Sydney for our family holiday, hard-working Jeff went straight to work re-editing 'The One Thing'. He felt the rough cut didn't take advantage of Michael's appeal, so he made a few well-placed edits.

Big, generous smiles. Thick waves of burnished hair rampaging into their brown eyes. Serious sides. And a huge sense of adventure. Michael and Michele were very much alike. It was his gentle side that drew her, she said. And how he was bright, empathic and funny. He loathed realising he'd hurt someone, just hated that. On the other hand, he could be steely and determined. He expected a lot from people, especially himself.

They were so into each other. They shared a place for a while with singer-songwriter Jenny Morris, who would later tour with INXS, and another lifelong friend, Nick Conroy. None of them were making much money. Things were a bit unpredictable, but they were great times all the same, a bit of a Camelot period.

Being with Michael, of course, brought with it some special challenges. He didn't have a driver's licence (possibly *ever*) but nevertheless adored cars. His taste was for European classics that, despite their stylish lines and sexy leather upholstery, were reliably unreliable. His car of the day would likely give up the ghost en route to or from a gig and Michael would have to abandon it by the roadside (with luck it would make it that far) and shout at passing taxis until one stopped. The road crew would go by the next day and get his latest vehicle operational again. This became something of a running joke in the INXS office.

Michael once bought an old Renault from John Polson, director of Australia's first indie short film festival Tropfest.

'We went on a weekend away once in it,' Michele recalled, 'and you know how much they toured—they never had time to go away. But we had the weekend and Michael was getting his pay, about one hundred and fifty or whatever, and we were going to stay in a hotel near the Jenolan Caves.' The area is in high, rangy bushland west of the Blue Mountains in New South Wales.

'And the first thing that happened was he didn't get his pay. He just didn't make the connection at the office and we had problems paying for hotels along the way. He didn't have credit cards back then. I only had some obscure credit cards and, as I remember, they only accepted cards or cash, and whatever they accepted we didn't have.

'So we'd go to different hotels and we'd have to keep moving on because we couldn't find anywhere that would take us and by this stage it was getting really late. We then found the only one in Katoomba that would accept us had only single beds at different levels and a window which was boarded up. It was horrible and so we left there and began making our way over to this place called Mount Victoria and on the way fog set in and you couldn't see the road ahead.

'I don't know what possessed us to do this, but I got out of the car and walked in front of the headlights so at least Michael had a sense of distance to see where the edge of the road was. I don't know why we didn't just pull over and give up because that's how low the visibility was. I did that for an eternity until the fog lifted. We got to this motel where the previous place had called ahead because they could take the card we had. There were no more misadventures until we took off the next day and we were heading down the mountain to the Jenolan Caves and the fanbelt broke on the Renault.

'So we pulled over,' Michele continued, 'and Michael was trying to fix it. A family pulled up and it was a carload of rednecks and for some reason Michael decided that he could take care of it and thanked them and said it was okay. So they drove off. And he did fix it and we took off again. And we passed the family and they passed us and we again passed them and then a tyre blew. And the same family pulled over again and offered to give us a lift to a service station.

'It was truly like *Deliverance*. No kidding. It was two brothers and a woman and three kids in the back with the two of us squished in.'

Michele and Michael got dropped at Lithgow by the *Deliverance* family and then had to hitchhike back to the stranded Renault with the replacement tyre.

'The only person who stopped for us,' Michele said, 'was a guy in a Monaro who looked like a Hells Angel and he just pulled over and said, "Do you want a lift somewhere?" And we hesitantly said, "Yeah, we need to get back to our car." He looked slightly dodgy.'

Michael jumped in the front and Michele got in the back where she noticed for the first time that two kids were crouching down silently in the foot-well beside her, behind the seats.

'They weren't properly clothed. One had a nappy on and the other had shorts on. I tapped Michael and he looked back and said, "Who are these children?" The guy said, "Oh I've just got issues with the missus and just taking the kids for a bit of an unsupervised weekend— quality time."

'I think he only picked us up because he recognised Michael— because why else would you compromise yourself?

'And it was like that little kid in *Mad Max* [the wordless Feral Kid in *Mad Max 2: The Road Warrior*, played by Emil Minty]—it was like having two of them in the back and they wouldn't sit on the seat, they had obviously been told to sit out of sight.'

Mr Monaro drove Michael and Michele back to the Renault where they replaced the tyre. Continuing on to Jenolan Caves, they were nego- tiating a really winding section of road when the fanbelt went again.

'This time a different family pulled over,' Michele said. 'It was a husband and wife and three teenagers in the back. He was a tradie and we didn't see the kids in the back because it was a panel van and the guy came out and he said, "Can I give you a hand?" By this stage I said, *over* Michael, "*Yes, you can*," because it was just a whole day of breakdowns ... alternating between the tyre and the fanbelt. Meanwhile all the time there was this one hillbilly family that kept passing us and wanting to help us and we just didn't get the right vibe so would never take up the offer, but *this* guy seemed like a straight-up tradie who knew what he was doing and I said, "Yes, please." And the wife was saying, "Ah, he can fix anything; he'll have you back on the road in no time."

'So he had a look at it, and he said, "Well, you do need a certain part but I'll see what I can cobble together," and he's under the bonnet fixing things and all of a sudden we hear this screaming and banging from the back of the car. The wife goes back yelling to the back of the car to the kids to shut up. You know, they had recognised Michael and were just going berserk and simultaneously we hear yelling from under the bonnet of the car and this guy has reached over something and he's got one of those metal spandex watches. And he's leaned over and it's melted the spandex together and his skin's got stuck in between and it's melted into his arm.

'And his wife starts yelling at him, "What've ya done?" And he's just hopping around trying to man up and not show he's in that much pain and she's going, "Oh, pull ya head in, it'll be fine." She looks at us like, he's fine! And we were horrified because it was quite a bad burn and meanwhile the girls had busted out of the van and just, you know, besieged Michael and the mother yelled back at them, "*Get back in the car!*" And she said to the husband, "You're fine; just fix it—fix the bloody thing."

'It was just the most surreal thing,' Michele continued. 'He fixed it. We didn't have money or anything, but we got their names and organised tickets for them for the next show.

'We finally got to this beautiful hotel and Michael had a joint with him and he decided he was going to have it after we booked in. I never did any because it makes me so paranoid. But this must have been pretty strong . . . We got down to the dining area—a formal one, quite a big room, everyone was dressed up. And we'd been changing tyres and fanbelts and hitchhiking and at any rate didn't have any formal clothes to dress up in. So at the door we already looked like we were completely out of place and then you had to walk across this hall to get to the dining area.

'Michael suddenly froze and said he couldn't do it,' she laughed. 'He couldn't walk across and I said, "Look, it's okay it's just—we're not dressed up, but it doesn't matter." And he said, "No, I can't do it. I just can't do it." I said, "No big deal—you've looked out of place before." He said, "It's not that, it's just walking all the way over there."

'And I realised I'd never seen him like that. Gone, he was. So I sat outside with him and tried to talk him down, and I was starving and they didn't do room service. So I had to walk him around the edge of the room, as if people weren't noticing us hugging the walls, to get to the seat—and he thought he would be really noticeable if he crossed the room! Then I had to translate for him. He couldn't talk to anyone so I had to speak for him to order the food—it was just . . .' She breaks up into helpless laughter. Hearing a story like this from Michele, it just makes me feel so grateful that Michael had her friendship and support. In my mind she was indeed Michael's 'one thing'.

•   •   •

'The One Thing' single was a big gear-changer for INXS too.

In 1983 they played a well-received set at the first Narara Music Festival in the New South Wales countryside along with the Church, Cold Chisel and The Angels on a huge, three-day bill in the sizzling heat of late January. In February there was an important anti-nuclear concert called Stop The Drop, with Midnight Oil, Men At Work, INXS and others packing out Melbourne's Sidney Myer Music Bowl.

Then they took off on their very first tour of North America. That year—1983—was such a golden year for the band in the USA. Their first show on US soil was in San Diego, California, on 25 March.

Wendy Murphy accompanied Chris for the first time and they stayed with Jeff and me while the band lodged at a so-so hotel a few miles away in Hollywood. Wendy and I were their only 'fans' at first but within days, after they joined Adam Ant and with 'The One Thing' on high rotation on MTV, it exploded: the girls went nuts over Michael. I remember it fondly as a crazy time for them. The support band from Australia was getting all the attention.

Chris left the band in the capable hands of Gary Grant as he and Wendy took a much-needed European break, while the band spent the rest of March and all of April and May winning hearts stateside: touring with Adam Ant; here and there supporting The Kinks and Stray Cats. On 26 May they headlined at The Ritz in New York and two days later slayed a big crowd at the gigantic US Festival in San Bernardino, California.

Jeff and I went along that day, and after returning from the festival with INXS and Gary Grant, we sat around my little 26-inch television in our den in Burbank, sharing pizzas and Jeff's famous margaritas, and turned on the news. We were all agog. Ten outfits played that Saturday, headlined by The Clash. Yet all the major networks were featuring the new little wet-behind-the-ears INXS from Australia.

8

the new world

AFTER WRAPPING UP the recording of their fourth album, *The Swing*, with Nick Launay producing, in late 1983 INXS could pop the champagne corks to toast 'Original Sin' becoming their first-ever #1— in Australia, fittingly. They were itching to make it overseas and the stars had aligned. Hundreds of thousands of dollars in international advances, including from their new music publisher MCA/Gilbey, buoyed the risk of this expensive first world tour.

INXS had already played overseas, of course, but their major odyssey beyond Australia was about to begin in earnest. It was as though Michael's 'mariners', as Tennyson wrote in the voice of Ulysses (1842), were 'pushing off' shore with him. The brothers Tim, Andrew and Jon Farriss, with Kirk Pengilly and Garry Beers, were like the 'Souls that have toiled, and wrought, and thought with me . . . The long day wanes: the slow moon climbs: the deep / Moans round with many voices. Come, my friends, / 'Tis not too late to seek a newer world.'

To send the mood stratospheric, 'Original Sin' would soon go to #1 in France too and make a big impact internationally. *The Swing*, a very fine album with finesse and variety that still makes good listening today, topped Australian charts for five weeks, delivering a string of singles that would pepper INXS set lists for the rest of their career. All of them: 'Burn For You', 'Dancing On The Jetty', 'I Send A Message' and of course (in my humble opinion) one of the greatest singles ever recorded, 'Original Sin', were co-written by A. Farriss and M. Hutchence, who were proving they had something pretty rarefied and true going on as co-writers.

• • •

On a more sobering level for me personally, Jeff and I went our separate ways. Fortunately he was okay about letting me take Erin, then six, to Sydney for a few months. Brent, who was now twelve, was at a critical point of his schooling and baseball commitments and chose to stay with his father in California. I could certainly understand that. Mother had just opened her latest business, the Advanced Make-up Academy, in a small, low-rise building in Kirribilli, which also held an office for Peter Garrett, of Midnight Oil. It was close to where Michael and Michele lived, in the penthouse of a block of flats owned by INXS with Chris and Wendy Murphy.

While we were there I taught some classes at the Academy as a visiting lecturer and tutor, Erin attended Neutral Bay Primary and we all hung out. Staying in close contact with our international ones was and is as natural as breathing to our family. Erin was able to develop important kinship ties, including with her beloved Uncle Michael, who adored and respected her right back.

When we got back to California I found a job that wouldn't keep me away from my little daughter for the hours that movie set make-up work demanded. And when I joined Continental Airlines in international reservations, happily the bonus was I could also sometimes jet off gratis to visit Michael on the road while Erin stayed with her dad.

Those first American tour dates sure left me with some of the sweetest and most precious memories of Michael I have. Although we were a dozen years apart in age, it didn't matter. We'd stay up till the threat of dawn, musing about anything and everything like teenagers on a sleepover. Sometimes I'd sew up a hem that had come loose on his stage shirt or iron away while we exchanged updates on our busy lives. We went to the cinema together and shopped for clothes. He had such a knack of picking things out, or having them made, that melded the hip with the classical. He made it all look like he'd thrown it together that morning—and sometimes he had. Michael wore clothes. They never wore him. His various 'looks' have aged so well. Dressing up was just another way he knew to entertain.

On this tour INXS added an extra singer-guitarist, someone who was already a friend and was being also managed by Chris Murphy at the time. Since Jenny Morris put backing vocals on *The Swing*—which became, in Australia, INXS's first #1 album—that made perfect sense. Jenny was already a smart and successful artist in her own right, both in her homeland New Zealand and then in Australia. Her clear, beautifully pitched and quite loud voice blended beautifully with INXS's chiming backing vocals, dominated by Kirk, and Michael's lead. The sight of her wielding an electric guitar on rhythm in the back line, all confidence with her black bouffant and big silver hoop earrings, added a new dimension and filled out the sound for bigger venues.

I think Michael quite enjoyed having someone so experienced at fronting an act there to reassure and back him. Jenny, on the other hand, got to tour overseas—with such a hot band who were also people she knew and respected. She and Michael had a lot of fun joining forces on 'Jackson', the cheeky duet that Nancy Sinatra and Lee Hazlewood—and also Johnny Cash and June Carter—used to do. The two sometime-flatmates recorded it as Michael's choice of a bonus track on *Dekadance*, the 1984 seven-track Australian cassette of remixes from *The Swing*. Not surprisingly, it made it into the country charts and was a live favourite. (Just to confuse everyone—I can't see any other reason for them to do this—INXS had put out a previous release called *Dekadance*, in the USA, in 1983. The first *Dekadance* was an EP of four remixed tracks from *Shabooh Shoobah*, available on 12-inch vinyl and cassette.)

In 1984 the band toured solidly through Australia, the USA, Canada, Europe, Guam and Japan—the latter two territories quite radical bookings for an Australian act. These adventurous incursions were another way INXS led the field. It certainly spread the seeds of their popularity to the four winds.

•

Christmas 1984 had seen the release of the Ethiopian famine fund-raising hit single 'Do They Know It's Christmas', by Band Aid, a group of British and Irish stars hastily thrown together by Midge Ure of Ultravox and Bob Geldof of The Boomtown Rats. The single was produced by Ure.

Inspired by this, an Australian furniture manufacturer called Bill Gordon (with major assistance from Zev Eizik of Australian Concert Entertainment, aka ACE) set up a day-long telethon concert to be broad-cast on television from Melbourne's Sidney Myer Music Bowl in January 1985. This, the first of the major Ethiopian fundraising concerts and the forerunner of Live Aid, was billed as the East Africa Tragedy (EAT) Appeal Concert. Midge Ure was invited to head the televised perfor-mances, with live satellite crosses made to stars from Band Aid.

Michael and Andrew represented INXS as many individual stars from various Australian groups, including Split Enz, Midnight Oil,

Divinyls and many more, combined to raise $1 million to hand to the Red Cross. Michael sang the first verse of the Rolling Stones' 'Gimme Shelter' as a massive Aussie super-group converged to cover the stage for the final song.

INXS toured Australia heavily after that, breaking to begin recording *Listen Like Thieves* in Rhinoceros in Sydney, the swanky hang-out studios with the great vibes and glorious sounds that seemed so much like home they bought into them. This was their first collaboration with producer Chris Thomas, the high-standards Englishman who had crafted unforgettable hits for the Sex Pistols (like 'Anarchy In The UK'), Roxy Music ('Love Is The Drug') and the Pretenders ('Brass In Pocket') among others, and would do so for INXS too. It's not too much to say that with his extraordinary history, Thomas is probably the world's greatest record producer. And he wouldn't have come cheap.

Meanwhile, Bill Gordon had followed up the successful East Africa Tragedy Appeal Concert in January with a visit to London in April 1985, to pitch to Ure and Geldof the idea of a UK Band Aid artists' concert, with an international satellite hook-up to a similar Australian concert for Ethiopia's famine-affected millions. Eventually this concept spread to encompass America and other nations, becoming the most complex and exciting live rock event ever coordinated. Gordon sold his furniture business to fund and manage the Australian end, assisted by music manager Brian de Courcy, with the cooperation of Geldof and the Band Aid Trust. It was all coming together, and the work and performances donated all around the world would soon show that the much-maligned music business was not all about hairspray and shifting units. Music could make a global difference in a way nothing had before.

In May, while the *Listen Like Thieves* recording continued, INXS appeared at the 1984 Countdown Awards, then Australia's biggest music awards. They walked away with seven wins including Best Album (*The Swing*), Most Popular Group, Most Popular Male Performer

(Michael), Best Songwriters (Michael and Andrew) and Most Outstanding Achievement. They shared Best Video ('Burn For You') with Mental As Anything ('Apocalypso') and also won Best Group Performance in a Video—again, for 'Burn For You'—the first in a long line of definitive INXS videos to be directed by Richard Lowenstein. INXS would continue to dominate Australian music awards for the next five years while gathering many others internationally.

The first day of Live Aid, 13 July 1985, featured performances at Wembley Stadium in London and John F. Kennedy Stadium in Philadelphia. Separately, INXS and sixteen other acts played in the charity concert billed as Oz for Africa; due to the time difference, the Australian concert began twelve hours before the Wembley show. The Australian section, four hours of concert/telethon, raised AU$10 million for the International Disaster Emergency Committee in Australia. INXS, Men At Work and Little River Band were the featured Australian bands integrated into the worldwide-televised concert. They played at the Sydney Entertainment Centre, with INXS headlining. Excited, I caught Michael's performance from my Studio City apartment in California. All up, Live Aid was a colossal charity event, watched by an estimated 1.9 billion people.

Listen Like Thieves had its final mix in London in August and INXS began a world tour the same month, from Australia. They visited Buenos Aires, Argentina, for a killer performance at the Rock & Pop Festival at Sarsfield Stadium in October to the biggest crowd they'd ever played to live: a reported 100,000 people. Appearing on the South American continent was completely radical for an Australian act in 1985, but it was a grand success. Chris Murphy was so proud of INXS and his team's efforts over that achievement he spread the word far and wide.

There were always unpredictable aspects to visiting unknown countries though. Michael's close friend Richard Lowenstein is a man whose dedication and passion for film-making is infectious. A conversation with him is intense as he'll want every detail of your story, much like Michael. He often visited Michael on tour and recalled one flight between South American countries—he wasn't sure of the year, or tour, but at this stage INXS travelled so much they'd rented their own private jet. Their plane landed and customs officers boarded for an inspection.

'Michael's still got a bag of cocaine,' Richard said, 'and he does the whole sneezing into it thing. He's like covered in cocaine, and the customs officers come on, and they sort of look at him and they just nod and walk off.' The guys were terrified that they would all be arrested and thrown into cells but nothing came of it.

The band always did a lot of benefits, and Rock Night For Greenpeace in Rotterdam, in the Netherlands, followed the Argentinian festival.

An unusual charity event would happen soon afterwards.

For what's colloquially known as Rocking the Royals, INXS were honoured in November 1985 with a rare invite to perform at a Royal Command Performance charity show in the Melbourne Concert Hall (now Hamer Hall) at the Victorian Arts Centre. The date coincided with the 150th anniversary of the state of Victoria and the International Year of Youth.

TRH the Prince and Princess of Wales, Charles and Diana, had the box seats. Molly Meldrum 'compered' in his own inimitable way, very much charming the bemused couple, while Models, I'm Talking and Kids in the Kitchen were also on the bill. Outside the Arts Centre on St Kilda Road, the tens of thousands who couldn't buy tickets thronged to watch on gigantic screens.

Mother was thrilled to be invited and so proud. Her seat was just behind the royal couple so she was able to watch 24-year-old Diana, mother to William, who wasn't quite two, and Harry, just a few weeks old, 'unabashedly rocking around in her seat' to her son's band. Michael himself looked unusually overawed. At one stage he scanned the venue almost nervously as he sang. No doubt that was one of the rare times he might have wished he could have actually *seen* Charles and Diana in the audience, so he could have delivered the songs directly to them. If he wasn't so completely myopic, that might have been possible. In his private life Michael wore glasses. He was extremely short-sighted and although he had taken unintentional dives off the end of the stage in the early years, he still refused to wear contact lenses onstage. He tried it once and found that seeing past the front row meant *far* too much distracting detail; he preferred his natural, more impressionist view of the audience.

Backstage later the band were introduced to the royals. After that, Michael and Diana remained 'friendly acquaintances' until her death, just three months prior to Michael's.

Charity work notwithstanding, Michael's bank account was bulging. The band was too successful, apparently. INXS used the 10BA tax program, designed to encourage investment in Australia films, to write off up to 150 per cent of what they expected would be their lost investment in a new Australian film. Alas, in 1985 INXS couldn't fail if they tried. They chose *Crocodile Dundee*—the second-highest grossing movie in the world the next year, to invest in. They had a track in it too, called 'Different World', which was also the B-side of the single 'Listen Like Thieves', but didn't end up on the actual *Crocodile Dundee* soundtrack record, just in the film.

After Rocking the Royals, INXS headed back to the West Coast of the USA to headline a run of sold-out shows, ending up in New York for more of the same. They'd improved out of sight, even in the last year. What had been a take-note bunch of youths had become a first-rate arts event.

Despite INXS's raised brio, 1985 was a stress test for Michael and Michele's relationship. Sometimes Michael must have rued what he'd wished for—that Michele would become a successful model. She was flying around on international shoots. They could rendezvous in foreign countries here and there, but as you'd guess, with INXS playing, writing and recording constantly, often their comet trails just criss-crossed in the sky. Michele missed so many of her partner's big events, although in early December, she did manage to fly from a job in Milan to meet Michael in New York to party for her 23rd birthday.

His diary gives a glimpse into the speed of his life back then. The first entry was for Tuesday, 31 December 1985. He and Michele had gone to see Sydney's traditionally orgasmic New Year's Eve fireworks off the Sydney Harbour Bridge. It's a spectacular sight, especially if you're lucky enough to be on a boat, as they were. That year Sydney synchronised the pyrotechnic display to INXS's music.

Two days later, Michael noted that his holidays had ended. They'd been fun, but too short, and this was so hard for him and Michele, he wrote.

The following day INXS flew to one of the hottest places on earth, outback northern South Australia, to film 'Kiss The Dirt (Falling Down The Mountain)' over three days. On the chalk-white salt flats of Lake Eyre and in the spiralling red dust of opal-mining town Coober Pedy, they kicked up dust and strutted in the cruel blaze of the inland summer air. The clip, directed by Alex Proyas, just looks amazing, with Michael's expressive moves filling whole frames, but gee they must have suffered for it. Great clouds of red and salt dust are blown over them and bonfires lit behind them. Hard work for a beautiful result, so Australian. After their flight out, the light plane's wheel 'exploded on impact'.

The next week Michael was back in Sydney for a couple of nights and he jotted down that he and Michele had 'planned a future—in it will be a child'. But despite his love for his 'brave and beautiful' Michele, on 8 January, with mixed feelings, he departed on a six-week global tour. As he left, he wrote in his diary of his longing for her. Four days touring New Zealand came first, with a double platinum record presentation and a good party, followed by a rare relaxing day with a swim and a sauna involved. In first class on the Pan Am flight to London he noted he was reading Simone de Beauvoir's *An Easy Death*. Arriving in London he discovered the airline had lost his bags, so he had no clothes and no money. Although an entire day of interviews loomed the next day, he found himself awake in the middle of the night again. *Aagh. I hate time*, he wrote. The next few days were consumed with interviews.

Michael was obviously caught up with band business, because the next entry, jumping to August, is about a property for sale in Australia. Then the final, November entry refers to having written three songs: 'Mystify', 'Monkey On My Back' and 'Tiny Daggers'.

On Friday, 17 January 1986, Michael noted, the band appeared live on London's hit television show *The Tube*, hosted by Jools Holland and Paula Yates. This was his first televised meeting with Paula. (Reports that Michael and Paula met in 1985 are, I believe, erroneous; *Listen Like Thieves* was not released until October 1985, and Michael did not travel to the UK after its release until January 1986, as noted in his diary and INXS tour dates.) On *The Tube*, Michael and Paula chatted on the bar-like set, while behind Michael's back, pretending to socialise, was Bob Geldof. Although he seemed to be taking no notice of his wife's outrageous flirting, he still remained close enough to eavesdrop.

Paula had previously referred to INXS as 'Rolling Stones wannabes'. Nevertheless, the YouTube clip of this interview shows just how smitten she was with the charismatic young Michael, who would be 26 in five days. Geldof, who was 34, and Yates, also 26, had been together for ten years at this stage. As a teenager, she had followed his band The Boomtown Rats around Europe. Bob and Paula had a child, two-year-old Fifi, but held off getting married until seven months after this interview took place.

Bob was still basking in honours over his groundbreaking organisa-
tional work on Live Aid the previous year. Back at their family home,
Paula put a photograph of Michael on their refrigerator and surrounded it with fairy lights. Bob scrawled something obscene across
Michael's face. Undaunted, Paula replaced the photo.

The *Listen Like Thieves* album's first single, the defibrillating 'What
You Need', was released to glowing enthusiasm in the USA, where it hit
#5 on the overall Billboard singles chart in April 1986.

In June 1986 I flew to London for ten days. INXS were on their third
world tour in two years, the pace was furious, and the band was about
to play London's princely Royal Albert Hall. I tagged along on a photo-
shoot and Michael and I chatted.

What he didn't tell me was that he and Michele were actually having
difficulty coming to a consensus about her career. She wanted to pursue
new professional avenues, and although Michael *wanted* Michele to
have a career, he also wanted her to be *available* to go on the road
with him. This devilish conundrum would eventually split them up
romantically, although they would always retain their deep, irreplace-
able friendship.

In mid-1986 INXS supported Queen on their Magic tour for six
shows through Europe, holding their own alongside the sensation-
ally talented and flamboyant English rock band, especially during the
Wembley shows. During INXS's set someone in the audience threw an
apple at Michael and he caught it; without missing a note, he took a bite
and tossed it back. Chris Murphy certainly had no reason to fret about
Michael's audience interactions after this tour: no doubt he learned
from the very best. One night after the show was finished, Michael and
Freddie Mercury raised the roof singing together in a hotel room just
for fun.

Tragically, Queen's Magic tour would be the last with their incredible
frontman as AIDS began to steal his strength. Freddie is the frontman

most likely to beat Michael, when all-time-greatest-frontman polls pop up from time to time in the media. As the two great contenders for the title caroused and sang together, caring little for such absurdities, Queen would only have a handful more concerts left to play.

Soon after the London trip I planned a return to Sydney. I sent Erin ahead and left three weeks later with my furniture for another new start. Brent was now fourteen and ensconced in high school studies. He was at that time very serious about his baseball; he was an exceptional pitcher. There was talk a college baseball scholarship might come his way, although unfortunately an injury would put paid to that. Again he stayed with his father.

One evening after attending an INXS concert at the Sydney Entertainment Centre, we were invited to a small reception where the band was presented with platinum records for *Listen Like Thieves*.

When Michael and Michele arrived to pick Erin up for lunch the following day, as usual she walked out the door with a book in one hand and the other in Michael's. This day she took a collection of Sam Shepherd plays, which does seem an odd choice of literature for an eight-year-old, but as a parent I was just thrilled that she loved to read. She was shy, and bringing a book meant she always had something to do, or discuss, when she felt awkward. Michael seemed to understand and appreciate this and over the years he would often suggest some reading material for her. Over lunch he flipped through the pages and showed interest in the book, prompting Erin to gift him with it the following Christmas.

Australian Made was a short-run concert series designed to prove that Australian bands could draw—and indeed, entertain—as well as the overseas raiders. From Boxing Day 1986 to Australia Day, 26 January

1987, nine very individual Australian bands joined together to play in six Australian capital cities. INXS, Models, Divinyls, Mental As Anything, I'm Talking, the Saints, former Cold Chisel frontman Jimmy Barnes and The Triffids, then making waves in Europe. Michael himself had insisted The Triffids join the tour. The line-up was notable for showcasing many female performers, including Chrissie Amphlett, Kate Ceberano, Zan Abeyratne, Wendy Matthews, and in I'm Talking, Barbara Hogarth on bass, and in The Triffids, Jill Birt on keyboards. This may not seem impressive, but as a contrast to even the early eighties scene, it was.

The costs and logistics of Australian Made were daunting. As well as all the publicity, the planning and organisation for the travel, accommodation, security and staging for nine bands, their crews, gear and companions, the shows would be recorded and filmed.

Meanwhile, for Michael some vital friendships would be struck up. INXS and Jimmy Barnes got together for a crème-de-la-crème version of a lesser-known Easybeats single of 1968, 'Good Times', written by Harry Vanda and George Young, which somehow ended up on Mushroom Records. That night I had the box seat, watching in delight from behind Mark Opitz in the Rhinoceros control room as two wild rock-star heads of hair bobbed and thrashed, Jimmy tearing strips off the studio walls with his unbelievable rock'n'roll voice while Michael got to play a damn good Stax Records Sam to his Dave.

A few days before Australian Made kicked off, Chris Bailey from the Saints popped up his erudite head at a press photo meet and greet and he and Michael hit it off like long-lost philosopher buccaneers who'd somehow mislaid a galleon in the Malacca Strait during a very big night. Their friendship would roll on and on. It's hard to believe that the plummy-accented Bailey was born in Kenya to Irish parents and grew up in Belfast until he was seven, when his family emigrated to Queensland. Like Michael, he was largely a professor of self-education.

He thought little of INXS. But if Michael was a charismatic romantic, Chris Bailey was rock'n'roll's Irish poet joker. Chris, his wife Pearl, Michael and Michele soon became inseparable.

The Saints singer, the only person I've ever heard call my brother 'Mick', found his new friend to be very happy with fame and his position but saw that this was by no means his only dimension.

Michael, for his part, had never been on the road with someone he had so much in common with. Both were gregarious and loved the classics. Fuelled by alcohol, they would talk all night about the great philosophers. Michael was impressed by Chris's vocabulary and intellect, and felt challenged to prove himself his equal.

Throughout the years after Australian Made, they remained close friends, threading in and out of each other's lives. I often received a postcard from somewhere in Europe, Michael writing to tell me he had been exploring some remote city with Chris, or how they were about to go to an outdoor gig together. The Saints frontman joined the short list of friends Michael would seek when he wanted to step out of the fame bubble.

By the mid-1980s Michael was spending very little time in Australia. He was touring and recording all over the world. In order to alleviate his tax burden, he took up residence in Hong Kong, along with INXS drummer Jon Farriss, on the advice of tax consultant Gordon Fisher, accountant Andrew Paul, and Colin Diamond, a barrister.

When Kell had his own company in Hong Kong in the early 1980s, he had come across Andrew Paul while using the services of a high-profile accountancy firm. With such a small degree of separation, it is easy to understand why his son Michael used the services of Fisher, Paul and Diamond.

In 1986, Sergeant John Thommeny was working out of Kings Cross Police Station with a young constable. Thommeny was manning a paddy wagon when late in the evening he took a call to attend the terrace houses in Victoria Street, Potts Point. The complaint was about a man climbing along the terrace houses' first-floor balconies, calling out a woman's name. When the police arrived, neighbours pointed across the street to a man struggling to make his way across the adjoining balconies. Thommeny ordered the man to climb down but he replied that he was having difficulty, so young Constable Fletcher climbed up and helped him over several balconies to the street below. Thommeny questioned the young man, who appeared to be intoxicated. He told Thommeny that he was looking for a girl who lived there, as he wanted to propose to her. He just couldn't remember which house she lived in. The sergeant explained that he had to take him in for trespassing and had Constable Fletcher walk him to the police vehicle; the young man was very polite and did not object. Fletcher had been quietly staring at the love-struck young man and when he returned to the front of the wagon Thommeny asked him what was wrong.

'Don't you know who he is, Sergeant?'

'No, who is he?'

'He's Michael Hutchence. He's in INXS.'

'What is that, a biker gang? Never heard of them.'

'No, Sarge, it's just Australia's best band.'

When Sergeant Thommeny arrived at the Kings Cross Police Station with Michael, he wasn't ready for the reception. He put Michael in the muster room. It seemed everybody on duty that night made it a point to walk into the room as he questioned him. While they stared open-mouthed, Michael smiled back at each one of them. Thommeny found an outstanding traffic fine under Michael's name for $80. But, having just got off the plane, Michael had only Hong Kong currency in his wallet. Sergeant Thommeny felt sorry for him, so he paid the fine himself.

MICHAEL

Michael in turn gave the sergeant a signed IOU written on the back of a Hong Kong one-cent note. Eight years after Michael died, Sergeant Thommeny, an honourable man, showed great class and kindness in sending that note to me.

He told me the name Michael was calling out that night was 'Michele'.

98

9

sometimes you kick

INXS MADE a pact with Michael and Andrew. Yes, since the two of them had come up with a whole slew of hits—'I Send A Message', 'Burn For You', 'The One Thing', 'Original Sin', 'What You Need', 'Kiss The Dirt (Falling Down The Mountain)', 'Shine Like It Does'—they now had free rein to co-write the band's material for *Kick*.

Michael had been obsessed with writing lyrics since he was a kid. He'd scrawl a line or two in his messy capitals across a serviette at dinner, reuse the backs of letters, rip the corner off a page from a phone directory. Some writers have a more carefully organised work style, but Michael was a jackdaw, a collector like another poet he admired, Emily Dickinson. When she died in 1886, Dickinson left among her unpublished writings 'the scraps': yet-to-be-used lines jotted onto chocolate wrappers, torn-off newspaper shreds and other bits of flotsam and jetsam she could repurpose. Michael's songs were generally developed from 'scraps' too. Clues to future lyrics peeped from between the pages of whatever he was reading, were tossed in suitcases as he rushed to make a flight.

His main co-writer Andrew Farriss, meanwhile, was an extraordinary musical talent—one in a generation. He used the full range of orchestral instrumentation in the synthesisers clutched to the chest of pop-rock in the 1980s, plus guitars, organ, piano, harmonica—you name it, he could play it. He could come up with music to the most heart-rending, classic ballad like 'Never Tear Us Apart', with its slow, throbbing waltz, then create the strange, playful, slightly alien funk landscapes of 'Need You Tonight' and 'Original Sin' with the funkiest Chic-style rhythms. Mind you, the *whole* of INXS would have everything to do with how sharp and minimalist that could roll. The driving yet floating, bounce-on-air rhythm section of Jon and Garry was undeniable as an invitation to the dance floor. The two of them had a great understanding of the positive value of emptiness versus clutter. It was what they left out that made them so damn funky. Kirk was one of the greatest sax players in rock, extremely emotive, and his vocals and guitar work were always spot on. And then Tim's sometimes humorous little guitar comments added to the sense of daring that was an INXS motif, while his slashing guitar-playing and adrenalin were what made the band rock more than anything—except perhaps Michael's vocals, which could also really tear things up. Credit where credit's due.

But Andrew was one of the most underrated talents around, and so prolific. He'd lay down a mass of ideas, riffs, melodies and feels on cassette tapes and send them from overseas to Michael, who was likely to be in Hong Kong, France or wherever.

Michael would then sift through his own fragments and clues of lyrics and begin to test them against sounds, like someone starting out on a jigsaw puzzle. Starting with an idea, a half-sentence on a scrap of paper, he'd work hard at it, crossing out, sing-testing phrases in his mouth out loud, searching for a new sound until he thought a song felt and sounded just right. Once they got into the studio, he might tweak that lyric further again, and again.

'Hutchence's instrument was his voice; he couldn't explain what he was thinking in musical terms,' Andrew Farriss told *Billboard* in October 2017. 'He would say things like, "It needs to feel like this." And I'd try to translate that into notes.'

Listen Like Thieves had already worked a treat, a step up into maturity and international embrace that proved the worth of the in-demand English producer Chris Thomas without a doubt. So INXS entered Rhinoceros confidently to record *Kick* with him, working through the experienced ears and hands of engineer David Nicholas, who made some good artistic decisions too, like how 'Mediate' works in the track sequencing. They created many good songs, but Thomas wanted a *great* album for them and knew they could do it. He sent Michael and Andrew away to Hong Kong to attempt to write an album of singles, and they came close. They also helped each other on songs they basically wrote alone—Andrew's 'Mediate' and Michael's 'Guns In The Sky'—and agreed to give each other 100 per cent of credit in return for the swapped minor input. They flew into Sydney with a cassette tape full of rough-hewn songs and took them to INXS to spin into pure gold. One of the gems from this collaboration intensive was 'Need You Tonight'. After they had put the finishing touches to the vocals in Paris, they took the recordings to London for the master mixer Bob Clearmountain to work on. Over the years Bob has mixed, engineered and/or produced some of the best work from Bowie, the Stones, Icehouse, Roxy Music, Crowded House, Springsteen, the Pretenders, Jimmy Barnes and many more. Around the same time that he was recording *Kick* in Sydney, Michael stopped by to see our mother at her make-up school in Kirribilli, not far from where he and Michele lived. He was very emotional that day as he shared with her that he and Michele had decided to go their separate ways. He blamed the hectic lifestyle that came with his career.

Michele Bennett would find career success as an award-winning producer of films including *Chopper* (2000, winner of five Australian Film Institute Awards); *I'm Only Looking: The best of INXS* (2004); *Leonard Cohen: I'm your man* (2005) and several films with director/producer Nash Edgerton.

As his star continued to climb, Michael's professional life not only kept him on the road, but 'necessitated', through the 'guidance' of Fisher, Paul and Diamond, that he live in the tax haven of Hong Kong. The trio had also devised schemes for the rest of INXS and Chris Murphy too initially, but Michael and Jon, the only ones who moved to Hong Kong to share an apartment, were perhaps the most affected. As time moved on, the pressures INXS faced, including this move, would open up splits between the band members, their loved ones and those they trusted to handle their affairs.

'To me,' Chris Murphy would later tell journalist Richard Guilliatt, 'that's where Michael's life changed: separated from the band, finances separated. He had to move to foreign countries to be protected in this web of darkness.'

Mother recalled how healthy yet unhappy he looked as he waved goodbye. She was deeply concerned for her son, who looked so forlorn as he walked away. Fortunately he was not going to be alone for very long.

While working on the vocals for *Kick* at Studio De La Grande Armée in Paris, Michael took a short break in Cannes. He was staying with his friend Michael Hamlyn, who would go on to produce *The Adventures of Priscilla, Queen of the Desert* for both screen and stage, and also U2's video opus *Rattle And Hum*. His father was UK publishing entrepreneur Paul Hamlyn, and the family owned a beautiful villa above Cannes, not far from where my brother would later purchase his own place.

It was the week of the International Film Festival (known later as Festival de Cannes, then simply nicknamed 'Cannes') and the streets were full of people-gazers. Strolling down Boulevard de la Croisette Michael suddenly saw a poised young woman walking towards him and realised he recognised her—the American model Rosanna Crash. They'd met once when he was visiting Michele, who was on a modelling assignment in Japan. He was so focused on this strikingly beautiful young woman that he didn't immediately recognise that her companion was *another* Rosanna—Arquette—who was there at a producer's invitation. The two Rosannas, both from New York, had more or less grown up together. They were in Cannes en route to Paris where Arquette was meeting up with her boyfriend, Peter Gabriel.

Michael invited Rosanna Crash to join him for dinner that night at the Hamlyn villa, then they met up again in Paris. After that, he and the girl he fondly nicknamed 'Jonnie' became more or less inseparable for almost three years.

After ten days in Paris, Michael was due in New York for a meeting with London-born Nick Egan, who'd designed artwork for The Clash and worked with fashion icons like Vivienne Westwood. Michael had met Nick backstage at a show and invited him to design the sleeve for *Kick*.

It was Nick's view that INXS's album covers so far had been a bit too 'democratic'. After all, an album cover is packaging, just like a book or magazine cover. It has the sway to sell—or *under*sell—the music inside. Nick believed that INXS were undercapitalising on their very appealing frontman. He recognised that Michael was a natural in front of the camera, with a rare bravura in styling his clothes and hair—no doubt partly absorbed through being around the fashion parades and movie sets that Mother and I worked on throughout his boyhood.

INXS were a great-looking band, undeniably. Nick just wanted to put their most charismatic asset centre stage. The cover he came up with is surely one of his best. INXS were shot by Grant Matthews, one of Australia's top fashion photographers, for the sleeve. Its sharp-focus portraiture, stark and striking, stands apart from the more colourful, abstracted early INXS album covers. Only one previous—*The Swing*—had even featured the band on the cover at all (albeit taking up about a third of the space, with Michael in the back row).

The *Kick* cover is predominately red, white and black. The big, half head-shot of Michael to the right on the front of *Kick*'s bold gatefold cover stands out. The smaller images of Kirk and Jon convey that this is collaboration while the other three band members wrap around the back, Tim dominant in a very rock-guitarist stance. Booted feet—Michael's—straddle a flying skateboard. Gravity appears suspended, with the strangely angled figures suggesting secrets and intrigue.

Chris Murphy hated it. He said he didn't want Michael to dominate. He would not use it. He demanded it be re-shot with equal space for all members. Michael stood up for Nick and in the end they used his design.

Beside Nick Egan's credit for art direction, design and cover art concept, Michael was also credited with 'cover art concept' and I think that was very important for him at the time. Expanding on Nick Egan's concepts, Richard Lowenstein and his crew shot groundbreaking videos for *Kick*'s singles.

Meanwhile, in America, Chris Murphy sat patiently while the man running Atlantic listened to *Kick* all the way through for the first time.

He hated it.

It was too black, too R&B. It would alienate the rock following that the band had built up; radio would get confused; INXS's growing audience wouldn't accept this sound.

He offered INXS US$1 million to record over *Kick*.

There were also unhappy noises from the top execs of their labels in Australia (WEA) and Europe (Polygram) over the band's proposed sixth album. Atlantic refused to put it on their release schedule. Chris, alarmed but not panicking—yet—thought they were all insane.

Luckily he *was* buoyed by one label manager, in France, who was absolutely having kittens over *Kick*.

Surreptitiously he met with Atlantic's radio promotion department for some inspiration and advice.

INXS believed in this album. Their seductive, lively combination of rock and funk had been gathering force beyond *The Swing* and *Listen Like Thieves*. Now ten years of sweat and the lion's share of their liquidity were on the line.

Atlantic's radio promo team said they'd help give *Kick* a shot. Based on the information he gleaned from them, Chris sent the band on a self-funded college tour, bussing them to universities and college towns across the USA. Hallelujah for American campus radio stations— partly, sometimes even wholly, run by the students themselves. Who better to have their fingers on the pulse of the buying public than young adults? Campus radio was more open to creativity. Ahead of the field in breaking bands, it regularly foretold what commercial radio would be playing next. And INXS were at home with the feel of alternative FM community radio stations in Australia, like Melbourne's 3RRR and 4ZZZ in Brisbane, who took risks, discovered and broke new music. In fact, that was very much the stations' raison d'être.

Across the USA, so many college stations loved various tracks on *Kick* and warmed to the friendly, funny interviews Michael and the others did with them. INXS started to score serious airplay. They played and sold out popular college bars and auditoriums. The students loved the band and word spread fast.

Atlantic soon capitulated and *Kick* was released to an avalanche of airplay and worldwide critical acclaim. The songs on *Kick* were all written by Andrew and Michael except for 'The Loved One' (Clyne, Humphrys and Lovett). Its first single, 'Need You Tonight', was put on high radio rotation across America almost immediately, hitting #1 on the main Billboard chart and also at home in Australia, while peaking at #9 in the UK. 'Devil Inside' (#2 in America) followed its lead, becoming a crossover hit before 1988 had ended. The album delivered four US top ten singles, their videos on high rotation on MTV, with third and fourth singles 'New Sensation' (#3) and 'Never Tear Us Apart' (#7) also big hits.

Less than two months after its release, the album was certified platinum by the Recording Industry Association of America. Altogether *Kick* spent 79 weeks on the Billboard Top 200 with 22 consecutive weeks in the top ten. After two years, in 1989 it went quadruple platinum in that country alone.

Over the years *Kick* has had several re-releases in various forms; remastered, with featured bonus tracks, in box sets and on vinyl. Over six million copies have been sold in the US and over 20 million worldwide. Following its 25th anniversary release in 2014, it topped the Australian charts again. I think that album must have purchased a lot of properties for a lot of people connected with the band.

Rosanna gladly had her name removed from her modelling agent's register and moved into the apartment Michael now shared with Jon Farriss and his girlfriend, Lisa, in the seething metropolis of Hong Kong.

That tiny apartment was so noisy, Rosanna said, you could hear the other residents through the walls as you walked up to the front door. And when you closed it behind you, not even the constant loud hum of the air conditioner could drown it out. 'Whenever I hear Michael's lyrics for "The Stairs", she said, 'I am always reminded of Hong Kong.'

In 'The Stairs' Michael writes of people brushing past each other in shared stairwells and corridors, their repeating movements mirrored on each side of a wall.

In Europe, Rosanna rode behind Michael on his Harley, hugging his warm, familiar body for dear life. The scent of his stirring hair, the nape of his neck and his leather jacket were comforting as they roared through south-eastern France en route to Gordon Fisher's new abode in Beausoleil, near Monaco.

In no time at all INXS took off on a tour that would stretch over a year and a third, travelling through Asia, Europe and North and South America.

Rosanna gave Michael the companionship he sorely needed and the support he wanted without a second thought. She was patient, kind and assertive. She'd speak up for him as he asked her to: for instance, with the crew if something needed attention, or helping his friends get backstage. Michael could actually be quite reticent, too reticent at times, about addressing things he had a problem with. He tended to claim he was ignored by INXS if he *did* speak up. He totally appreciated Rosanna's personal and professional support and I have to say he performed extremely well on this tour.

The couple took small forays into the real world, away from the interviews, sound checks, performances and the air-conditioned artifice of hotel life. They ate macrobiotic food and practised tai chi and yoga in their daily routines, even with the tour's rigorous demands.

Nicole Bartleet, Garry Beers' girlfriend at the time, now a photographic artist, kindly shared her memories of the Kick tour.

'I had an instant connection with Rosanna, an exquisite beauty who was so down-to-earth,' she said. 'Rosanna had substance. She wore simple, classic, casual clothes and Doc Martens with a camera slung around her neck, all of which suited Michael just fine.

'She took a juicer on the road to keep him healthy, despite this sometimes being a big ask, with such extraordinary demands on him and virtually no downtime. She adored Michael and he adored her.

'I have memories of them wrapped in each other's arms asleep on yet another American tour bus, to yet another bizarre town. Rosanna seemed to fit perfectly inside Michael's leather jacket. She would disappear and look so vulnerable. They would sleep most of the way, exhausted,' said Nicole. 'I came to understand that Michael lived for those two hours on stage; the rest became a pain and a blur after so long on the road.'

To keep him on his toes, and also as a kind of personal dare, Michael would ask Rosanna to wake him from a deep sleep just a few minutes before he had to go on. Being easily bored, he liked the challenge.

'She would thread roses into his ponytail, and like a cat he would leap onto the stage and nobody knew the difference,' Nicole recalled.

The two girlfriends had a favourite routine, every concert, of making their way down to the front of the stage for 'Never Tear Us Apart'.

'There was such beauty in that song, and that moment it was palpable in the audience. That never wore off. It gave me shivers.'

Things weren't always easy though. 'I remember walking out of the hotel with Michael and Rosanna in New York during the tour when he was trapped by hysterical fans. For all his talent, his beauty, inside and out, I knew he hated that feeling. Deep down he was an ordinary man who adored his family and had lost his privacy. He hated that, and Rosanna was always thinking a step ahead trying to protect him.'

Despite being so short-sighted, Michael was often without glasses, so he needed visual guidance too from his partner at times. Once they were seated at the same table as Madonna and several other celebrities, but Michael couldn't make them out across the table; he could have easily come across as a snob if Rosanna hadn't subtly interceded.

Nicole remembers INXS had dinner with Mick Jagger and his solo backing band three nights in a row at one stage. They were all invited up to Mick's room, where the two lead singers were engrossed in conversation for hours. This led to an ongoing friendship between Michael and Mick.

Another strong friendship Michael formed in the music business was with U2's Bono. 'It felt like an amazing connection to witness,' said Nicole, 'and they seemed equally fascinated with each other. Their mutual affection was beautiful to see.'

She loved the thrill of travelling with such a stunning troupe of rock'n'roll performers and their companions and the eye-boggling this could arouse in fellow travellers. 'What amused me,' Nicole recalled, 'is when we got on a commercial flight every morning in Europe, dressed in our black leathers, designer and colourful clothes along with these very serious businessmen. They looked at us over their newspapers with disdain as we entered the plane. We then took a sharp right into first class and the champagne was delivered with the daily faxes, distributed by the ever-patient tour manager. Loved that.

'There were such highs and lows on that tour, in particular in Japan where it was a strange time and band relations were strained. Every morning when we left a hotel to get back on the road, there always seemed to be arguments and stress over the bills and mini bar, of all things. A lot of us dreaded it.'

There was also quite a food fight in an expensive Japanese restaurant with the record company at the table.

'There were so many egos in the band, including Chris Murphy. It was a constant struggle to find peace,' sighed Nicole. 'The gigs, though, they were breathtaking.'

Sometimes for Michael, dangerously so.

Rosanna was closest of all to the toll taken on Michael as the demands wore on. Playing so many open air festivals through the European summer was hard on his vocal cords. He was in the habit of carrying inhalers, never having fully shaken off his childhood asthma, and was prone to allergies. Sometimes he experienced a major asthma attack.

'There were times,' recalled Rosanna, 'when he was putting so much into the performances at the outdoor festivals that he would barely get to his inhaler on the side of the stage. Once he couldn't find it fast enough on the afternoon before a show and he almost passed out. It was a very scary situation.

'The Kick tour was long and gruelling,' she said, 'and, yes, we did take off sightseeing when he got the chance; and, yes, he did socialise with celebrities after a performance—they would naturally gravitate to Michael—but that didn't give the band licence to tear him down.'

'When Michael's vocal cords began to give him problems during the latter part of the Kick tour, it was because of the pace,' she said. 'He was exhausted. The other band members admonished him, accusing him of partying too much. There is a big difference between playing an inanimate musical instrument and relying on your voice.'

'But there was only one show,' Rosanna said, 'when he insisted that he honestly didn't think he could go on that night.' That was on 30 June 1988, when INXS played at Denmark's Roskilde Festival alongside Sting, 10,000 Maniacs, Billy Bragg, Bryan Adams, Hothouse Flowers, John Hiatt and Leonard Cohen, to a crowd of around 60,000 people. Nicole witnessed a big argument fly out of control before the concert. 'Michael had a sore throat and was exhausted,' she recalled. 'The band had a big fight; they blamed it on his partying. It rapidly deteriorated into a screaming match.

'Somehow Michael did perform that night and was amazing. That night was unforgettable and the audience was hypnotised. Rosanna and I danced euphorically in that big European crowd, close to back-stage and I fell completely in love with her and knew why Michael had done the same.'

There were also 'fun times, earlier times when [band] relations were better', Nicole recalled. 'Michael bought his custom Harley-Davidson Softail, and not to be outdone Garry had to buy one too. Our bikes would be rolled off the planes and Rosanna and I would jump on behind our men. In Melbourne we jumped on our bikes and took off straight from the tarmac.

'We rode to the Dandenong Ranges the next day and called ourselves Harley Honeys, lifting up our tops in the breeze and laughing. Michael complained about the insects he swallowed on the ride and was concerned that it would affect his voice later. But the day was fun and carefree. Michael had eluded the press.'

• • •

Kick had a hybrid vigour that was right of the moment and songs that only INXS would write. It had funk, melody, moving performances and the highest of production values. These were helped along by clips bursting with the band's lusty, high-energy charms, igniting a passionate new MTV fan base. Worldwide fans were further whipped into submission by impressive live performances during INXS's constant international touring. *Kick* became a phenomenally huge, worldwide success, with the tour ending at the Sydney Entertainment Centre in November 1988.

10

maximum dynamic pressure

IN JUNE 1986, in Strasbourg, Germany, Michael's friend Bruce Butler, who'd known him since he was a teenager, was visiting INXS on tour when a long-awaited cassette arrived. It was Nick Launay's final mix of Michael singing 'Rooms For The Memory' for the independent Australian film *Dogs in Space*, written and directed by Richard Lowenstein.

'Michael quickly went into the tour bus,' said Bruce, 'and we all listened to the finished song for the first time. Everyone was speechless. It really was a turning point—the band heard what Michael could do without INXS. Michael was like, "*Fuck*, this guy's *so* good! Ollie is just the man." Because Ollie wrote that song, and that was the start of the Max Q project. It was "Rooms For The Memory" that sealed it.'

Michael did a great job—he was proud to sing it, along with three other tracks co-produced by Melbourne's electronica savant Ollie (née Ian) Olsen. 'Green Dragon' is a kind of spoken word storytelling, and then there is 'Golf Course', and an actual song called 'Dogs In Space'.

Richard Lowenstein's first-ever video clip was 'Leap For Lunch' by The Ears in 1980. INXS had done gigs with the band and Michael's inhabitation of their lead singer Sam Sejavka's mannerisms, tortured bed hair and kohl-rimmed eyes was just uncanny. It was all so incestuous but somehow Ollie was the key to it all.

'Rooms For The Memory', which reached #11 on the singles charts, was Michael's second solo single, following 'Speed Kills' from the Don Walker–produced soundtrack to *Freedom*. By now he knew he wanted to collaborate with Ollie again in the future.

Then *Dogs in Space* scored an R (18+) rating for showing sex scenes and heroin use. This shocked its makers, who unsuccessfully appealed the decision. With most teenagers—a good part of its prime audience—now locked out, it closed quickly on the screens brave enough to show it. It raised US$49,000 in the USA and AU$189,000 during its eight-week run in Sydney and Melbourne cinemas in early 1987. Nevertheless, in this soon-to-be cult classic, Richard captured the glaring-eyed anarchism and tribal, music-locked heart of Melbourne's post-punk party in a way no other director could.

Down the track his documentaries *We're Livin' on Dogfood* (2009) and *Autoluminescent* (2011, co-directed with Lynn-Maree Milburn: his tribute to Rowland S. Howard of Boys Next Door, Birthday Party and Crime & the City Solution) explored how the little band scene of inner Melbourne with all its charm and tragedy flowered in many ways. *Dogs in Space* hooked Michael on acting and proved for Richard that if you really, really want it hard enough, you can make it happen. As I write, Richard is still fighting the monsters movie-makers have to face to complete a documentary on Michael's life called *Mystify*.

•   •   •

By 1989, Michael was pretty burnt out after touring *Kick* for sixteen months. Nevertheless, there was a certain project he'd been thinking about ever since doing *Dogs in Space*. Michael called Ollie and invited him to collaborate on a fresh set of recordings—an album, if things panned out. They didn't waste any time. Ollie suggested they call the act after his blue heeler dog, and they did. Max Q, as it was now known, would be major escapism for Michael after a decade in INXS with the same line-up.

The musos of Max Q were quickly summoned by Ollie. They actually shared a few things in common with INXS. For instance, some of them had been to school together, and lived or played together for years. Curiously, Max Q guitarist Michael Sheridan and Kirk Pengilly were close friends as young boys when they both lived in Almond Street, North Balwyn, then one of the newer suburbs in Melbourne's east. They went to kindergarten and primary school together and even recorded three songs together as little kids, one an original, before the Pengilly family moved to Sydney.

Overall though, Max Q was a very different assemblage to INXS indeed. Apart from Michael, Max Q's members' common history was to have been in bands that got together to play one kind of music, warped into something else, then broke up before success could overcome all their efforts to escape it. Every one of them—Bill McDonald on bass, Ollie on keyboards, programming and vocals, Gus Till on programming and keyboards, John Murphy on percussion and Michael Sheridan and Arne Hanna both on electric guitars—had played on the soundtrack to *Dogs in Space*. Marie Hoy, who did backing vocals and had been with Ollie in Hugo Klang, also had a strong presence in the film and soundtrack. The pedigree line to Melbourne's post-punk world was direct and pure—just the kind of credibility Michael craved. Experimentation and originality fuelled them far more than commercial success.

It is astonishing how the *Max Q* album sprang together in a few short months. It's as though the parts of this infernal machine (and it is rather infernal-sounding music at times) were just waiting for the right moment to assemble. Ollie went into Powerplant Studios in Carlton and laid down some programming with Gus Till putting his own guide lead vocals over it, then took most of the members of Max Q into Rhinoceros and quickly put down roughs of 'Buckethead' and 'Way of the World'. Michael loved the two tracks, so he invited Ollie to fly overseas for some co-writing sessions, and to sort out what other tracks to record.

'It all seemed to work so smoothly,' Rosanna said. 'Everybody was happy and excited about the project. We decided to stop off in Tahiti on the way over to California, because Michael hadn't really had much time off since the end of the tour. After being so concerned about Ollie having all the right documentation, ironically Michael was the one who arrived without a visa, but we were able to negotiate something with the authorities. Tahiti was really good for him because he loved anything to do with water activities.'

She mailed me a postcard from Bora Bora, Tahiti, dated 25 May 1989.

Michael is very relaxed . . . This place is beautiful, the water is too much—shark feeding very exciting—boats, bikes—lots of photos. Ollie broke one toe last night the men were having too much fun. Love you all a lot,

Love Rosanna, Michael and Ollie x

Meanwhile, Ollie wrote to Richard Lowenstein.

'I do remember getting a few messages or postcards or whatever,' Richard recalled, 'saying, "I'm stuck here in amazing luxury while Michael and Jonnie disappear into their bedroom for hours at a time".'

When they got to Los Angeles Michael rented a house on the beach in Malibu and a 1966 Thunderbird convertible. Neither of the guys would attempt to drive it on the 'wrong' side of the road, and 'Los Angeles is impossible without a car', said Rosanna, so she drove them everywhere.

'The Malibu house backed onto the surf beach. The sun would rise from behind the mountains in the front of the house', Rosanna said, 'and in the late afternoon we could sit on the balcony and watch the most glorious sunsets disappear into the Pacific Ocean and then the moon across the water. Beautiful.'

The soothing ocean sounds were the perfect co-writing and arranging backdrop. 'Michael wanted to learn to play guitar so I called my friend Richard Ortiz, who was so knowledgeable about stringed instruments,' she said, 'and he came up with this gorgeous, cherry-red, Gibson vintage Al Caiola. Michael loved it and began strumming right away.

'Ollie and Michael would sit across from each other,' Rosanna said, 'writing, singing and going back and forth with possible lyrics. Sometimes Michael would jot something down on a pad next to the bed in the middle of the night or wake up before anyone else and I would find him on the balcony overlooking the beach, head down, writing away.'

Knowing there was no time to lose in creating Max Q's repertoire, Ollie took some of his own favourite compositions and, adding contributions from Michael to his own reimaginings, deconstructed, then reconstructed them. Frank Zappa used to do this with his compositions all the time.

Some of the songs on *Max Q* were reworked from (very different) versions previously recorded by one of Ollie's recent ensembles, Orchestra of Skin and Bone, which also featured Marie Hoy and John Murphy. 'Like "Sometimes" and "Ot-Ven-Rot"—which means "red friend" in a Norwegian dialect,' said Ollie. 'This carriage of skin and bone is my home,' he quotes from his own lyrics, 'I'm in need of new tissue but I ain't gonna get it. That whole lyric is in "Ot-Ven-Rot" on the *Max Q* album, but the music is completely different.'

Rosanna remembered the strange jangle of Ollie Olsen meets USA. 'One day Michael had a meeting on Sunset so I first drove to Melrose,' she said, 'where it's a great people-watching boulevard. I thought it would be a good place to leave Ollie while I drove Michael to his meeting. Ollie got out of the car and we were making arrangements as to where we would meet up with him, but he hesitated, so nervous. Michael asked him what was wrong and he said he wasn't sure he wanted to stay there as he was afraid to walk around by himself, afraid of maybe getting shot! We finally soothed his nerves and I think when he really looked around he could see he was surrounded by mostly young adults window-shopping and drinking coffee. It may have been the sheer number of people and all the activity on the street that unnerved him.'

They returned to Rhinoceros Studios in Sydney, with the band and engineer Paula Jones, to finish recording the album. It must have cost Michael a fair bit of money all up—although *nothing* like INXS had spent on their last album, *Kick* with Chris Thomas—because Michael flew up most of Max Q from Melbourne to record; then he and Ollie flew to New York to do some mixing and remixing with New York house DJ-mixer-producer Todd 'the God' Terry. (Terry also mixed some Max Q B-sides and 12-inch club mixes on his own.) In England some other mixes were done with red-hot acid-house DJ and producer Paul Oakenfold, who would soon be named NME Producer of the Year (in 2000) for producing Happy Mondays' #1 in England album *Pills 'n' Thrills and Bellyaches*.

The Max Q kingpins were in New York for around a month. Michael and Ollie liked to take the track they'd been working on and get the driver of the black Lincoln Town Car Michael had hired for the duration to put it on while they were driving around, to see if it still sounded as good on the little speakers.

Ollie was overwhelmed one time when someone from Atlantic Records came into a mix session for a listen. 'I basically walked into the studio,' Ollie recalled, 'and kind of screamed. I recognised one of the "suits"—I think it may have been Ahmet Ertegun—and I freaked out. I was pretty grungy/psychedelic-looking, so I guess they kind of freaked out a little too. But then we got introduced and all was fine.'

After Nicole broke up with Garry Beers, Rosanna invited her to come to New York to stay with them. Michael was at this time also preparing for his role as the poet Percy Bysshe Shelley in Roger Corman's *Frankenstein Unbound*.

'He was worried,' Nicole recalled, 'about his weight—needlessly— and anxious about the role as it was new territory but in a healthy, perfectionist kind of way. He was simultaneously working on *Max Q* with Ollie Olson and was loving the process, inspired and enjoying the connection, collaborating with a kindred spirit. He was free for the first time ever. I know boredom was torture to Michael so it was lovely to see his liberation. I remember he was furious with Chris Murphy at this point. I understood.

'One night we went out to the most amazing underground club. After tunnels and twists and turns we found ourselves in a club/ restaurant that was themed on first-century AD food and styling. Those were heady days and in beautiful company.'

Michael had been so happy with Nick Egan's *Kick* cover for INXS that he'd commissioned him to design *Max Q*'s too, although he did not stay around to give input. He assumed his manager would protect him.

The cover *was* very stylish indeed but it transmitted no idea *whatsoever* about the artist(s). The music it packaged might as well have been completely programmed by a single nerd computer, based on the look of the cover. And actually Max Q were a knockout, visually. Check out *Sometimes*, their performance-based clip on YouTube, if you haven't already. They had a great look, Michael lighting the way into their strange, eccentric galaxy. It seemed like such a lost opportunity to throw all that visual attraction away.

When Nick designed the *Max Q* album cover, 'I suggested creating one face out of all seven musicians,' he said. 'Ollie may have said, "Like an identikit" and that is why I made the face in sections, as opposed to one face. I know I wanted it to have no torso—a bit like Big Brother from Orwell's *1984*.' Ollie confirmed to me that he had indeed asked for something resembling an identikit.

I vividly remember a call from Martha Troup in mid-1989 regarding the Max Q project. Chris had appointed Martha the band's representative in New York. She had ferociously supported Michael's decisions outside of the band and had high hopes for Max Q. Now she was concerned about the album cover.

Michael wasn't on it.

Rosanna remembered the controversial sleeve design too. 'When Michael saw the final album cover we were in Morocco,' she said. 'He was furious. Although he agreed that Max Q was a band, he had made it clear that he at least wanted to take advantage of the following he had built up with INXS. It didn't even feature his name, let alone his image.

'Obviously if Michael was kept busy with INXS, and the album cover had nothing on it to associate him with it, it had little chance of getting promoted. Michael had funded this album and it was clear that Chris had not stood up for him in his meetings with the record company. Michael said it felt like sabotage,' said Rosanna.

Whether or not this was a true reflection of Chris's input on the cover, rather than what happened when other creatives stepped in while he was otherwise occupied, Michael had *other* reasons to be angry.

His old mate Bruce Butler had worked as an Australian music industry executive in record companies and elsewhere for some time by then and had many connections.

'Sony Australia, or CBS as it was still known then,' Bruce said, 'was frustrated with the lack of cooperation and participation by Michael in the promotion of the album.

'As a friend of Michael's I had been in touch with him during this project as I was music producer and talent coordinator on ABC TV's *The Factory*. I was able to get Ollie on the show performing with his band NO [which also contained Michael Sheridan and Marie Hoy]. Before its release, *I* was even interviewed myself on *The Factory* about the Max Q project, but I was not able to get Michael on, with or without the band, even just for an interview. Michael told me he wasn't "allowed" to do the publicity and CBS promotions told me they received no joy approaching MMA either.'

Martha has talked about a meeting she was at with Michael where Chris bounced in and said, 'I've got this great idea! Let's not even tell them you're on the album, you know—*Max Q*.'

Which went down like a death at a party.

There was another, even crueller blow.

The cover of US *Rolling Stone* is what artists all around the world have wet dreams about from the age of thirteen on.

'*Rolling Stone* wanted Michael, because of Max Q, on the front cover,' Richard Lowenstein confirmed. 'The *Kick* thing had come and gone, it'd been his number one, and so his kudos was high.'

It would have been a great chance to promote both the wife (INXS) and mistress (Max Q). But INXS was off the road, between albums; show-biz thinking is to do the promo when you've got an album to flog.

'I think at that time, Chris and the band may have been worried about Michael going the way Sting did when he left The Police,' said Richard.

'I was in the studio when Michael *heard* that Chris or someone had said, no cover of *Rolling Stone*, in his name, without the band,' Richard recalled. 'And then he just slammed the phone down and smashed or kicked the wall and said, you know, "Fucking arseholes." Because—not so much that he wanted it to be just him, but he wanted the Max Q thing to have the publicity.

'And he *knew* that INXS would be on the front cover of *Rolling Stone* at some stage down the track . . . And he probably had the power to ring up and say, "Yes, I'll do it." But he didn't. He sort of toed the line. The actual thing of the cover of *Rolling Stone* is, you know, it's better than a Grammy. You may not get it again. You're in the pop world. It's all very well to say yes, we're going to be like U2, and in five years' time we can get it.' (A year later, in November 1990, a US *Rolling Stone* cover for INXS *did* emerge to push *X*—with Andrew Farriss looking not a little awkward, poised above INXS's always perfect-cover-fodder singer.)

In a fury Michael called Chris, telling him he no longer needed his services as manager. He asked Martha to be his personal manager.

It was obvious that the band was concerned that success for Michael on this project might discourage him from continuing with INXS. I had thought this might be at the heart of the problem. Martha skirted around the subject but refused to actually nail what she suspected, or knew, was going on. Over the years, and certainly during this year, 1989, when there was downtime for INXS, the other members had each worked on outside projects. Nobody seemed to have a problem with that. Michael felt strongly that it should not have been any different for him. Martha suggested I speak to him about it. I did encourage him to speak up about whatever he was aiming for, although the complexity of the music business was not something I was all that comfortable with.

On YouTube there's a sound-only recording uploaded by 'futsal1958' called *INXS Interview 1988—Michael Hutchence and Andrew Farriss* that is very interesting in terms of Max Q's emergence. The recording is described as reporter Steve Harris interviewing Michael and Andrew in October 1988, at the Roppongi Prince Hotel in Tokyo, during the Kick tour. Michael commented in the interview that if an established band like INXS stopped exploring outside avenues of creativity, that would be where most bands 'screw up', through being so 'scared of each other's abilities' that they stifle themselves.

'One of the best things that you can do is say *go* off and have a bloody good time and good luck, get it out of your system,' Michael said. 'It's when someone has to think that they have to *secretly* do them . . . that sucks, you know. You don't have to break a band up to let somebody do something.'

Michael obviously thought he *did* need to keep Max Q on the QT though, as the album was recorded, and its videos, and for the most part, he did. So did Chris Murphy, who was involved on the business side, having previously signed Ollie to a music publishing deal during the *Dogs in Space* era.

So then when Andrew Farriss was watching a music show one day in 1989, and Max Q's debut single 'Way Of The World' came on, clearly sung by Michael, he was totally blindsided. By some accounts he got on the phone to Chris Murphy and gave him a piece of his rather furious mind.

Rosanna, who was with Michael through this time, believed INXS were constantly concerned that he would take off on his own. 'What is it they say about holding on to something? Relationships are like birds: if you hold tightly they die; if you hold loosely they fly,' she said. 'But if you hold with care, they remain with you forever.'

If Max Q remained a studio band and Michael's hands remained tied, there was little chance that his fans would hear it. 'There was a definite push in that direction,' Ollie said, 'from management, who didn't wish to promote Michael in it so much.'

'I think, quietly,' Nicole reflected, 'Michael and Ollie hoped and planned to go on tour and promote the album but they both knew there was little chance that Chris Murphy was going to allow that.'

At least they were able to get Richard Lowenstein on board for some videos. Over the years, apart from directing Michael as an actor in *Dogs in Space*, and directing the clip of his solo single 'Rooms For The Memory' (1987) from the same film, by this stage he'd also directed him in INXS videos 'Burn For You', 'All The Voices' and 'Dancing On The Jetty' (1984); 'What You Need' (1985); 'Listen Like Thieves' (1986); 'Need You Tonight/Mediate' (1987); and 'Never Tear Us Apart', 'New Sensation' and 'Guns In The Sky' (1988).

All the chemistry, connections, insight, artistry and experience made Richard the perfect match to shoot Max Q's first two videos, 'Way Of The World' (1989) and 'Sometimes' (1990). 'Sometimes' is a particularly great example of the pure performance clip. He'd also go on to direct more INXS videos over the coming years: 'Suicide Blonde' (1990); 'By My Side' and 'Bitter Tears (1991); 'Heaven Sent' and 'Taste It' (1992); and 'The Gift' and 'Cut Your Roses Down' (1993).

Creating Max Q's hotted-up, industrial disco while flying under the radar in a few brief weeks was an ambitious ask. For the most part, it really comes off. There's a strong songwriting backbone under the studio skill-sets of both Ollie and Michael, boosted by the musicality of the rest of Max Q.

And *Max Q* the album is cohesive, impressive. It's pop, rock, electronica, house, psychedelia, soul and noise on the rocks in a cocktail shaker. All credit to the strength of the personalities involved that it does hang together so well.

The seven Olsen–Hutchence co-writes, whether brand new or recalibrated, are effective. 'Zero-2-0', with its dark metal riffs and cut-ups of Michael on the phone, sleepy, playful and blue-tongued, and the B-side of 'Sometimes'—'Love Man'—are excellent experiments of the moment. The track 'Everything' is restrained. A smacking snare and bold approach to vocal mixing leave the lethal funk of the bass (Bill McDonald) and interplay of two exceptionally fine guitarists (Michael Sheridan and Arne Hanna) to rule there. 'Concrete' and 'Ot-Ven-Rot' sink deeper into the pleasure centres with each repeated listen. 'Soul Engine' and 'Tight' work well too, although the fast and furious recording does leave some ends and sounds a little underdone here and there. It would have been interesting to have heard John Murphy play live drums, rather than have most of them programmed, for instance. Two 100 per cent Olsen compositions are 'Buckethead' and the floating psychedelic fantasy 'Monday Night By Satellite'.

An article in *Juice* stated that Max Q was 'killed in a series of political moves'. Certainly Michael was discontented and disappointed with what felt like a derailment of the project.

Ollie agreed. 'He was really pissed off about it. Yeah. Yep.' If Max Q had been able to continue recording, or play live, 'I would have really loved to see Michael be able to extend himself further,' he said.

Apart from this frustration, did Ollie think Michael was happy? 'Oh yeah. I think, like most singers, he had insecurities. He was moody, yeah. He'd crack it sometimes. Get a bit angry and pissed off. He smashed a guitar once in the studio.' Ollie has a deep belly laugh. It belonged to Michael himself, according to Ollie. 'It was a very *nice* acoustic guitar, too! Like, what the fuck! What a waste of a *damn* good guitar! He got all moody because he got frustrated . . . And threw a bit of a turn . . . But he never *argued* with me, you know.'

Bill McDonald confirmed that Michael did indeed smash up a guitar in the studio. He was no wiser than Ollie as to the cause. Obviously it had been something Michael didn't want to discuss.

"No big deal. You know, it was guitar, and . . . He smashed it,' shrugged Bill. 'The worst thing was Gus spilled a glass of wine onto the mixing console. *That* was the worst. It was Rhinoceros. Gigantic mixing desk and . . . But that was back in the days when you could just take out modules, so they took out modules, and you know, hair dryers and . . . These days if you did that, it's digital, the whole thing's gone. You can't take out components.

'I wish Max Q had gone on,' sighed Bill. 'It would have been good. It's just a pity that it was *just* an album. Rather than an album *and* some performances—that would have *really* come together. Because Michael performed the songs as we were recording them.'

Being in this first-rate studio, playing, seeing and hearing Michael singing in the control room, his microphone lead plugged direct into the mixing desk, flying live with the band, triggered an unsatisfied appetite to play live with Max Q for the bass player. 'It wasn't like we'll patch together some vocals,' said Bill. 'He'd just do—takes. You know, a whole performance of the song, then he'd do another one.

'So it would make it come alive, obviously. Good singer, you know, he could sing in tune—good road-hardened voice. I appreciate those guys like him, and like Paul [Kelly], you know, who've just got that voice, kind of grungy, that can cut through a bad PA and a bad crowd, through a band. Just a really good guy. Friendly. Funny. He was really generous . . .' One of the things Bill took from the sessions was a new bass, one he still treasures: a 1976 Musicman Stingray with a tobacco sunburst finish.

'You know,' the bass player mused, 'him and Ollie, they were just like, in love with each other. They were just—off. Doing their plans. So we were yeah, kinda like the hired guns. We weren't cut into the deal too much. But yeah, it was Ollie and Michael—it was their baby.'

With fragments of publicity, Max Q aced the 1989 Rolling Stone Australia Awards, voted by readers and critics, with thirteen gongs. The band won Best New Artist; Michael Hutchence Best Singer and the coveted and serious Artist of the Year. John Murphy (who has since died, sadly) was gonged Best Drummer by the critics. And while John had played very fine drums and other instruments in most of Olsen's bands, due to the programmed nature of the album, his credits on *Max Q* include 'only' screams, percussion, bowed cymbal, Tibetan Thigh Bone (!) and trumpet, although his played drum loop formed the backbone of 'Love Man'.

At the 1990 ARIA Awards, although they didn't win anything in the end, Max Q had five nominations: Best Australian Single and Best Debut Single ('Way Of The World'); Engineer of the Year (Paula Jones); Best Debut Album (*Max Q*); and Video of the Year, 'Sometimes'. Then at the 1991 ARIAs the following year, Michael and Ollie were nominated for Producer of the Year for 'Monday Night By Satellite'. They didn't win that either, but gaining six ARIA nominations for one album was an outstanding achievement.

According to Bruce Butler, the album sold round half a million copies worldwide, going gold in Australia. It reached #13 on the ARIA album chart. In the USA, the album made #182 on the Billboard Top 200, while debut single 'Way Of The World' made good impact, peaking at #6 on the Modern Rock chart and #44 on the Dance chart. 'Sometimes' spent three weeks in the UK charts reaching #53. In Australia, 'Way Of The World' got to #8 on the ARIA charts, 'Sometimes' #31 and 'Monday Night By Satellite', the third single, missed the ARIA Top 100 but reached #91 on the Kent Report chart.

The chart positions show the optimistic spunk of a well-launched rocket starting to shudder, falter and fall around the time Michael was told to cease and desist media appearances to promote it.

Jen Jewel Brown spoke to Chris Murphy in 2013, prior to the INXS television mini-series *Never Tear Us Apart* (which frankly I found exploitative and insulting to our family, particularly to Mother; and not one family member or close friend of Michael's was invited to an advance screening, although the press was).

Chris said that for him, Max Q was 'just continuous controversy the entire time'. Would he like to see the album re-released?

'I think definitely,' he replied. 'When the timing's right—I think I *know* when the timing's going to be right. And I think at that stage, we'll put it back out. And quite frankly, all great music never dies. And you know, it was always a project that I had control of, and I had control of the masters . . .

'So all the people who sort of say, "Oh, it's a shame about the *Max Q* album"—well, I don't know if it's a shame because I think it might still have its heyday. If we get the timing selected right, and there's a bit of a reason, a bit of momentum, it could do quite well.' Jen asked Chris if he had a sense of when the right time might be.

'Around the end of 2013, early 2014 could be . . . I'm just waiting to see . . . A whole bunch of projects are in the works at the moment, and lots of spin-offs around those projects, and quite frankly, it'll just be obvious. And once those gates start opening up, well, then it's time to take the opportunity, so you know, I'm not really miffed by whatever tax haven, estates, whatever they are.'

As I write in 2018 there appears to be no slated rerelease of *Max Q*. Fingers crossed that situation will change.

Back in Los Angeles Michael distracted himself by looking for his dream car. His friend, photographer Andy Rosen, had a sideline brokering prestige automobiles and at Michael's request he tracked down a silver 1964 right-hand-drive DB5 aluminium-bodied Aston Martin, just like the one in the 1964 James Bond movie *Goldfinger*. Michael and Rosanna took it for a spin above Sunset Boulevard. What a thrill to drive the curves of the Hollywood Hills' Mulholland Drive in this gorgeous piece of machinery! Michael told Andy he would take it. No haggling; they would meet him the following day with the asking price of US$152,000. When Andy met Michael and Rosanna next, he expected a certified cheque. Instead Michael handed him a brown paper bag full of cash. He didn't even ask for the keys or certificate of title. (Andy told me this was highly unusual; he has never conducted a deal this way before or since.) It was such a special day in Michael's life that his favourite designer (and by now also good friend) Nick Egan went along and videoed the transaction; perhaps that served as a kind of Michael-style receipt. Then he asked Andy to store the car until he could send for it. He began checking into hotels as Mr Aston Martin, like some kind of realised Walter Mitty, but in truth his lifestyle wasn't settled enough to enjoy the car. It would be almost a year before he found a home to settle in so he could send for the beautiful vehicle.

The title of *Frankenstein Unbound* (1990) is stitched together from Mary Shelley's original novel *Frankenstein; or, The Modern Prometheus* and Percy Bysshe Shelley's drama *Prometheus Unbound*. The movie was co-written, directed and produced by Roger Corman, known as the 'Pope of Pop Cinema'. Nobody had churned out movies faster than Corman in the 1950s and '60s. He led the charge in the indie movie business and jump-started the careers of Robert De Niro, Dennis Hopper and Jack Nicholson to name a few.

As Michael's personal manager, Martha was on alert for roles that would suit his range and time constraints. After an initial meeting with Corman, Michael was offered the role of Mary Shelley's husband, Percy Bysshe Shelley, in this science-fiction horror movie, which would be Corman's last as a director. Bridget Fonda was cast as Mary Shelley.

Coincidentally, when we lived in Studio City and Michael was at North Hollywood High, Mother had worked on a Corman-produced movie starring Bridget's father, Peter Fonda: *Fighting Mad* (1976), directed by the great Jonathan Demme (*Silence of the Lambs*).

Others already signed to *Frankenstein Unbound* were John Hurt, Raúl Juliá and Jason Patric, whose acting Michael particularly admired. Jason and Michael got along immediately.

Rosanna was with Michael at the time. It was the middle of 1989. 'During filming we stayed at a gorgeous hotel in Bellagio, Italy,' she said. 'Michael was feeling quite confident about his work; he had his lines down and looked forward to each day on the set on the banks of Lake Como. Most evenings the whole cast and their partners along with Roger Corman would meet for dinner. The setting was so beautiful it really was a magical time. I think Michael was disappointed with the overall result of the movie when it premiered, but he looked upon it as experience.

'Whenever possible,' Rosanna continued, 'Michael and I took every opportunity to travel and sightsee when he didn't have commitments. After filming was wrapped, he, Jason Patric and I met up with Martha and her husband [entertainment attorney] Bill [Leibowitz] and we headed off for a tour of Venice, Rome, Sorrento and the Amalfi Coast.'

But Michael's relationship with Rosanna was coming to an end. Throughout the highs and lows of the worldwide Kick tour, the early excitement and later disappointments of Max Q, she had assumed important roles for him. She'd played his protector, personal assistant and travelling companion. She'd had his back, and he'd sorely needed that. They would always be friends but the romance had run its course. Michael encouraged Rosanna to spread her wings and explore life beyond his side, as he craved new adventures too. She opened a successful casting agency and continued to be one of Michael's closest friends, and mine.

11

suicide blonde

SOPHISTICATION had not yet entered her lexicon but she was working on it—and Michael was doing his damnedest to help her along on that path.

I liked Kylie—how could I not?

The five-foot-tall 21-year-old he introduced me to as his next girl-friend—although I admit I was shocked beyond belief to hear it—was quite impressive. Although self-conscious and vulnerable at times, like Michael himself, Kylie Minogue was open-hearted and polite. She had many other attributes too. Apart from her obvious beauty, she was family-oriented, bright, ambitious, a fast learner, self-aware and eager to please. The cherry on top was that she was talented.

Kylie's *Neighbours* character, Charlene Robinson, your everyday girl mechanic in overalls and a flannelette shirt, had been a big drawcard on the huge television soap opera *Neighbours* for two years. By the time she 'married' her real-life boyfriend 'Scott' (Jason Donovan) and left *Neighbours* to pursue pop, she also had one of the most recognisable faces in the UK. Kylie blazed a path a string of other *Neighbours* alumni would follow over the years, although none would have such eyebrow-raising success on the charts.

Right out of the box, her very first single, 'Locomotion', spent seven weeks at #1 in Australia. A rerecorded version reached #2 in England; #1 in Belgium, Finland, Ireland, Israel, Japan and South Africa and #3 on the US Billboard Hot 100. (Wouldn't INXS have loved to do that right off!)

In fact, in the eighteen months before meeting Michael, Kylie had grinned her way through a whole cavalcade of dance-pop videos that became hit singles around the world.

Affectionately nicknamed 'the Singing Budgie' (short for budgerigar), Kylie had even won the Gold Logie for Most Popular Personality on television in Australia in 1988! But you could have knocked me over with a budgie feather to think that a Logie would impress Michael.

His previous girlfriend Rosanna had told him, in the first blush of their relationship, that although their love was strong, the day would come when his career would take a natural dip. Then he'd feel the tug to move on; maybe fall for someone famous. Naturally Michael denied this could ever happen. But in some ways Ro was foretelling the future.

Of course the English and Australian media went into a frenzy over the 'odd' and very famous couple. For the first time Michael began to be troubled by stalking paparazzi with telephoto lenses.

We met up at a Japanese restaurant in Sydney. Kylie was her adorable, blonde, curly-haired, spunky self while her 'older man' (by eight years) Michael was wearing a dorky hat which, coupled with his black thick-rimmed everyday glasses, gave him the appearance of Inspector Gadget.

Heaven help the man attempting to hide out next to Kylie Minogue.

When she excused herself to go to the bathroom all eyes in the restaurant trailed her to the door. It was my birthday and, after dinner, the three of us went to see a movie. That ended in a fan pursuit so hysterical it was like the chase scene in The Beatles' *Hard Day's Night*.

Actually I came to see how Kylie was very clever when it came to the media and public relations. After several years in the limelight with an effective management machine behind her, she understood the career value of the right 'photo op' at the right time. She was frugal with the opportunities she offered the professionals and she shared the depth of her publicity experience with her new boyfriend. She warned him how easy it is for them to turn on you.

Michael had never known bad press. He couldn't imagine it becoming a problem. INXS had always been on the up-and-up trajectory. His feeling was that you, the interviewee, have the power to control the information. It had always worked for him so far. He mused about the hundreds of interviews he had given, how he'd steered the flow and the content with his thoughtful answers and disarming humour.

True enough.

But Kylie had worked in London. The big time. In the domain of Fleet Street. She was familiar with the perils of wowserish, scandal-addicted front-page journalism. Like the tabloid *News of the World*, for instance, founded in 1843 on the trail of vice, outrage and sensation. Before it crashed to earth in 2001 (following its self-inflicted, unsurvivable phone-tapping scandal) at times it was the biggest-selling English language paper on earth. In the USA, it was the *National Enquirer* which came sniffing after celebrity drug and alcohol shenanigans, more gossip and scandal: a licence to print money to the paparazzi. So much power in the hands of so few.

Attack was always better than defence; that was the power of committing to the right exclusive at the right time. Michael shook his head.

Doing media campaigns was a hard slog sometimes, and repetitive. But he was superb at it and he knew it. He simply could not see the pitfalls.

• • •

In November 1989 INXS returned to the site of their greatest recording success, Rhinoceros, to start the process of recording their seventh studio album. They welcomed back producer Chris Thomas to the big chair for the album that would be *X*.

X: ten in Roman numerals. Ten years since their first album. X for ecstasy, some might guess. And, of course, the essential X of INXS.

This would be the third of Thomas's trilogy of INXS albums. Music that keeps playing on radio stations scattered like confetti around the world. Songs strangers sing as they wander past you on the street.

But before *X* could sit in the classic racks alongside *Listen Like Thieves* and *Kick*, there was much to be done. Since Michael, Andrew, Tim, Kirk, Jon and Garry last made a record together they'd been awarded so much silverware they didn't know where to put it. Yes, there had been side projects, but it was time to reopen the chronicle of INXS and see what the next chapter could bring.

The band had taken a whole year off after the utter brain-grinder of the international Kick tour. Now they were back working together again, the gloves were off in some respects too. Instances of paranoia and insecurity ran rife. Andrew was still offended Michael hadn't discussed Max Q with him. On the other side, there was a rumour that it was Andrew who pushed Chris Murphy to shut Max Q down promotionally.

Now, after the success that had come from the other band members giving the green light for Michael and Andrew to co-write their last album *Kick* alone, the musical powerhouse of the group discovered he was no longer automatically co-writing everything. Michael, never one to be tied down, had co-written two tracks in the running, 'Faith

In Each Other' and 'Disappear', with Andrew's little brother Jon while they were hanging out being residents of Hong Kong together earlier in 1989. There was friction over whose songs would go on the album.

By Christmas 1989, when Michael and Kylie's romance was new, our family's nomadic impulses were on full display. In our regular chats with each other we were all preoccupied with new pastures, future plans. Of course this probably seemed normal to Kylie. It was a good fit. She regularly flew back and forth across the world in search of new markets herself.

Rhett, who'd always been resourceful and artistic, was visiting from Los Angeles. He'd been working on music videos there with the help of Nick Egan and others.

Rosanna had given Michael a parting gift. She'd arranged for Rhett to move in with her friend Lovey, an actress with an apartment near the Hollywood Bowl. Michael was constantly trying to find ways to settle our younger brother into something that would inspire him to find his niche. It seemed to be working out well.

Meanwhile, our mother was making a new life for herself on the Gold Coast in Queensland with her new love, Ross Glassop. We'd all become really fond of this loving, gentlemanly man too and it was a joy to see her so happy. She'd opened yet another make-up academy and published a book in 1988: *Make-up Is Magic: From the 1920s to now, corrective, fantasy and fun.* Kell was in Hong Kong with his Susie and they seemed pretty happy together as well. They hadn't made it back to Australia for the holidays that year. Michael, Rhett and I were very pleased that our parents had found life partners who suited them so much better.

I was planning a return to LA, and soon we'd be scattered across the globe once again.

Kylie, meanwhile, was rehearsing—in her case for her second major tour; this one called Enjoy Yourself, after her second album, due to start in Australia in February 1990. She and Michael met up when they could, all the while being tracked and troubled by the goss-hounds of the paparazzi.

In late 1989 Michael rented an apartment at the gracious Connaught, overlooking Hyde Park in downtown Sydney, for a while. He and Kylie stayed there together when they could. She was very close to her stylist Nicole Bonython-Hines, 'the stylist's stylist', who had worked with her from her early days. Nicole was designing stage gear like the Australian flag jacket, silver shorts and outsize red cap Kylie would wear for the upcoming tour, so there were heaps of clothes stashed at the Connaught. One time when Kylie was off doing something else, Michael asked me to come and get a Hard Rock Cafe jacket Kylie wanted Erin to have. We found the tiny thing in the bedroom. Unopened shopping bags of new clothes spilled all over the floor—no doubt part of the cache of things Nicole had brought in for her to try, or that she'd bought out shopping with Michael.

After Kylie enjoyed Christmas with her own family in Melbourne, she and Michael hosted a small get-together at the Connaught on New Year's Eve. That would be a launching pad for various other parties our small group hopped in and out of together through the night.

At the last party of all, I finally got the chance for a quiet one-on-one when Kylie sat herself down next to me. I asked her how she and Michael met.

Apparently Nicole, who was the daughter of gallery-owner Kym Bonython and his model wife Julie Bonython, knew Michael, and she had offered to arrange a date.

But Kylie didn't raise the precursor incident, repeated on many Tumblr pages (although its original source has proved elusive).

'I was eighteen, standing in a corner by a wall, really scared, sur-rounded by three bodyguards,' Kylie said. (This was three years before they got together.) 'He came staggering over, really drunk, wasted on something, and he said, "What are we going to do first, have lunch or have sex?"

'Those were the first words he ever said to me.'

I rather suspect that instead of the two words 'have sex', there might just possibly have been a single four-letter word in that question. But if so, the ladylike public persona of Kylie Minogue wouldn't have been likely to repeat it.

When Michael arrived to pick Kylie up at her hotel in Hong Kong for their first lunch date, he told me, he was 'very late and slightly inebriated'. He wasn't concerned until he knocked on the door of her suite; but when it opened, there sat her parents formally arranged like a judging panel alongside her manager Terry Blamey, inspecting him with great interest. Fortunately, Michael's mastery of social niceties got him through but it was a near thing.

Kylie revealed herself to be a well-raised young woman from a close-knit, watchful family. Michael was very sweet on her and he always called her 'my baby'. Before then, his partners were always taking care of *him*. This time, *he* was the protector. He tried to have a private life with her and let things develop naturally. But people were intrigued by the whole 'innocent' Kylie–'rampant rock-star' Michael angle. Those who adored the goofy, naive side of Kylie were quite suspicious of Michael's intentions too, at times.

My brother had never dated anyone this famous before. He was shocked by the insistent paparazzi, their subtle reconnoitring. The telephoto lenses you couldn't see trying to catch you taking off your clothes, bathing at the beach or kissing your girlfriend in a park when an affectionate whim crossed your mind, the results plastered across some magazine in the doctor's waiting room when you went in for a sore throat.

This was the time when the price of catching somebody famous off guard started to skyrocket. Magazines outbid each other for romantic new celebrity couple pics. And frankly, the sight of Michael and Kylie cuddling on the grass on a sunny afternoon got everyone excited. It was sort of like the Loch Ness Monster—a photo proved that 'Michael and Kylie' really *did* exist.

Michael had painstakingly learned, tour by tour, how to stir up an enormous crowd and keep them happy for hours, how to play to the back row at stadiums. Kylie was just beginning to move into that phase of her career and there had been no 'pub tours' or 'support spots' for her to break in her show-woman tricks. Michael took great pleasure in helping her find key musicians for the backup band she was about to tour with. James Freud from Models would play bass and, in the Australian leg of this world tour, Greg Perano was on percussion. When the songbird needed some confidence to face a live audience, they set up a small, private warm-up show with Michael front and centre.

Their relationship was new and exciting and the two of them spent a lot of time on the phone. Michael had been trying to come up with the right lyrics for one of Andrew's new instrumental recordings when Kylie rang one day. It was around the time she was filming her first lead feature film role as sixteen-year-old Lola in *The Delinquents*.

'Hey, what's up?'

'Well, in the next scenes we shoot, Lola has dyed her hair. So I'm having it done now!' she laughed.

'True? What colour?'

'Suicide blonde!!!'

As well as the colour Kylie's honey-coloured tresses turned that day, 'suicide blonde' is an expression with a history. It traces back to 'blonde bombshell' Jean Harlow, star of the 1931 comedy *Platinum Blonde*, who regularly had her hair treated with ammonia and household bleach. The resultant toxic vapours were suspected of causing kidney damage. A star with genuine talent, Jean sadly died from complications of kidney failure at the age of 26.

Anyway, INXS's 'Suicide Blonde' (A. Farriss, M. Hutchence), inspired by Kylie's dye job for *The Delinquents*, became such a fresh, infectious romp racing out of speaker systems around the world. The first single off *X* sounded like nothing else with its syncopated, sampled harp riff from Native American blues artist Charlie Musselwhite blazing away.

INXS had found out that Charlie was in Sydney while they were laying down *X*. He came in and played some great stuff that was used on three tracks. Charlie's 1967 album *Stand Back! Here Comes Charley Musselwhite's Southside Band* announced a legend, and INXS adding some of his harmonica raunch to *X* was a master stroke.

'Suicide Blonde' reached #2 on the Australian charts, #9 in the US top 10 and #11 in the UK.

The Delinquents wasn't a hit movie but Kylie was well reviewed and even did a topless scene (!). At its premiere in Sydney, waves of music and film names parted like the Red Sea when she entered hand in hand with her beau. They looked very comfortable together, exuding a mix of Pearly King and Queen splendour and streetsmart Aussie hip. Michael was in an outfit he wore for the Max Q 'Sometimes' video clip: jewel-patterned black pants, combat boots and a black vest with pearly button strips that showed off his dancer's chest. Kylie was in a thigh-scraper mini-dress that looked like black velvet with a giant, sequined crossword puzzle on it and a platinum waif bob. He looked like the cat that swallowed the canary. She grinned like the cat that got the cream.

In a *Sydney Morning Herald* story in 2015, Kylie said, 'Michael was Byron-esque, he was poetic, he was cultured and hilarious and tender. He was all of these things. I guess I was the perfect age, I was 21 years old, to get the butterfly wings and go out into the world and we collided at that time and I guess he just fast-tracked some of it. Anyway, it was a glorious time. I loved it.' And you know, so did he.

Here's to butterfly wings.

• • •

In mid-1990 Michael and Kylie dropped by to see me in LA where I'd returned to live yet again. Michael raved about a place he'd snapped up in the South of France for US$1.5 million cash—a bargain!—from the manager of Duran Duran. Apparently he'd been there before. Years ago, when holidaying with Michael Hamlyn at Cannes, just some obscure upstart Australian hanging on the coat-tails of Richard Lowenstein, he'd gone to a party there. The villa was called Vieille Ferme des Guerchs. Later Michael's caretaker told me that Simon Le Bon often called during summer months, to ask if it was vacant. But I think mostly Simon just came when Michael *was* there, later, and they hung out and were what the English call 'naughty', whatever that means.

Michael asked me if I'd move into the front cottage and manage the villa. He wanted to let it out for photographic shoots, and it was hired out that way for a while too. My eldest, Brent, had left home by then to attend college in Oregon, and if Erin hadn't been only twelve years old and dealing with some crucial years of school, I would have done it.

Michael had his dream home. He began referring to it as 'the family home' pretty quickly too. He finally had a private garage for his Aston Martin and bought a black Mercedes jeep for running around in and a yellow Peugeot convertible for staff and visiting guests. Some wonderful family times were to be spent there, and some bleaker days too.

Chris Bailey of the Saints and his wife, Pearl, joined Michael and Kylie in the south of France that year. There had been two months touring Europe with INXS for Michael on the Suicide Blonde tour, including four nights straight at Wembley Arena (a feat of drawing power and performance). Finally, he had three weeks to himself.

The little village of Roquefort-les-Pins was surrounded by a pine forest in the Alpes-Maritimes, Provence. The views from the two largest upstairs bedrooms of the villa were enthralling. On a clear day you could see all the way to the Riviera coast. With all the surrounding villages, it was impossible to be bored or uninspired. Whether your medium was paint, words or music, it was an artist's dream.

And Michael's 'farmhouse' itself was rather grand, set as it was on just over one-and-a-half hectares of lush land overlooking the Cote d'Azur. The main villa was nearly four hundred square metres. There were five bedrooms upstairs and a vaulted basement with a sixth bedroom downstairs. The ceilings were low, fitting the period history. There was a fully equipped kitchen and a graceful swimming pool that Michael would later redevelop (as it was a little run-down) set in beautiful natural gardens.

Most of the lounge and dining furniture was in situ when Michael bought the villa but Kylie helped him with the rest. She was eager to try out some recipes, comparing notes with Pearl while the two vagabond minstrel poets, 'Byron' and 'Shelley', did what *they* always did when they got together—drink and talk all night. The foursome did some sightseeing, exploring local villages and eateries, picking up last-minute Christmas gifts and checking out various cities on the French Riviera including a daytrip to the principality of Monaco.

Pearl sensed that things didn't quite feel right between Michael and Kylie on this visit. Although there was no hostility on display, their body language had cooled.

In fact, Michael had already begun romancing Helena Christensen. He had 'met' her (albeit over the phone only, so far), through Herb Ritts. Although most people did not know her name at this stage, Helena had made quite a splash in the 1989 Chris Isaak video 'Wicked Game', which Ritts directed. Often voted one of the sexiest videos of all time, it features the camera following the magnificent twenty-year-old Helena slowly in close-up embraces along the beach.

As the new decade dawned in January 1991, INXS played two sold-out indoor shows in Mexico City's Palacio de los Deportes, before heading off to Brazil's Rock in Rio with its sensational line-up of Ziggy

Marley, George Michael, Billy Idol, Donna Summer, Run DMC, Guns N' Roses and Robert Plant. At those three concerts alone they played to more than 150,000 people.

For another big show in Buenos Aires, a stunner in just shorts and stilettos kissed Michael happy birthday onstage with a cake for his 31st. This seven-month tour would wind from South America up through the northern continent to Canada, then jet down to the southern hemisphere and Australia before travelling through many of the countries in Europe.

The INXS X-Factor tour started in Los Angeles on 1 February with a warm-up at the Whisky Au Go Go and a great after-party in Michael's suite at the Four Seasons. They left California for four more dates on the east coast and on Saturday, 9 February, appeared on *Saturday Night Live* playing 'Suicide Blonde' and 'Bitter Tears' in New York City.

By this stage Michael and the rest of INXS had become quite socially fragmented. Because 1991 was the year Mark Opitz spent on the road with them as musical consultant, he remembers it well.

'I noticed on the tour that Michael definitely lived in his part of the tour and the band lived in their parts of the tour,' he recalled. 'Like Andrew did what Andrew did, was just solo. Tim did what Tim did after shows, which was get on his computer and look at cars, or whatever. Garry had Jodie there so they'd be off doing what they were doing and Jon would be confused about what he was doing but Michael would be going off, sometimes taking Jon with him, to parties. And I'd go off with Michael too when I was there, *heaps*, to parties, thinking "I haven't done *this* before", said Mark wryly.

His role was one only a visionary band and management might have come up with. 'My main job on that tour was to be the first person backstage—with the tour manager, Michael Long—to comment on the show. To give technical advice on how songs are running into each other, how the set was working, how the songs were working . . . You know, anything that I could see, while they were fresh. It was quite fun doing it because everyone was in an up mood then.'

Helena and Michael arranged to have their first face-to-face contact. She was coming to New York for a modelling assignment.

Michael was nervous about their first date. A few days before she was due to arrive, to alleviate his nerves, Michael asked if Mark would come along, and also invite their mutual friend, New York-based artist Kay Mahoney (sister of both Jimmy Barnes' wife, Jane, and also Jep Lizotte, coincidentally the caterer for the *Max Q* album sessions at Rhinoceros) to dinner too.

'And so Michael's first date with Helena,' Mark said, 'was with myself and Kay at the New York Plaza Oak Room. It was a fabulous, palatial, oak-and-velvet kind of old-English room, with massive casement windows overlooking Central Park and snow falling under light outside. It was beautiful. Just stunning. INXS fans huddled across the street in the snow. But there it was. Plaza, New York—you know, it was just like being in a James Stewart movie.'

Helena had never been to an INXS concert, had never seen Michael perform live. The first time she did was at Madison Square Garden on 16 February.

What an amazing showcase that was! Michael did not disappoint; he never did. But in the audience was not only Helena, but also our mother and her new husband (of two weeks), the gorgeous Ross (the boss) Glassop, retired and highly decorated Royal Australian Air Force commander. Mother and Ross were on their 'round the world' honeymoon, having married in Reno, Nevada, on their first leg.

The band and our mother were staying at the Plaza, a Manhattan property that its owner Donald Trump called 'the Mona Lisa of hotels'. That and the private Learjet that the band was touring in were signs that they had indeed come a long, long way from those days of dingy motels with four to a room, sharing soggy hamburgers and fish and chips.

In fact, at this stage INXS stayed at the Plaza for an entire month.

'We all had these amazing, palatial, *huge* rooms,' Mark said. 'Just massive. I had the benefit of knowing the head chef of the Edward VII room, the restaurant. And so we used to get a private table down in the kitchen every now and again, as well, which was quite interesting. But I really count myself lucky to be able to say, yeah, well I spent a month holed up in the Plaza, in a great room, in the snow. Getting paid for it. How good is that? That's what it was, for a year. Chicago, Toronto, shit, so many places, you know. Kentucky. Just incredible.'

Mark witnessed firsthand how much Michael was enjoying himself at this time.

'We'd get back from say Philadelphia, one car would take the band, who didn't want to go out—mostly everybody—back to the Plaza with the bags. And those who wanted to go out, which was usually just me and Michael, would take one of the other cars, and head off down the Village or to clubs. Like I remember going to clubs once with him and Michael rang ahead and Peter Allen was waiting for him, for a private party. It was full on. Going out most nights, coming home late and going, wow, did that really happen?'

•   •   •

When Mother and Ross were escorted backstage by INXS's hefty head of security, Jeff Pope, before the show on 16 February, the only other person in the room was the former Miss Denmark herself. Helena was standing there in a long white dress, hair cascading around her bare shoulders, unsmiling and statuesque. Mother didn't immediately recognise her and wondered who she might be with. Before she could introduce herself, Michael appeared and made the introductions. It was also Ross's first time at a concert—any concert, in fact—and I'm sure he was glad for his hearing loss from 40 years as a fighter pilot and instructor in the air force, because the reception at the 20,000-seater was overwhelming.

After the show Mother and Ross retired to the Plaza and slipped a note under Michael's door, inviting him for lunch the next day and suggesting that he might like to bring Helena along. Imagine their surprise when he showed up to the restaurant with Kylie instead. It was a meal laced with uncomfortable pauses. Mother gathered that Kylie was staying in Michael's suite, but when had she arrived? Mother had no way of knowing if Kylie had seen the note to Michael, inviting Helena instead of her. To be fair, we had no idea Kylie was there at the time. The frostiness was only interrupted by Michael's questions to Ross about his career, as he was keen to get to know his mother's new partner better. None of us met up with Kylie again after this and she left New York the following day.

12

rue des Canettes

ON A COLD, EARLY EVENING IN PARIS, the jet that had just flown us across the North Atlantic touched down. It was 18 December 1991; Erin and I were flying together and it was the very first time that either of us had set foot in France. Michael was hosting Christmas at his villa for the whole family and we were the first to arrive.

He met us at the airport, just as excited as we were, and we took a taxi to the little apartment he and Helena shared in Saint-Germain-des-Prés. On the drive into Paris he shared the considerable knowledge he'd picked up on the Parisian histories flashing by our window. Apparently both Helena and his housekeeper had been teaching him French. He was keen to practise speaking it; I had never seen him so committed to acquiring a new skill.

We arrived at rue des Canettes—the charmingly named street of ducklings—a street no wider than an alley that dated back to the thirteenth century. Michael gallantly struggled with our luggage, overstuffed with winter clothing and Christmas gifts as it was, into an old building and up a winding staircase to the first floor. With many a dramatic flourish he gave us the grand tour of the tiny yet enchanting two-bedroom apartment. There was a self-portrait of Frida Kahlo as you entered and a mirrored armoire to the right where family photographs and other memorabilia were on display. Michael enjoyed relaying how he and Helena had gone to the local market and bargained for the beautiful old furniture.

The apartment's eclectic approach was charming. Ahead, the gleaming wood floors of a generous living room were scattered with expensive-looking rugs, flooded with light from floor-to-ceiling windows, looking down onto the tiny street. A range of beautiful tapestries and paintings, including some of Helena's own work, adorned the walls. It was quite stark, with French slat-board cafe chairs and small, odd tables with books resting invitingly on them.

The floorboards creaked and the hallway ended at a spiral staircase that went nowhere. It was clear that the whole building had once been a single grand house. Across from the building was a restaurant that Michael and Helena frequented. Outside its entrance lay the matted English-sheepdog-in-residence, liable to howl at various times of the day or night.

The bathroom was tiny, with a claw-footed bathtub. Every surface was spilling over with product, no doubt gathered from many fashion shoots and runways. Helena had the latest and best of everything cosmetic and a smorgasbord of perfumes. In the centre sat the largest bottle of Michael's favourite cologne, Guerlain's rich, sensual Habit Rouge.

Michael laid out delicious French cheeses and crisp rolls, uncorking a gorgeous local vintage to go with it. We were counting our blessings when in strode the femme now in the centre of Michael's life. Twenty-two-year-old Helena Christensen had the green-eyed gaze of a

In the backyard of our Frenchs Forest home, Sydney, in 1964: Michael was four, Rhett eighteen months and I was sixteen. Caring for my little brothers while our parents worked was both blissful and challenging.

Michael, Mother, Rhett and I upon arriving in Hong Kong in January 1965: taking in the view from Victoria Peak.

Michael, at seven, looking very serious in his uniform for Glenealy in 1967—the second of his three Hong Kong primary schools. We were already onto our fourth residence in Hong Kong.

January 1970: Michael celebrating his tenth birthday at our home in Kowloon Tong with his close friend Tim Stewart.

Michael at eleven with some medals he won in the pool in competition at the Hong Kong United Services Recreation Club. He was a strong swimmer and fearless diver.

Michael and his talented and prolific writing partner Andrew Farriss (seated in front of him) on an early INXS tour crisscrossing Australia.

INXS at the ABC Studios in Melbourne, 20 December 1981, to perform 'Stay Young' in a *Countdown* Australian hits 'Summer Special'. L–R Andrew Farriss, Jon Farriss, Michael, Kirk Pengilly, Garry Gary Beers and Tim Farriss.

Michael, myself and Rhett—who had two broken wrists after totalling Michael's motorcycle. We always found something to laugh about though.

TINA HUTCHENCE COLLECTION

SERGE THOMANN

Michael in a newly acquired hat in West Hollywood in 1983. INXS supported Adam Ant on their first Southern California dates.

Looking fierce as a post-apocalyptic steampunker on the set of the 'Listen Like Thieves' video at the Palais Theatre, Melbourne, in 1985. Michael enjoyed every minute.

MIRANDA BROWN

INXS in Paris in 1984 on their first European tour, photographed by their then overseas publicist Miranda Brown (Jen Jewel Brown's younger sister).

RENNIE ELLIS

Michael with the beautiful, intelligent and sweet Michele Bennett at the 1986 Countdown Awards. They were similar in so many ways—not the least of which was their shared addiction to literature.

SERGE THOMANN

On the set of Richard Lowenstein's cult feature *Dogs in Space* in 1986 with his co-star Saskia Post. She would later rent Michael's Sydney house.

The eight-band entourage for Australian Made (Boxing Day 1986 to Australia Day 1987) made travel arrangements a nightmare. Here Michael and Michele arrive for one of the concerts.

Australian Made bonding was fun. Michael is sandwiched between Divinyls guitarist Frank Infante (ex Blondie) and singer Chrissy Amphlett—Australia's greatest-ever female rock star.

Michael and the stunning American model Rosanna Crash (here with Tim Farriss and Chris Murphy) spent almost three years together; she was good for him.

When Michael was on stage, connecting with his audience was assured. He had that special something that made everyone feel he was singing directly to them.

IAN GREENE, 1988

TINA HUTCHENCE COLLECTION

Michael and me in 1989. In INXS's 'I'm Just A Man', which tells our family's story, he referred to me as 'Sweet Sister T'. That song meant so much to all of us and many tears were shed over it.

The Calling All Nations tour came to Melbourne on Halloween, 1988. Four shows there (playing to 60,000) and six in Sydney (80,000) underlined how huge INXS had become.

The lighting crew set a moody indigo vibe around INXS's lead singer on their Si Lo Tienes Muevelo Australian tour. Festival Hall, Melbourne, September 1986.

Holidaying on the secluded island of Bora Bora, Tahiti, in 1989; Michael in a reflective mode.

Max Q performing in their 'Sometimes' clip in 1989. L–R Arne Hanna (in wheelchair, partly obscured), John Murphy, Ollie Olsen, Michael, Gus Till. Members not shown are Bill McDonald and Michael Sheridan.

Ollie Olsen and Michael listening to their Hit Factory Max Q mixes in the black Lincoln Town Car Michael hired for their stay in New York.

Michael as Percy Bysshe Shelley with Bridget Fonda playing Mary Shelley in *Frankenstein Unbound*; on location in Bellagio, Italy, in 1989.

Michael and Kylie Minogue during their blissful and (for once) press-free days on the *Orient Express*. In 2015 she recalled this as 'the most incredible adventure'.

Vieille Ferme des Guerchs, the French villa Michael bought from the manager of Duran Duran, looking from the luxurious cabana back towards the house.

Helena Christensen and Michael at a family gathering in Denmark in 1992. She nursed him with care after an assault left him with a significant brain injury that changed the course of his life.

Michael and Helena had a very playful relationship. Here they are clowning around backstage during the 1993 Get Out Of The House tour.

Our house-proud, generous host preparing a traditional Australian-style barbecue in 1994 for guests in the grounds of his beloved villa.

With Paula Yates in Byron Bay, for Rhett and his partner Mandy Nolan's little Zoe Angel's naming ceremony in 1995. The complicated Englishwoman clearly intrigued Michael.

Mother was charmed by Paula and her children at their first meeting in 1995.

Michael's last summer, 1997. Snapped by the ever-present paparazzi with Paula and Tiger in Beverly Hills, LA.

Mother's home in Main Beach, Christmas 1996. L–R Peaches Geldof, Michael, Tiger Lily, Paula, Pixie Geldof, Mother and Ross. Paula later upset our mother by claiming her nanny was writing a book about her.

Michael performing with INXS onstage at Wembley Arena on the Elegantly Wasted tour, 18 June 1997. He was exhausted but still giving his all.

A combined party—for Tiger Lily's first and Erin's nineteenth birthday—at my home in Burbank, California, on 26 July 1997.

Main Beach, Easter 2006. Tiger Lily on the only visit she was allowed to make to her maternal grandmother as a child after her parents' deaths.

JIMMY STEINFELDT

Michael's last ever gig, at the Viper Room, Hollywood, 12 November 1997.
L–R Black Grape's Danny Saber, Rolling Stones singer Bernard Fowler, Michael and
Stevie Salas. He sang 'Suffragette City' and returned for a big set closer of The Faces'
'Maggie May' with Ivan Neville and ZZ Top's Billy Gibbons on guitar. Michael
adored Black Grape, and now he was recording solo tracks with Danny Saber.

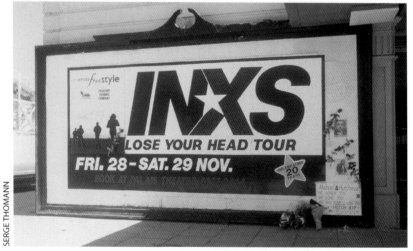

SERGE THOMANN

The gig, the tour that was not to be. Moving fan tributes for Michael begin to
gather beside the giant INXS billboard outside the Palais Theatre in St Kilda
on 22 November 1997.

jaguar and a powerful presence. With her perfectly balanced body and natural, unfussy style, the daughter of a Peruvian mother and a Danish father was such a golden-skinned beauty she seemed other-worldly. But right now she was in a real mood. Her hair had been tightly curled, being half up, half down, and she was upset about that—along with the lashings of make-up they had trowelled on her for the shoot.

In all honesty I don't think Helena could look anything but enchanting, but I guess if your face and body are your livelihood you want every photo session to show you at your best. We would discover that, in private, she never seemed the least bit fussed about her looks, so perhaps it was the uncomfortable artifice that irritated her that day.

It might be hard to understand how a model can complain about her job, but we're all human. First-world problems, perhaps, but it's all relative, whether you wait tables for a living or stand in front of hot lights for hours posing while people squirt water spray or blow wind machines at you and fuss with your hair, face and clothes—except most definitely regarding the pay!

Helena announced that she was starving and did not feel like bread and cheese.

We were happy to go anywhere for dinner; after all, this was our first night in Paris! But Michael took us to a magnificent place. La Coupole ('the dome') is an enormous old restaurant on the Boulevard du Montparnasse. It is steeped in art history, and Michael had chosen it for just that reason, for Erin's sake. She was only thirteen then but she had already won several art competitions and had her heart set on being an artist in some capacity. My daughter was (and is) soft-spoken and somewhat shy, but if you touch on a subject she feels passionate about she'll give you an earful—not unlike her famous uncle. Taking in the Art Deco decor and beautiful works on the walls of La Coupole made it easy to imagine you were seated next to Hemingway, Dali or Picasso—all of whom actually frequented La Coupole in the past.

Michael was so droll and entertaining that night. Clearly he loved the laissez-faire Parisian attitude towards fame and was enjoying just being able to be himself. When he hailed a taxi to take us home, the driver pointed to a sign in French. Only three passengers allowed— and there were four of us. So Helena, whose ravenous appetite that night had been vanquished and who was therefore feeling much more playful, jumped in after Erin and me, slamming the door on Michael who for once was summarily abandoned. As she imperiously ordered the driver to take us to rue des Canettes and we departed, I turned to see Michael's expression through the back window change from surprise to amusement. Helena laughed most of the way back home and fell into Michael's arms when he arrived in his own taxi. Their relationship was very loving, spirited and at times competitive. She challenged him.

The next morning Helena had another modelling assignment and, despite the fact that she hadn't been feeling well, having eaten something that did not agree with her, she was gone before we rose. I thought it very professional of her.

On the day we were leaving for Nice, Michael woke us with breakfast and lugged our bags downstairs again. We ran behind him as he hailed a taxi. He opened the door for us, then jumped in too, directing the driver to the Paris-Gare de Lyon in perfect French.

Not content to let us stumble around the huge multi-level train station (the third busiest in France), Michael insisted on getting us seated on our train, then darted off to buy a stack of magazines and snacks for our trip as well. I was grateful he deposited us safely on the right train, because with the confusion of announcements and signs in a foreign language, who knows where we could have ended up? As we pulled away from the platform he waved us off with a big smile on his face.

'See you down there,' I lip-read in the grand noise of Paris-Gare de Lyon.

The French landscape we took in as we travelled by rail almost the whole length of France, winding south to Nice on the Cote d'Azur, was stunning. Many of the views out my window looked like Impressionist masterpieces you might come across in the Musée d'Orsay. Honestly, I didn't dare put my nose into the magazines Michael had laid in my lap for fear of missing something.

Rhett arrived in the black 1991 Mercedes-Benz G class Michael called 'the jeep' to pick us up from the train station. From Nice we still needed to be driven west, through the less settled countryside of the French Riviera to the little village of Roquefort-les-Pins, a succession of small rural hamlets and secluded wild areas around Roquefortoise forest. As I sat in the front seat of the relatively new luxury SUV, I glanced down to see cigarette burns in the leather upholstery and wires hanging loose where the stereo ought to be. Rhett just shrugged and described a 'hilarious night' when he had driven down some steps in the middle of town. I didn't want to know any more—and I sure as heck didn't want to be around when he explained this to Michael.

13

Vieille Ferme des Guerchs

IT WAS DARK when we reached the house but I could still read the sign across the main gate: 'Vieille Ferme des Guerchs'. The old farmhouse had originally belonged to a family called the Guerchs. It was a magnificent, rambling place. It would be Michael's home, for all intents and purposes, for seven years, until he left us, and it will always be Michael's home to me.

As we drove through the main gate, we came upon the two-bedroom caretaker's cottage, surrounded by gorgeous trees and flowers. Sunflowers, Australian bottlebrush and grevilleas were scattered around. Michael had replaced the previous ageing pool and cabana and taken great pains to make sure that the surrounding grove of old olive trees was kept intact and healthy. At the same time he had ordered a new double garage, avoiding modern touches, of course—even in the garage doors—and his contractor had purposefully used large rocks and beams like those the villa already featured as well. Later would come a pool house, its style also in keeping with the architecture of the low-ceilinged, vine-wrapped villa.

The main building was an old farmhouse, although that description belies reality, as the villa, while earthy and simple in style, was rather grand. The numerals over the door suggested it was around 400 years old. There were six bedrooms, two upstairs with sea views. The kitchen, dining room, living room, playroom, music room and three more bedrooms were on the ground floor. The basement was extensive too, large enough for a two-bedroom apartment, and there were plentiful bathrooms throughout.

Even though it was winter, a tracing of bougainvillea in a brilliant magenta surrounded the front-door entrance. Michael's house manager, Carol, greeted us and led us upstairs to choose bedrooms. Michael had requested that I take the second-largest bedroom, next to his. That way, when our divorced parents arrived with their new partners, the couples would have the choice of any *other* bedroom. Michael was being the diplomatic middle child and peacemaker that he was; he wanted both Kell and Mother to feel equally loved and valued. The fact that the remaining bedrooms were all similarly sized, he hoped, would symbolise that, and prevent either from the fear of looking as though they had 'grabbed' a superior room, thus snubbing the other. He was very concerned about this holiday being harmonious.

Before our arrival Michael had been away two months, so Rhett was occupying the master suite until his brother arrived. He raised the subject of why Mother had chosen to taken Michael to California all those years ago and not him. I knew Michael did not want any drama clouds over the villa, especially with his new romance, and Helena's parents would be joining us too, so I discouraged the timing of that conversation needing to happen over Christmas.

Michael and I had agreed to take turns to cook, but I was in charge of Christmas dinner. He had given me a list of wines and liquors he wanted to stock up on. Haig's scotch for Kell and Johnnie Walker Blue Label for Ross, and several bottles of Châteauneuf-du-Pape, the luxurious red that had been a family favourite ever since Kell imported it all those years ago to Hong Kong. And of course it was the holiday season, so it was imperative (!) that we stock the house with Moët & Chandon and Bollinger champagnes. Carol took us grocery shopping and I filled the pantry, the refrigerator and the liquor cabinet and with satisfaction went to bed.

Rhett had bought a Christmas tree and hung stockings for us all, which was so endearing. But I was mad in the morning when I realised he and some rowdy friends of his who were now comatose on couches around the place had attacked the liquor cabinet overnight, so I stashed the replacement stocks elsewhere.

All at once the remainder of the family was arriving. We were very busy as we shuttled back and forth between the villa, the airport and the train station as everyone came in dribs and drabs. Mother and Ross arrived first, and we barely had time to catch up before Michael's driver and caretaker Claude came back from the airport with Kell and Susie.

After providing Michael with that lovely guitar in the Max Q days, Richard Ortiz, who had slowly become my friend, then my partner, arrived too. He brought Shawna, his daughter from a previous relationship, and Brent. The three of them had been dazzled by being swooped up by Michael and Helena in a limo from Paris airport the previous day and taken to a Christmas party at Helena's modelling agency. Brent was nineteen, in his second year at college. I could just imagine his friends' faces when he returned to school and they asked him, 'Hey dude, what did you do on vacation?'

Since Helena was a Christmas Day baby, she was in Denmark to share her birthday with her family and wasn't expected in Roquefort-les-Pins with her parents until Christmas night.

The dreadful toothache Michael arrived with necessitated a trip to the dentist en route to the villa. But this wasn't enough to stop him dousing himself in Nice and Cannes night life with Rhett and Brent for the next few evenings.

The three men would arrive home in the early hours of the morning and sit in the kitchen, raiding the refrigerator, drinking more and laughing loudly. Early one morning I was shocked to see Brent with a deep, bloody cut on his forehead.

'Uh oh,' laughed Rhett.

Looking at my horrified face, Michael grinned and broke into a machine-gun James Cagney accent.

'Okay sis, you got us. Dere were dees tree guys wid dere girlfriends see and one of der girls made a play for Brent and one thing led to anudda and *we had to run for our lives!*'

Actually Brent had just collected a low doorway leaving a club. As I helplessly watched these three young men I loved so much bonding so well, I couldn't help feeling secretly delighted.

One night everybody turned in one by one till Michael and I were the only ones left standing talking in the kitchen. He raided the wine cellar as Richard joined us. Michael pointed out the site of his plans for a coming pool house with a shower, sauna and wet bar as we walked the slumbering garden under the moon.

'We should . . . *I* know,' said Michael suddenly. 'You know what we should do? We should drive to Saint-Paul-de-Vence and wait for the sun to come up.'

We jumped into the jeep and drove up to a little village on the hill. Halfway up the winding road he pulled over and stopped and got out; Richard and I followed. We sat on the side of the mountain in the chill night air and took in the view. It was around two in the morning. The moon was quite bright, but there was nothing to see below except for the tops of trees and distant yellow lights from a small village.

Michael began to speak softly, spinning us a story of horror and the heightened sense of smell. I'd have to say he enjoyed even our very small audience of two. We were spellbound, and never suspected that the tale of a perfumer's trainee who lacked body odour himself but tried to create the perfect scent from the blood of virgins came from *Perfume*, the novel by Patrick Süskind. (Until later, when Erin dug out *Perfume* from his library and began reading it and the ruse was revealed.)

We continued up the mountain to sleepy Saint-Paul de Vence where we parked and followed Michael up and down the narrow walkways, round the church tower, resisting the urge to ring the church bell. Michael showed us the town cemetery where Marc Chagall lies. Michael and Richard kept hiding from me. We were children again, only now Michael was the carer, the teacher.

Saint-Paul de Vence is a tiny village, approximately seven kilometres square, but it didn't take long for us to tire. We gave up on waiting for the sunrise and as we headed for home the men discussed music, and the future direction of INXS. Michael was feeling restless and uncertain about the band. He made a crack about the other band members getting too comfortable on their farms and in their cocoons, far away in Australia. He was ready for a new sound and was very concerned about what he felt was inertia.

They had already begun working with Mark Opitz on *Welcome To Wherever You Are* and there had been disagreements in the studio. Having habitually hunted down anything new, anything with a different polarity, Michael wanted to keep up with contemporary disruptions and felt the others weren't much interested in that. In fact it was mainly only himself, Andrew and Mark showing up to work in the studio.

I wonder if his next chain of thought was inspired by the fact that the Nirvana song 'Scentless Apprentice', from their album *In Utero*, had been inspired by Süskind's *Perfume*. He sighed with admiration as he raved about the Seattle band and their leader, Kurt Cobain. Not that he wanted to turn INXS into a grunge band. It just unnerved him that the other band members might refuse to move on from *Listen Like Thieves*, *Kick* and *X*—their trio of mega-successful albums produced by Chris Thomas. And he didn't want to lose the fresh, experimental, slightly dangerous edge INXS had hit the ground running with, and had embraced on tracks like 'Melting In The Sun' from *The Swing*. His free-handed explorations with Ollie Olsen in Max Q had let in enticing visions and sounds, opened a door to musical freedoms that now seemed to be closing to him.

Despite the many good things in his life, professionally Michael was beginning to feel irrelevant. And that is dangerous for a performer.

Even if it is not true.

The sun was almost up by the time we arrived back at the villa. We three retired exhausted as everyone else was wandering down to breakfast.

•

The next couple of days were spent in a flurry of last-minute gift hunting and finding the ingredients for the familiar side dishes and desserts that would make us all want to do this again. It was going to be the best Christmas dinner ever. In my heart I was going for a typical American Christmas for my family, but I knew there were extras that would bring it home for the Aussie side. Erin was making her famous pumpkin pie and, since she was also adept at meringue by this time, I put her in charge of the pavlova shell. I had asked Mother to bring some tins of passionfruit—so difficult to find outside Australia back then. I tried out a sweet potato pie and a peach cobbler, and of course we did not forget the obligatory plum pudding and brandy sauce. We found some cranberries and I borrowed some sturdy sewing needles and thread from Carol, then sat Mother down with Shawna and got them started on a cranberry garland. A domestic goddess Mother was not.

'Ouch . . . Darling, do we really need this? . . . Oh no look, I've got blood all over my white Chanel . . . Ouch! . . . Is it long enough now?'

Erin and I were doubling over with laughter in the kitchen. As well as tucking into doing some cooking, Michael took the men out to see more of the surrounding countryside and local taverns.

• • •

In Cannes Rhett spotted a poster for a Lenny Kravitz show that night. Lenny's first album *Let Love Rule* had started as a slow burner in 1989, but had gradually taken off in Europe and indeed around the world. And his second album *Mama Said*, released a few months before this gig, contained the marvellous single 'Always On The Run', co-written with Guns N' Roses's Slash, who also played guitar on it.

Lenny was another act some music business honchos tried to push and pull around, like they did with INXS. They wanted him to conform, to fit into either rock or R&B pigeonholes. There was no need for that. Luckily both INXS and Lenny proved that thinking was passé. True artists make their own rules!

Michael was a fan. He made a call and we all (minus Kell, Susie, Mother and Ross) headed to the venue. When we got there, Rhett jumped out of the car first with Michael following closely and the rest of us running behind. There was a lot of noise and jostling as we made our way through a crowd in front of the venue, Michael incognito in a heavy jacket with the collar pulled up around his face. When Rhett got to the entrance he said something to the men on security and Michael flipped his collar down for identification. His face was our passport—thanks, Michael (and Lenny). They waved us all in.

Lenny Kravitz is a crackerjack performer and we adored his show. We mingled with the performers afterwards and Michael invited Lenny and his girlfriend to visit the villa, late on Christmas Day.

Christmas morning was ridiculous. We are not one of those families who sit around calmly opening one gift at a time. We were all so excited about playing Santa that the living room became a maze of discarded gift wrapping. Michael topped up mimosas all round while I followed up with plates of frittata in the hope that everyone wouldn't be too bombed before we could finish opening our gifts.

We all took special care in dressing for a mid-afternoon dinner. Rhett was resplendent in the red, white and black striped suit that Michael had given him. It suited his effervescent flamboyance, fitted his tall, lean form perfectly and would become his go-to choice.

The long table was set for fourteen. Carol and Claude joined us with their little daughter, Marie, and Rhett had invited a girlfriend who was now staying at the house too. We began the meal with (very Australian) Sydney rock oysters, which Michael had had flown in. The wine flowed and there was much laughter, storytelling and forgiving. Helena called several times that day. I imagined she and Michael were anxious to see one another.

Actually, the phone hardly stopped ringing with calls from all over the globe. Michele phoned through her love and Christmas greetings.

'Yep, getting out the cookbooks,' Michael joked with her, 'doing all the cooking for the family.' He was so obviously relishing his new 'patriarch' role and had made a beautiful toast before dinner. I don't think we have ever been happier as a family.

After we had stuffed ourselves, it was Ross, of course, who chased us into the garden with his camera. We might have complained about his insistence on capturing the moment, but thank goodness he did. That photograph of us all, lined up on the grounds of the villa, brings back one of the most joyful, fulfilled shared moments of our lives.

Helena and her parents, Fleming and Ilsa, arrived that evening, their luggage filled with traditional Danish Christmas treats: canned pickled herring, smoked salmon, klejner (deep-fried pastry strips sprinkled with sugar), a cabbage dish made with spiced fat and whipping cream, then finally sprinkled with cinnamon and sugar (how did Helena keep her figure?) and a potent drink called Akvavit, which was consumed liberally to the shout of 'Skål!' All extremely tasty and fun, but three hours later I woke up on the bathroom floor with Richard mopping my forehead with a cold washcloth.

Ilsa had arrived with many glossy magazines featuring Helena to show us. Naturally, she was very proud. Not only was Helena at the pinnacle of her trade, she was well educated, spoke five languages and kept up with global current affairs. Michael was very proud of her for all of that too.

The following day they drove to Nice to pick up Lenny and his girl-friend. We were all delighted to see him again, as he greeted us like long-lost friends. He wasted no time in getting to the house phone to call his little three-year-old daughter Zoë, who was in the USA with her mother Lisa Bonet—herself a real talent and recently Lenny's musical collaborator. 'Little' Zoë Kravitz is now a sought-after actress (*Big Little Lies, Californication, Mad Max: Fury Road*), singer and spokesmodel (Vera Wang fragrances). Anyway, there was lots of gaiety and joshing each other as we shared the virtual second banquet of leftovers in the kitchen before Michael took the visitors off to his music room for a while. Lenny turned out to be a fun guy and we all ended up in hysterics, particularly about the tiny clip-on koalas he'd clipped all over himself, including on his massive dreads.

One day we watched a recorded interview with Helena on Michael's television, which ran off a huge satellite dish. She was typically out-spoken (one of the things that Michael loved about her). This time she was asked about her future plans, and what she thought about models continuing to work into their thirties. She referred to models over 25 as 'old cows', noting *she* would not stay in the business that long. Mother of course did a double-take. She herself had been on the catwalk modelling maternity outfits at 30, six months pregnant with Michael and looking fabulous!

I had purchased a movie camera and brought it to the villa specifically to get some footage of our big Christmas in the south of France. Richard shot a video on it in the crowded kitchen while I was cooking a meal. There's dancing, singing, lots of ribbing and laughter. Rhett does his impersonation of a breakdancer and Kell flies by with a bowl on his head. Michael joins Rhett in the dancing, and, referring to my ancient history as a go-go dancer, yells, 'Tina, get with it, on the table, baby, come on, you can do it!' I did *not* jump on the table, not even for Michael, but I'll admit to breaking out some go-go moves.

One evening we were invited to a magnificent home that belonged to a neighbouring family. They owned an art gallery in Saint-Paul de Vence. In the living room hung an amazing contemporary abstract that was somehow *moving*. Ripples of paint seemed to brim up to the side of the frame, ready to spill out, then just as they reached the top they'd drop down. There were no visible tubes or wiring. We were fascinated. Helena couldn't help herself. She touched it lightly and a healthy portion spilt out onto the floor, which, luckily, was hardwood. She and Mother got such a shock. They instinctively huddled together to shield the damage from the rest of the guests. Luckily again, at that moment the hostess announced that we were to move to the dining room where her chef had a surprise. As guests began walking towards the door, Mother chivalrously removed her white cashmere wrap and dropped it onto the ooze on the floor. Helena bent down as if to scoop it up for her, surreptitiously wiping the red and purple mess into the centre of the ruined cashmere. Oblivious to the disaster, Michael approached them offering each an arm. In the adjoining room the chef wheeled out a large cake bearing the message, 'Welcome to the Michael Hutchence Family' in gold lettering.

We never heard anything about the artwork, so either it had happened before or the family was just too polite to mention its downfall.

Everyone was still at the villa for New Year's Eve. Michael and Helena along with her parents, Ilsa and Fleming, spent the afternoon in the kitchen preparing hors d'oeuvres for the celebrations at the villa. Michael planned a barbecue and was very specific about the seafood and beef marinades—he insisted on making his own. A lot of tasting went on, of course, the sign of a good cook. It was worth it as the meal was delicious.

At midnight a great ruckus began on the balcony as Rhett and Brent set off the fireworks. It hadn't rained for ages so the firewood stored below ignited and within minutes a very stressed-out Claude was running to hose down a blaze at the side of the pool. Considering the surrounding dry shrubbery, neighbouring villas and woods, it could have been disastrous, but there was actually very little harm done in the end. Michael laughed it off.

New Year's festivities over, we all arrived back in Paris, where Richard and I planned a week of sightseeing with the children. Michael called our hotel and invited us to dine with him at the little restaurant on rue des Canettes with the resident English sheepdog. He had chosen it just for Brent's benefit as they served delicous steaks. Surrounded by all of that rich, unfamiliar, gourmet French food, he knew his nephew had been craving a plain steak.

Michael was due back in Sydney to record *Welcome To Wherever You Are* with producer Mark Opitz. He and Helena were only staying overnight at their Paris apartment, so he gave me the keys and an open invitation to use his driver. It was very generous of him and I was overwhelmed.

Soon after Christmas Michael needed to replace his villa staff. He eventually hired Linda and Nestor, a wonderful couple from the

Philippines, helping them obtain their papers to stay in France. Nestor came to love caring for the garden and Michael's cars, while Linda's cooking and cleaning was highly valued. Together they brought a whole new dimension and warmth to Michael's appreciation for his home. One time when he returned home they had a surprise for him. Cherie, a golden labrador, had belonged to a neighbour who couldn't care for her anymore. They begged him to let her stay on the property and of course he acquiesced. A dog was another first for Michael, who hadn't had the time or stability to own a pet since having Tinkerbell and her kitten Tabitha as a boy in Hong Kong.

Michael had never had a garden before either. He took every opportunity to tend to it, side by side with Nestor, who patiently taught him about planting and cultivating plants suited to the region. There were paths lined with rows of lavender bushes and ivy-covered lamps leading you through gardens of herbs, vegetables and roses.

Michael had the olives pressed and their oil bottled, while Helena gave her personal touch to the labels. Together they seemed invincible there. Although both of them travelled for their careers, La Vieille Ferme was their primary residence. Michael was never more relaxed, more content than he was at his home in the French countryside and he made it abundantly clear that it gave him great joy to share this picturesque sanctuary with his family and friends. He was even in the habit of offering it to guests when he knew he was going to be away. He just wanted people to enjoy it. He thought it a waste if the villa was empty.

When Michael *was* in residence he was always up for guests, and Helena was his perfect partner and mistress of the house. She was unflappable. Bono's arriving with how many people? Well, I'll take Linda to Valbonne and we'll pick up some supplies, and you get the wine. Music producer Mark Opitz said he always called if he was in France; he said you never knew who was going to answer the phone.

Helena often filled the home with her friends and Mark remembered having a long conversation with Christy Turlington one day who passed the receiver to Yasmin Le Bon. In an interview with the Sydney *Daily Telegraph*, Helena's friend, model Gail Elliott, said, 'It was the '90s and all very glamorous in a "Rock Star and Supermodel" kind of way. We'd go to his concerts and he'd come to our fashion shows. But Michael also enjoyed cooking and chilling out. I would stay with them in his beautiful house in the South of France.'

Four months after Christmas, Michael was at the A&M Records studios in Los Angeles, working again with Bob Clearmountain. Back then A&M, said by some to be the finest recording studio in the world, was located on the grounds of the historic Charlie Chaplin Studios on North La Brea Avenue, near Sunset Boulevard.

Michael and Bob were doing some final mixing on 'Baby Don't Cry' and Richard and I were invited to take a listen. I sensed the rich history of the lot as Richard drove us through the gates. We sat quietly as Michael asked Bob to crank up the volume. Richard has pretty good ears, as they say in the trade. We listened twice and when Michael asked him what he thought, he replied that he thought the track would be even stronger if they cut out the fourth round of the chorus, in the intro. Michael immediately asked Bob to try it. The edit worked and the track stayed that way. That incident just shows you how inclusive and generous Michael could be, and what an open mind he had as to his music.

14

this changes everything

ONE NIGHT IN August 1992 Michael and Helena had been night-clubbing in Copenhagen. As they remounted their bicycles in the street and rode into the night, the lovers decided they were hungry. They decided to get some takeaway food to bring back to Helena's apartment and dismounted in a narrow street to order their food. There wasn't much room, really, when a taxi appeared with a driver impatient to get past. He sounded the horn but Michael wasn't fast enough making way for his liking. Enraged, the driver leapt out of the cab and shoved his impediment backwards with great force. Michael—in a rare occurrence for a man with the poise of a cat and the strength of a dancer—lost his balance, reeling backwards. Surprised, he had no way of saving himself. When the back of his head hit the road it fractured and he was knocked unconscious. The taxi driver, wary now, jumped back into his vehicle and sped away. He was never caught because the focus was very much elsewhere at that moment.

Helena took charge, caring for Michael with all she had and helping coordinate the arrival of the ambulance and paramedics.

She was extremely protective and nursed him for several days. Michael complained of a persistent splitting headache. Sometime later, in London, a specialist diagnosed that he had sustained injury to the olfactory bulb, the neural structure of the forebrain near the eye socket that translates chemicals entering the nose to smell. In Michael's case, he lost two of the five senses—smell and taste—in that calamitous assault. The medical profession had no way of predicting if or when they might return.

At first Michael did not speak about it very often, but as his missing senses remained elusive, and the damage seemed permanent, he let us know with sadness how deeply he missed them. He had always been such a sensual man. Now the taste and special scent of his partner as they kissed and made love, or the heady aroma and subtle aftertaste of a great cabernet sauvignon, had gone. The mingling of fresh herbs, the twist of cracking peppercorns in a plate of spaghetti with napolitana sauce. Even the hypnotic scents of the deep black-red and flushed pink petals of the roses in his own garden were forbidden to him.

The changes in his personality did not go unnoticed either. He often became short-tempered. In fact, he suffered powerful mood swings. He seemed to go off the rails easily—even became physically violent. We were all so used to the easygoing Michael that this new, unpredictable one was disconcerting. I really don't believe his doctors told him that the injury he sustained could manifest itself in poor impulse control, even in violently losing his temper, because he actually seemed confused by this himself.

Then again, physicians and emergency responders knew less about traumatic brain injury in the 1990s. The repercussions of a hard blow to the head were not so well researched. Nowadays, those with suspected concussion in a sporting match are taken from the field, prevented from returning and likely spelled. Sufferers of such injuries are now counselled on the dangers of getting into stressful situations and given tools to deal with impulse control.

Over time I've read some powerful statements from people who, like my brother, have had a traumatic brain injury (TBI) inflicted on them.

TBI survivor Amy Zellmer wrote in the *Huffington Post* in 2015 that she was 'up and down emotionally like a rollercoaster, and exhausted beyond comprehension':

> I have felt an entire spectrum of emotions; anger, rage, fear, sadness, depression, hope, joy, frustration, contentment—
> I struggle in crowded restaurants or shopping malls. I cannot handle stimulation from multiple sources including light, sound, and vibration. I grab for words that seem to have disappeared into thin air. My personality has changed, and I am aware of my mood swings. I have anxiety and panic attacks.

It was impossible for someone in Michael's line of work to avoid crowds, noise and harsh, dynamic lighting. From that day on it must have been very difficult for him to handle the very atmosphere he had worked in for fifteen years. He had genuinely *revelled* in being onstage and in his ability, fronting INXS, to make huge crowds sway in ecstasy. Now the assault on his remaining senses might have become hard to take. No one knew or understood the injury's damaging hold on his emotions, not even Michael himself. Did he feel he was mysteriously losing the ability to do, and to enjoy, the job he had felt was in the palm of his hand?

After the birth of his daughter, Tiger Lily, in 1996, he would complain that he couldn't smell her, couldn't breathe in that incomparable new baby smell. Even his creative palette as a writer was tied up with his senses. The world must have overnight seemed a duller, less promising place.

Meanwhile, Helena was at the pinnacle of her busy career. During this period of Michael's life I was more likely to see them in fashion magazines, photographed together on the runway, or just Michael seated in the front row of the audience at a fashion parade alongside fellow supermodel 'handbags' Richard Gere (dating Cindy Crawford) or Johnny Depp (Kate Moss). Various designers asked Michael to become part of Fashion Week in Paris with Helena. As the son of an ex-model, he clearly felt comfortable surrounded by Helena's friends and their actor partners. Of course he remained keen to pick up whatever he could about the world of movies and the craft of acting, and was able to relax around other people who understood the strange, limiting aspects of fame (such as not being able to walk into a public space without being the centre of attention). He enjoyed this time in his life, socially speaking. He and Helena could do no wrong. They were such an impossibly photogenic and accomplished couple, with lots of time to play and travel in their lives together, and they took advantage of it.

However, even though he looked great—physically very healthy—Michael was dealing with the side-effects of brain damage. This hidden disability can be quite confusing and debilitating to others as well as to the sufferer. His fellow band members didn't understand how the assault in Denmark had changed Michael. His jet-setting lifestyle further distanced him from the other five band members, especially Tim and Kirk, who were more into fishing and farming, which didn't interest him. Gradually Michael and the other members of INXS drifted apart, becoming more and more estranged.

The worldwide X-Factor tour ran over ten months and 121 shows. With ongoing media interviews for Michael (everyone wanted to talk to the singer, of course), live shows and constant travel, it was a fairly exhausting process. A fifteen-track live album *Live Baby Live* was released, and despite being a genuine, undoctored recording, was criticised by some (including Molly Meldrum) for not sounding 'live'. In fact, the band was probably simply so tight, such a well-oiled machine after years on the road, that it was hard to tell the difference.

The recording of their eighth album, *Welcome To Wherever You Are*, in Rhinoceros studios from November 1991 to mid-1992, was fraught with difficulty. New material was worked on and rehearsed at the Sydney Opera House beforehand, perhaps, partly at least, as the Australian Concert Orchestra would be brought in to play on two tracks including, to great effect, 'Baby Don't Cry', later.

Mark, who had become so familiar with the band on the road through their X-Factor tour in 1991, was producer. The album experimented with some eastern feels and applied some heavy distortion to vocals and guitars.

'With *Welcome*, Michael was still living in his own world,' Mark remembered. 'But everyone had different things going on. Kirk and Karen were splitting up. Garry was having a baby. Tim had the worst arthritis he'd ever had in his life. That carpal tunnel thing had really taken a toll, in his arms and hands, whatever. And Jon was about to get married. So no one was on the case for recording *Welcome To Wherever You Are*, except Andrew, Michael and me, and the engineer, Niven Garland.

'Andrew and I would make loops up, and do different things, and Jon would come in and play on a lot of things, and then he'd go off and do wedding stuff. Or Kirk would have problems doing what he was doing . . . It was all different. We brought in Deni Hines to sing on a few things. But basically it was Andrew and me, building up bits of music. Michael would come in from partying the night before. Basically wheel him in, say, do anything in front of the microphone—just scat. Just scat five or six tracks, just like the old days, when you don't have lyrics.

Just make up stuff on the fly. He'd go, then I'd make up all the melodies from editing together the best takes of what he'd been singing, then the lyrics would be written to that, at a later point. A lot of it was done like that. They'd be pre-set lyrics; they just had to be fitted into the new melodies. But that's the way that that album was pretty much created. Fragmented, but also even so, Andrew and I were really working hard on it the whole time, Michael was coming in and working on it as well, and then there were contributions from all the rest of the band. Other times it was the whole band, but most of the time it was just a very small core for that record.' Despite this, the album was listed as being co-produced by INXS.

Welcome To Wherever You Are would be released with a cover abandoning the principle of putting INXS up front. There was a quirky photo of The Artane Boys Band from Ireland on the front cover so, at first glance, the artist was anonymous. It went to #1 in England, a breakthrough for the band, but reviews and sales were comparitively patchy. After completing *Welcome To Wherever You Are*, Mark took a break in Paris, staying with Michael and Helena at the rue des Canettes apartment. One night Michael invited Chris Bailey over and the three of them polished off a bottle of cognac as they discussed poetry, literature and politics. Mark said that the subject of music did not come up—although touring did.

Perhaps because they were somewhat burnt out from touring, INXS decided not to tour to promote *Welcome To Wherever You Are*, but to go straight into recording its studio follow-up, then tour to promote them both.

'When INXS tour,' Michael told Mark and Chris that night, with a certain amount of sadness, 'I have to put the Michael Hutchence coat on and be Michael Hutchence. I'd rather be the Michael Hutchence who wakes up late on a Sunday morning with his girlfriend Helena, and has breakfast of scrambled eggs at some restaurant and strolls around the bookshops for the rest of the day. That's the Michael Hutchence I'd like to be.'

'You could really tell at that point INXS was the farthest thing from Michael at that stage,' Mark said. 'The band did not tour after *Welcome To Wherever You Are*, which was a big mistake. They should have done *one more tour*. And that way they could have incorporated *Welcome To Wherever You Are* with this lavish stage set that that required, plus all the hit songs. It would have been a huge tour. They would have got "Baby Don't Cry" in there, "Beautiful Girl", whatever; three or four songs off *Welcome* would have easily got in there if not more. And that would have made a difference to that album.

'But having not toured, they were now in trouble. Because they had two more albums to do for Atlantic, so they had to figure it out.'

It had been while they were working on *Welcome To Wherever You Are* that Michael had told Mark about a studio that was being built on the island of Capri, in the Tyrrhenian Sea south of Naples in Italy. They ended up recording the next INXS album *Full Moon, Dirty Hearts* there in November 1992. Michael was initially excited about this as he felt that transplanting the other five band members to this luxurious, isolated setting would breathe fresh creative air into minds and bodies.

He was wrong.

'It was very discordant,' Mark Opitz remembered. 'There was Michael's camp and the INXS camp. Michael and I shared a place, he was upstairs and I was downstairs. And the rest of the band was around in different buildings or hotels. But every night I could hear the furniture being smashed or I would go to Michael's room and he'd say he was going to leave the band, all that sort of stuff, he was just so over it.

'He was still passionate about his music and even though he was separated from the band he was not separated from his music. One night he and I had a poetry session. Michael considered his lyrics to be his poetry and he had the lyrics before he had the music a lot of the time. He was into Sylvia Plath, that kind of thing. Michael had written a poem he called "The End of Rock'n'Roll" so we went into the studio and recorded it and I later put it to music but it was never used.

'We still had work to do on *Full Moon, Dirty Hearts*, but we'd used up all our studio booking at Capri, so Michael, Andrew and I went off to France to Studio Guillaume Tell—located in a beautiful 1930s building, which was formerly a movie theatre just outside of Paris. And it was while Michael and I were getting a guided tour of the studio that we were told Ray Charles did all his stuff there. What, Mark asked, Ray comes in? Oh no, Ray doesn't come in here, we're told, it gets recorded here, then sent to his studio where he does vocals. And we thought, wow, Ray Charles should be singing on *our* album! They forwarded Mr Charles two tracks, "Make Your Peace" and "Please, You Got That". He passed on the first but that's how he came to sing on "Please, You Got That", said Mark.

When it came time to shoot the cover for *Full Moon, Dirty Hearts*, Chris Murphy thought they needed something strong to grab the attention of the buying public. He contracted controversial photographer Helmut Newton, who was known for his sadomasochistic erotic images. Michael hated the results. He threatened to pull out of any tour for the album if any of those pictures were used for the cover. They weren't, although they did pop up here and there illustrating various articles and got plenty of exposure. Michael was under contract, of course; I felt he might have been railroaded into the Helmut Newton shoot. Photographs emerged of a sullen-looking Michael roped to a chair and grouped with rather objectified-looking women in underwear, along with extras-looking INXS who seemed somewhat confused about the whole thing—with good reason.

After being off the road for so long, the band then had to promote their Get Out Of The House tour, even though they had planned a scaled-back itinerary. Before they arrived in Los Angeles to play at the

Barker Hanger at Santa Monica Airport on 8 May 1993, Michael called the very popular DJ Richard Blade and suggested they take a helicopter from Van Nuys in the San Fernando Valley and land in front of Barker Hanger. They could meet the press and do a live broadcast from there. It was a brilliant move because they sold out the show in a matter of minutes. Nevertheless, there was something very unfriendly about that tour. Hard times had beset Michael's charmed career. Band and crew seemed out of sorts.

• • •

Christmas 1993 was spent on the Gold Coast with Mother and Ross hosting Helena's parents, Ilsa and Fleming. Helena and Michael and their guests, model Gail Elliott and her first husband John, were staying at a nearby spa hotel. Mother and Ross had great style when it came to entertaining. Michael and Helena were definitely together but there was a shift.

In January Michael sent me a fax from the villa. He and Helena had spent the holiday season in Denmark with Chris Bailey which had been 'hilarious' but he said he was getting 'cabin fever'. Whether it came from his nomadic childhood, his frequent touring with the band or perhaps something else, he was often restless and needed to be on the move.

He often seemed unsettled by Helena's playful, verbal sparring. Perhaps the ribbing had gotten old, or maybe we simply missed the cues to Michael's brain injury.

As it was Helena's birthday on Christmas Day, we were invited to gather early for an unusual Danish tradition. In Denmark it is customary to wake your loved one on their birthday by flying the Danish flag in front of the house and serving them breakfast in bed. If you fail to do this, it's bad luck. Rhett took off with Ilsa and Fleming to the hotel early on Christmas morning to knock on Helena and Michael's door, but the rest of the family held back. I just thought it would be uncomfortable to bust into my brother's hotel room while he was in bed with his girlfriend. I couldn't picture how this would work with us all standing around their bed while they ate breakfast.

Except for the occasional intrusion of the press and completely erroneous stories in the local news, it was another great Christmas holiday. But things could not stay that way.

Just before his 34th birthday in January, Michael fell onstage in Melbourne. He suffered a badly sprained ankle, a pulled tendon and a hairline fracture in his foot. He was restricted to crutches, unable to walk on his foot for a couple of weeks. Mother conveyed the news to me and added his contact details on the end of her fax. However, all was not gloom. As was often the case, Michael had some fun with his pseudonym, checking into the Como Hotel under the name Mr Dick Shake.

A few days after the accident, he went to the Gold Coast, where Rhett was staying with Mother and Ross. Arriving two hours late for lunch, Michael apologetically explained to Mother that he had just purchased the Paradise Lanes Bowling Alley in Labrador, only fifteen minutes from her home, for AU$2.25 million—cash. Paradise Lanes was on a large block of land with a view across the water to Bribie Island that could not be blocked.

As usual he arrived with a load of dirty clothes, and added them to Rhett's, which were already in the wash. When the brothers opened the machine to retrieve their clean jeans, Michael had one pair with a bulging damp back pocket. Upon inspection he found a little over AU$6000 in hundred-dollar notes that he had forgotten. True to his sharp sense of humour, Rhett made a crack about money laundering.

While on a small-scale tour that year, INXS were joined in Europe by music journalist Dave Simpson, who later wrote about his experience in *The Guardian*. Of course he talked about Michael's expertise as a frontman, how he was obviously born to be onstage. He wrote that of all the concerts he had covered, he had never before seen a crowd whipped into such a frenzy; in fact, one couple actually began 'shagging against a speaker'.

After the gig he joined the band at a party. He and his friend, who had a small record trading company, an outlet where lovers of vinyl traded and purchased records, talked into the night with Michael and recorded the conversation. Simpson wrote about how surprised and impressed he was at Michael's interest in his friend's modest business; not the sort of thing you would expect from a frontman used to playing stadiums and mixing with the elite of rock and roll.

'Here was a rock god', wrote Simpson, 'who was utterly interested in music and the lives of ordinary people. He was also very funny. I remember Michael Hutchence not as a strutting rock animal, nor tabloid caricature, but as a sensitive, fragile soul and fundamentally a very lovely man.'

Michael was also quite forgetful. One evening in London in October 1994 when INXS was playing the Brixton Academy, he walked out of his five-star hotel and, as he was climbing into the limousine that would take him to the venue, remembered he'd left something in his room. The band complained. They were ready to leave. Two fans who had followed the band for years were nearby and Michael looked over and asked if they'd take him to the venue. Of course they agreed, so the limos departed.

The two young men pulled their vehicle up to the front of the hotel. 'We had our work vehicle, an old jalopy of a transit van,' recalled Gary Lilley. 'Mike came out and said, "Fucking hell, what's that thing?" He got in and we were crying with laughter. It was like a kangaroo going down the road and we dared not stop even at the traffic lights in case the van clapped out on us. When we got to Brixton Academy it got worse. The security would not let us in. What it must have looked like, one of the world's top performers in this clapped-out old knack of a van. The security were not having it at all. We had to go get the tour manager to the rescue. I think Michael made the show by twenty minutes and Jeff Pope, Michael's head of security, was not pleased.'

As he was driven to LAX to catch a flight to San Jose, on 8 April 1994, Michael called to tell me he had just heard that Nirvana's Kurt Cobain had been found dead, apparently through a self-inflicted gunshot wound. He expressed his sadness and disappointment that such a talented man would take his own life. He could not understand how he could leave his little daughter, twenty-month-old Frances Bean.

'We've lost the poet laureate of our generation,' he said sadly.

After completing the US leg of the tour, INXS continued on to Caracas in Venezuela for one night, took a three-week hiatus and then played one night in Japan, after which Michael returned to his villa and called me. Unsurprisingly, he was having trouble sleeping. He wanted to talk about his favourite retreat. It was spring and the foliage was bursting into glorious colour all over the French countryside. Nestor was doing a masterful job with the garden and Michael was looking forward to working right next to him on his six-week break.

After another conversation, towards the end of that break, I faxed him a letter:

May 24, 1994

Hi Michael,

It was good to 'feel' the relaxation in your voice last night. The view outside of your bedroom window (at the villa) must be a slice of heaven. I remember seeing photographs of the sun deck when it was covered in vines, so different from winter . . . it must be getting that way now—I promised Brent and Erin that we would make a trip over there during spring or summer of next year. Take care and keep in touch,

Love Tina.

The break had been good for Michael, and as we kept in contact over the next couple of months, I was so relieved that he seemed more at ease with life; I had been quite worried about him. After the latest set of tour dates, he went sailing with some friends. In June he sent me a postcard of a Greek god with an enormous appendage, writing that he was reading Socrates on the way to the Temple of Poseidon, and felt that 'life had just begun'. He signed off 'love from the Ionic sea + me'.

Erin told her uncle that she was going to attend the 25th anniversary of Woodstock. We received a fax from him on 8 July 1994 in which, quoting Lewis Carroll's *Alice's Adventures in Wonderland*, he wrote that Woodstock sounded 'curiouser and curiouser'. He and Helena had found time for a Danish festival, where they'd 'said hello to Bjork'. He was thrilled with the beautiful bounty in his garden of pears, apples, plums, lemons, pink grapefruit, cherries and corn.

Michael was happiest at his beloved villa. He said it was the best investment he ever made. It was hard to find among the surrounding little hamlet villages—the perfect private retreat. Many people from the music, fashion and movie world and even royalty—Prince Albert of Monaco—frequented the property over the time he was there.

INXS may not have been in the public eye all that much in 1994, but Michael was never invisible with Helena by his side. Among other events, they were invited to the World Music Awards in Monte Carlo, where Michael presented Ray Charles with his Legend Award for outstanding contribution to the music industry. After recording alongside the genius of 'Brother Ray' during the making of *Full Moon, Dirty Hearts*, Michael was happy, and so honoured to make the presentation.

Also appearing that night were Prince, Ringo Starr, Billy Joel, Placido Domingo, Whitney Houston and Kylie Minogue. She greeted both Michael and Helena with warmth.

One of the highlights of the year came in the first week of October. Michael flew to Nashville, Tennessee, to perform solo at the Pyramid Center in a special, multi-artist Elvis Presley tribute that had been organised by Priscilla Presley. Priscilla and her daughter with Elvis, Lisa Marie, had requested that Michael perform. He was introduced to the stage by John Stamos and sang a wonderful, sexy rendition of 'Baby Let's Play House'.

Some time after Michael's passing I received a heartfelt letter from Maureen Martin, a professor of international human rights in Canada. She wrote that in 1994 when she and her family were living in Monaco, she started up an organisation she called Artists for East Timor. She wanted to raise awareness about the ongoing East Timor genocide under the Indonesian regime. She took a chance and dropped off some flyers at the Hotel de Paris, where most of the musicians attending the World Music Awards were staying.

She said that much to her delight, Michael called her and suggested a meeting. He surprised her further by being familiar with the drastic situation in East Timor. Michael was well aware of the brutality there and had long been an ardent supporter of the East Timorese people and their plight.

'He was a young man with a big heart and proposed to use his fame to help the cause,' she wrote.

After their initial meeting, Michael and Professor Martin met several times at Helena's apartment in Monaco. Once she was amused by the sight of his boots drying in the oven there; it had been raining and he had arrived on his motorcycle, drenched. They also met in Amnesty International's office in London, and at his villa, where he took the professor for a tour of his fruit trees and wine cellar, and showed her a mural in his dining room titled *Orion '94* which his friend Kay Mahoney had painted.

She wrote that on a later occasion at the villa, after he and Helena had parted ways, she was surprised to see Helena drive in with a boyfriend and make herself at home by the pool. Everyone seemed quite comfortable with the situation.

Fellow musician Paul 'Paulie' Stewart, singer, songwriter and trumpet player for the rhythm & punk Melbourne band Painters and Dockers, had tragically lost his brother Tony Stewart, one of the 'Balibo Five' journalists murdered by Indonesian forces in Balibo in 1975. Paulie became a powerful advocate in the push for East Timor's independence from Indonesia. He helped form (and still plays in) the activist touring band the Dili Allstars, a mixture of Australian and East Timorese musicians. (Paulie later became a mentor with the Artful Dodgers Studio in Collingwood, Melbourne, working through the arts with young people at risk.) He spoke about how Michael became a major supporter of the East Timorese cause.

'When Michael died, he was just about to narrate a big documentary about East Timor,' Paulie said. 'I'd always feel incredibly guilty when people made him out to be a bit of a dill, just into drugs and fucking, if I didn't speak out. My experience of Michael was very different because I interacted with the activist side of him.'

Paulie and fellow Dili Allstar Gil Santos got together a charity compilation album in 1994 called *All In The Family*, produced by David Bridie, the top producer of world music in Oceania. The Dockers had a track on it but couldn't afford to fly up to Sydney to help launch the album, which was a fundraiser for the widows and children of the Fretilin resistance fighters. One of the organisers of *All In The Family* was a friend of Michael's and mentioned it to him. Michael then went along to a Painters and Dockers gig—always a wild experience—to talk to Paulie about it.

'At our gig,' Paulie recalled, 'Michael sort of had his hair all over his face, hiding behind it—he was *so* shy! What a contrast with when he hit the stage!

'He paid for us—the whole band—to fly to Sydney and didn't want anyone to know about it. He's really into Timorese liberation. In *Dogs in Space* there's a poster, do you remember, up on the wall, "Free East Timor"?' Paulie is certain Michael put it there. 'And *any* mention of East Timor was gold back then too, because so few people knew about the situation. Michael was interviewed once on TV and he said, "I lean towards the ALP and I believe in Amnesty International. And we all have to do something about the East Timor situation."'

Paulie knew the origins of Michael's interest. 'Once he was delayed for hours at an airport. He sidled up to a guy at the bar there who turned out to be [popular East Timorese ex-leader and co-recipient of the 1996 Nobel Peace Prize] José Ramos-Horta. Apparently they sat there talking about East Timor for three hours or something.

'I was talking to José Ramos-Horta one day and he said, "Oh yeah, Michael's a really nice guy, I met him and we talked at an airport for ages."

'So Michael ended up paying for the Dockers to all fly up to Sydney and launch this album, and it was a big success and so we were able to send the money to the war widows of the Fretilin resistance.'

A few years later, in February 1998, U2 were in Australia for their PopMart tour. 'Bono came to town and he needed to meet us and so we all went out to Waverley Park [stadium in outer Melbourne]. As soon as he saw me he threw his hands up in the air and said, "Don't start on me about East Timor! Michael wouldn't shut up about it!" Then this woman pops her head around the door, a very beautiful one, and pipes up, "Oh yeah, Michael talked about that all the time!" Helena Christensen was on tour with U2 as a photographer at that time.

'I ended up putting it on Kylie,' Paulie continued in his enthusiastic manner, 'saying "Hey, your boyfriend was really into this cause, did you know?" And talking to her about it. And then the Dili Allstars which is a half Timorese band, half not, went up to Timor to play with Kylie and John Farnham.

'Yes—before liberation, Michael was a fanatic for East Timor.'

* * *

The Australian press once again reported Helena and Michael's upcoming wedding plans as they often did when they had space to fill. Speculation rumoured a venue in Paris, suggesting that Helena had commissioned Gianni Versace to design the gown. Michael *was* a neighbour of Versace in Roquefort-les-Pins and they were friends, but there were no wedding plans. Helena did buy a fabulous full-length, satin antique wedding gown. She happened to like beautiful, pre-owned treasures, and perhaps it was to remind Michael of her wishes.

Actually it was another brother who had the truly exciting family news to spread at this time. By late 1994 Rhett was seeing Mandy Nolan, the brilliant and beautiful stand-up comic and artist. Michael said that she was just what Rhett needed, someone with a good sense of humour. Rhett called in late December with the news that Mandy was pregnant and they were expecting their baby in August 1995. He asked me to relay the news to all. This was very exciting, so unexpected, and we all hoped that it would be a new pinnacle of fulfilment for him.

15

tabloid storm

MICHAEL CALLED in the first week of 1995.

'Let's have dinner at the Ivy. You'd better, because I had to resort to using Helena's name to get a table,' he laughed, mocking his relative obscurity in LA. Actually, I sensed, being a nonentity for a change was comforting to him.

The Ivy had drawn a regular roster of A-listers, surrounded by avid paparazzi hovering for their daily scoop, since it opened in 1983. I was hungry, and the Ivy's fresh, Californian mélange of seafood, fruits, salads and divine desserts was almost as appealing as another chance to see my brother. The gaps between our catch-ups were longer these days, now he was spending so much time in Europe with Helena.

Mother and Ross were in town. They had joined us for Christmas, and they were waiting with Erin, Brent and me at the entrance to the Ivy when Faye Dunaway leapt out of her car. Shoving Ross aside, she called out to the *maître d'*, 'Where is my order to go?'

Ross was not in the habit of recognising Hollywood royalty. 'What a rude woman!' he proclaimed loudly.

Michael found this extremely amusing when we told him over a satisfying dinner. The atmosphere at the Ivy was casual, the décor pretty: so Californian, really. Helena told us about the photoshoots she was in town to do and Michael seemed content to take a back seat for once. The previous year, in an interview with the *South China Morning Post*, he had referred to her as 'the breadwinner of the family'.

After dinner we headed back to the very rock'n'roll Sunset Marquis bar in West Hollywood and settled around a corner table. Helena phoned Kate Moss and then suggested heading off to join her and Johnny Depp at the Viper Room. Michael, on the other hand, was happy to stay put this time. He suggested she take a cab; obviously the Viper was no place for a family get-together. Helena was not overjoyed. The atmosphere changed. Clearly this dilemma was uncomfortable for everyone and, knowing how stressed out Michael got about being a drawbridge between different tribes, I feigned fatigue. I reminded everyone we had a whole week to catch up anyway, and started the exodus.

Actually, it wasn't at all onerous to go home 'early' that night. Something had just happened out of the blue at Christmas time that made the idea of an early night strangely exciting.

By that stage I was a single mother again—Richard and I had parted amicably a year before. Erin was then sixteen and halfway through her junior year at high school. Brent was working his way through college and I was helping as much as I could. I'd been renting for some time.

Mother and Ross arrived on 18 December—and within two days they purchased a luxury penthouse in my name! It was in a three-storey building on tree-lined Riverside Drive, bordering Burbank and Toluca Lake; walking distance from the back gate of Warner Brothers. This was a huge surprise and outrageously generous. We moved in in record time.

Michael had suggested he buy me a home himself in 1988, but I was proud and wanted to be self-reliant. I'd thanked him profusely but turned it down. Perhaps this was why Mother and Ross had more or less ambushed me. I *knew* how fortunate I was for their incredible gift though, and returned the hospitality other family members had shown us in my new place.

So it was that four nights after our dinner at the Ivy I had a house-warming party. Michael looked relaxed, savouring a Cuban cigar a friend of mine offered him as he sat overlooking the LA skyline, talking about spending more time in California looking for some new roles. I was happy; I loved the idea of having him close.

Michael's birthday (22 January) was coming up and I was looking forward to a family lunch with him and Helena to celebrate, at the Four Seasons on Doheny, before they left town later that day. Knowing he was serious about acting, I found a copy of the original script for *Citizen Kane* at one of our little bookshops in Burbank, one that collected used scripts donated by studios, production houses, actors and crew. These often had extra dialogue and scribbled notes on the side, and if you were lucky, a famous name attached. No 'Orson Wells' scratched inside this time, but knowing how Michael treasured great film classics, I was sure this historic script would intrigue him anyway.

He arrived, rock-star style, an hour late, minus Helena, looking handsomely dishevelled. He stumbled over words trying to explain her absence before finally admitting that he hadn't been to bed at all the night before.

'I was celebrating my 35th by dancing naked on a friend's coffee table,' he explained, drawing himself to his full height. 'You come into the world naked . . . why not celebrate your birthday the same way?'

Mother and Ross weren't too sure about this proclamation but Erin and Brent enjoyed it. Michael spotted his old friend Michael Hamlyn in the restaurant and waved. Hamlyn was at the bar with Terence Stamp, lead actor *in The Adventures of Priscilla, Queen of the Desert*, which Hamlyn had co-produced. He was consoling Terence for narrowly missing out on the Best Actor in a Comedy or Musical award at the Golden Globes two nights earlier, for his unforgettable take on the poised, witty, tragicomic transsexual Bernadette.

Hamlyn had originally offered Michael the role of estranged husband and father turned drag queen Anthony 'Tick' Belrose/Mitzi Del Bra, which eventually went to Hugo Weaving, in Stephan Elliott's fabulous film. But after numerous meetings and negotiations, Michael had been advised by INXS's office to turn it down as it would have interfered with their plans. The hit movie's eventual co-stars Stamp, Weaving and Guy Pearce experienced great career boosts after *Priscilla*, while still being recognised as serious actors.

Michael very much regretted having to turn down the part. He knew that such a risk-taking, stylish film would probably have been the kind of turning point in his acting career that might now escape him. It was another instance where he felt that INXS's management had not looked out for him and it smarted. In fact, he was never offered such a good part again. That day he gloomily told me how his longing to surpass his tentative early acting achievements seemed pointless. He felt held to a higher expectation of creative self-denial than the other band members. Rock'n'roll did not marry well with making movies, he sighed, compounding his other frustrations with the band.

But this was his birthday, and Michael wasn't going to be stuck on a downer. We were there to celebrate as a family, just happy to be spending these last hours together before he and Helena left for Nice, and that's what we did.

About two weeks later, when Michael was alone at the villa and unable to sleep, he called me. I made a cup of tea and settled in because he wanted to talk about someone new. Paula Yates was a journalist and a British television personality. A terrific mother, he said—and a real wit.

He spoke about her daughters and mentioned she'd authored several books on raising children. Suddenly I recalled Rosanna talking about a 'Paula' who showed up on tour sometimes. They had known each other 'for years'. I guessed that Michael had been seeing her covertly for some time.

Publicly, Michael and Helena presented themselves as their usual loving and superbly photogenic selves. But Paula made her own plans and moved out of her marital home with Bob Geldof, taking their three daughters Fifi, Peaches and Pixie and their nanny, Anita. For around three months she and Michael saw each other secretly on and off. Then she proposed a quiet, supposedly secret weekend away. In her book *Paula, Michael & Bob: Everything you know is wrong* (2003), Paula's former publicist Gerry Agar wrote that, from her press contacts, she learned that 'Paula had engineered the initial "discovery" of their relationship to separate Michael from Helena'.

Michael had no idea he'd been set up when he and Paula entered the dining room of the Chilston Park Hotel in Kent, which was heavily sprinkled with members of the tabloid press. When a journalist friend of Paula's came over to the table, she and Michael immediately returned upstairs to their room, attracting even more attention. Attempting to leave early the following morning, while the inn was surrounded by press, he had an altercation with a photographer who filed assault charges.

Michael, who had been juggling his feelings for both women, had the choice made for him. For all his faults, he just adored women. He was a romantic, but monogamy was not one of his strong points. Mother once asked him why he didn't settle down and get married and he replied, 'Because there are too many wonderful women.' His vision of Bob Geldof was of a controlling ex-husband and father. He had watched our parents' simmering war for years and the memories of the fallout never left him. (To be fair, he had only heard the story of the Geldof marital breakdown from Paula's side.)

Soon after the Kent hotel fiasco, Michael began explaining to friends and family how, after his great work fighting famine through Live Aid's worldwide rock music broadcasts, Geldof exerted enormous influence with the press. Let's face it; Live Aid catapulted Geldof to international fame, way beyond his fronting Irish rockers The Boomtown Rats.

Sensitive, moody Michael, fearless about experimentation with life itself, but passionate about his private life being kept that way, meets outrageous Paula, with her seemingly unslakable thirst for making headlines. No surprise that the shaken cocktail of these two could be volatile.

Paula Yates was a complicated woman: bright, sharp-witted, seductive and sometimes perverse. She wrote that she'd hated being a child and couldn't wait to grow up. She was raised by English show-business parents in Colwyn Bay, Wales. Her mother, Hélène Thornton-Bosment, born Elaine Smith, worked as a Bluebell Girls high-kicking, feathered dancer as a teen, and later as a film actress and romance novelist under the name of Heller Toren.

DNA tests would eventually confirm that Hélène conceived Paula, her only child, to *Opportunity Knocks* television host Hughie Green, weeks after marrying the man her daughter *thought* was her father, the much older religious television presenter Jess 'the Bishop' Yates.

Jess himself had bipolar disorder and was often dosed up on laudanum, Paula wrote. Hélène travelled to pursue movie roles, frequently leaving Paula, as a young girl, in the care of her erratic father, according to her. Paula also claimed she became anorexic at eight, which was also around the same time that Jess Yates left the family for a much younger showgirl. Paula would only discover who her real biological father was after Michael's death. Needless to say, the double impact was devastating.

Her mother, Hélène, has claimed she never *knowingly* had sex with Jess Yates's then friend (later sworn enemy) Hughie at that time, but said Jess liked to spike her drinks—so it is possible Hughie fathered Paula when Hélène was drugged, without her knowing it (in other words, via rape). It sounds like a traumatic family history, no matter how you look at it, much affected by alcohol, drugs, abandonment and psychological problems.

In her 2006 book *Big Girls Don't Cry*, Hélène says she now regrets not seeking medical help for what she later believed was Paula's mental illness.

'Paula's problem was Paula', Hélène told an interviewer from *Wales Online*, 'lack of true identity and solid reality and that's a very difficult thing in life. If Paula hurt a lot of people it's partly my fault for not having realised that even small children can need a psychiatrist.

'It was clear then she had behavioural problems,' Hélène continued. 'I should have put her into therapy, and I feel very disappointed with myself that I didn't. I can only plead catastrophic ignorance.'

In a June 1998 interview with the *London Sunday Times*, Dr Oliver James, a clinical psychologist who worked with Paula Yates on a television series, spoke about her.

'[Paula] is liable to feel that she does not exist unless she is at the centre of a crisis, which she likes the tabloids to chronicle because they make her feel significant,' said James. He believed she suffered from borderline personality disorder.

Despite his restless ways, by his mid-thirties perhaps Michael was considering that he might finally be ready to grasp the nettle of fatherhood. Someone who was as enthusiastic about motherhood as Paula appeared to be a good match. Her three bright children were a bonus of a kind no other partner had brought. It seems he fell for all four of them: Paula, Fifi, Peaches and Pixie.

And of course when Tiger Lily arrived, she would change everything.

In many ways, though, Paula was the worst possible partner Michael could have chosen right then. She was a creature of the media, living off it with her columns, television presenting and interviewing roles. Yet the 'straying' mother (in the media's eyes) virtually had a combination of explosives packed around her, whether she liked it or not.

Her abandonment of the widely respected Bob Geldof, father of their three young girls, who was also her employer at the time, was immediately condemned. He had been awarded an honorary knighthood by Queen Elizabeth II (being Irish, this was the only type of knighthood he qualified for) as a powerful anti-poverty campaigner. Paula was firmly ejected from her identity as a fun, quirky, flirty mum and recast as a shallow Jezebel. She was fired and furthermore entangled in long, costly legal struggles with her ex over custody of the girls.

Paula's life then had to be in lock-step with that of the girls' father, regarding her residence, which had to be London. This trapped Michael in Britain at the mercy of a pernicious and sustained Fleet Street attack. Meanwhile, he was cast as the homewrecker, the upstart colonial stud who would shatter the finest family to put another notch on his belt.

Broadminded as Helena was, she was not going to stand for this humiliation. Their four-year relationship was in tatters and his reputation was in ruins.

The photographs that made the newspapers showed Michael standing over a fallen photographer as Paula dashed to a waiting car. Of course what most people did not know was that while one tag-teaming photographer baited Michael, another stood by waiting to snap his reaction. With his acquired brain injury, Michael's impulse control was left wanting. He was fairly easy to bait.

From now on the paparazzi would always be lying in wait, ready to hit the bear and make it dance. Thus began Michael's slow-growing contempt for the British press.

Paula hired Gerry Agar, a publicist both she and Bob had known and considered a friend for many years. Boosting Paula's image must have been a daunting task at that time. Michael took to calling her 'Gerry-berry'. Gerry said that Paula planted stories in the tabloids suggesting that she and Michael were about to be married partly as a strategy to keep him.

When Paula sold a story to a magazine or tabloid entity she generally knew when it would be published. Knowing that marriage was something that Michael was quick to deny and also hiding the fact that selling stories was how she now made a living, Paula went to great lengths to make sure Michael did not see the stories she planted, according to Gerry, especially if she was quoted. On one occasion when Nanny Anita was about to take the children for a walk, Michael offered to tag along. This caused some alarm for Paula, who pulled Anita aside and warned her not to allow Michael anywhere near a newsstand.

Paula came across as a successful, independent author living off her royalties. In fact she was massively overdrawn at the bank after losing her television work. It's understandable that she would want to keep up the facade. Michael probably took her at face value.

It was a difficult balance for Gerry and Anita, though, especially when Paula had Michael's ear and was so quick on her feet. Gerry soon found herself covering many bases and unwittingly covering for Paula too.

I empathised with Michael. In the past the press had always been on his side and now he found himself at the centre of a painful, confusing scandal. I wonder if Kylie's forewarnings played in his mind at this time. His physician increased his dosage of Prozac, which he had been taking since 1994.

In May 1995 Michael sent Mother and Ross a brief fax letting them know he had to face court in August for assaulting that journalist. 'Ah Well!' he commented.

The house Michael had bought on Smith Terrace, Chelsea, was being extensively renovated, so when Mother and Ross arrived in London in June to meet Paula for the first time, they stayed with Michael in his Belgravia apartment. Paula arrived wearing pink Chanel and a sweet smile. She carried an armful of flowers, a shy young mother sharing anecdotes about her three girls. Mother and Ross were totally captivated and disarmed. They spent the day shopping at Harrods, Chanel and Dolce & Gabbana, where Mother purchased a beautiful pale blue suit. She never suspected that day that two and a half years later she would wear it to her elder son's funeral.

Mid-afternoon they met up with Anita and the Geldof girls for afternoon tea. Twelve-year-old Fifi was friendly and intelligent and looked most like Bob. Peaches was six at the time, naughtily pushing boundaries and her nanny's patience on that first meeting. Four-year-old Pixie was so endearing. She told Mother how she had attempted to colour her hair red the night before, in honour of their first meeting, and in fact Mother remarked on the patches of red and blonde. Peaches said that they had been warned to be on their best behaviour. Mother and Ross thought all three were gorgeous, observing Michael's playful interaction with them as they showed their affection for him.

Throughout their ten-day visit they spent more time with the Geldof girls and Paula, who struck them as quick-witted, bright and attentive. Michael was very relaxed and laughed a lot when she was around. She showed interest in both Mother and Ross and found ways to let them know. For instance, when she saw Mother reading Sarah Miles' autobiography, she showed up the following day with the author's latest book. When Ross mentioned that he was addicted to dark chocolate, she excused herself and was back in no time with a beautifully gift-wrapped box of rich dark chocolate. Paula truly won them over.

One night halfway through their visit Michael made reservations at San Lorenzo, his favourite Italian restaurant. He invited his friend

Michael Hamlyn and his wife, Sara, and let Paula know he would come by for her at seven. But Paula insisted on meeting them at the restaurant. Michael's driver had alerted him to photojournalists regularly following them around London but had managed to give them the slip. So far, nothing had been mentioned in the tabloids. Michael was very pleased to have this break, especially as it was family time. That was about to change.

After dinner they stepped outside the restaurant to a blinding flash of lights. Voices behind the cameras yelled questions as they chased them a block to their waiting car. I can't imagine how frightening and disorienting this would have been for our mother and Ross. Mother said that for the rest of their stay, no matter how secretive they were, how often they changed cars or met up separately, the press was always there.

During the visit, Michael took them to see his house in Chelsea, explaining the renovations that had been done so far and his future plans for the property. He also told them about a house he'd bought on the Gold Coast, not far from where they lived. Colin Diamond had found it for him as he'd been too busy, but he was looking forward to seeing it on his next visit.

Far from being estranged from his mother, as so many uninformed journalists and authors have claimed over the years, Michael sent repeated invitations and requests to spend time with her throughout his life. On this trip she and Ross continued on to Roquefort-les-Pins, where they were joined at the villa by Chris Bailey and, finally, Michael himself. Music filled the house as Chris and Michael spent many hours in the music room. Together the two were hilarious; Mother described this as one of the happiest breaks they'd ever had.

Paula called often, and Michael laughed a lot during their conversations. Nevertheless, Mother worried about the conflicting press coming Michael's way in direct response to this relationship. She asked

Chris about it and he answered, 'I wouldn't worry, Patricia, as far as Michael's concerned, this thing with Paula is nothing serious.'

After the seduction period cooled down, Michael shared with me how Paula told him how much her children adored him; that they had never responded so lovingly to a man before. Gradually his sense of responsibility towards Fifi, Peaches and Pixie grew.

While staying on the Gold Coast with Mother and Ross in August 1995, Michael expressed a desire to see his house at 15 La Spezia Court nearby, on the Gold Coast's Isle of Capri, set among artificial canals. Diamond had described a house in disrepair but having potential. He said they couldn't ask much in rental until it was fixed up. All of this surprised Mother; she had driven by the waterfront property that spanned three house blocks. It was big and seemed to be well cared for. Michael had paid $1 million, with a Bentley thrown into the deal for him as well.

After escaping some of the bitter English winter in Queensland, alas Michael returned to London just days before Rhett and Mandy's little Zoe Angel was born. Michael was thrilled to be made an uncle.

In late November, there was news of an impending birth much closer to home. Paula told Michael she was pregnant with his child. He jumped on a flight to Los Angeles to think about it. Then he returned to London a few days later with gifts for everyone. He did not immediately share the news with the whole family.

In December 1995, Michael and Paula arrived on the Gold Coast for a visit with Mother and Ross. The Geldof girls would enjoy Christmas with Bob in London, and then their father would put them on a flight to spend ten days in the Australian sunshine.

Michael had always been really intrigued by Ross's stories and medals from his life in the Royal Australian Air Force, so Ross arranged a flight in a Tiger Moth for the two of them. The following Christmas Michael gave Ross silver Tiger Moth cufflinks to show his appreciation.

Michael made the plans for Christmas dinner himself. He wanted it served in a private room at the Hyatt where they were staying in Sydney. Every detail was pivotal to him, as he planned to announce Paula's pregnancy to the family. It was quite a surprise to all, especially as her divorce from Bob was not yet final.

Then Bob called Paula to tell her that Peaches was ill, so he was keeping all three girls in London beyond Christmas. Naturally she felt torn: Michael had rented a beautiful home in Palm Beach in preparation for the children's visit, and now she would be in chilly London for New Year's Eve without Michael. But a mother's instinct is to be near her children, especially if one is ill.

16

and when thy heart
began to beat

ONE DAY IN APRIL 1996 a two-page fax printed out, as our commu-
nications did those days, with a great fanfare of beeping and whirring.
It was from Michael, who had just moved in with Paula Yates.

Paula was about six months pregnant and Michael was 'very excited'
at the prospect of having a daughter. They had been going over names
and 'Heavenly' seemed to be at the top of Paula's list but Michael was
specifically looking for a Polynesian name like 'Herani, Lani, etc'. In the
midst of this idyllic picture, Michael was going through 'an unimag-
inable hell with the press, the police, a fire, four burglaries, litigation,
and at the moment Paula is on the verge of being made bankrupt . . .
we have 7 or 8 writs on our hands'.

I was stunned to hear about this level of difficulty. I couldn't imagine
how hard this confounding mess must be for my brother to face. He
was standing by Paula, a mother of three with such a depth of legal and

financial problems, it seemed. And to be honest, for Michael the day-to-day needs of playing house had been pretty straightforward. He had remained largely footloose and fancy-free, able to take off on a whim. His success had led him—for better or for worse—to delegate the management of the practicalities of life to others.

Now his new reality was a family life with three children, a nanny and a pregnant girlfriend trapped in a house surrounded by dozens of photographers and journalists. At the same time, he was trying to co-write the INXS album that would become *Elegantly Wasted*, as well as working on his own solo collection, which meant so much to him.

I recognised that the impending birth of his child was all-powerful motivation. Still I was amazed, frankly, that he was able to cope with all this. In hindsight I can see that he was putting on a brave face. Meanwhile, behind the scenes his life was spinning more and more out of control.

It was sickening. At the time, we, his family, didn't understand how much.

The latest in the Geldof–Yates legal saga was that Paula wanted to move back into the family home. After three days in court, Bob agreed. But (despite owning a country estate in Kent) he told the judge that he and his girlfriend Jeanne Marine had nowhere to go and could not afford to move.

To keep the peace, Michael generously handed over the keys to his home in Smith Terrace, Chelsea (which despite a year of costly renovations, he had yet to live in) and Bob and Jeanne lived there rent-free for six months.

As you can imagine, the revelation that Michael had turned his home over to Bob Geldof titillated the journalists no end. But researching the property, they could not come up with any public records connecting Michael's name to it. They hit a brick wall at Citipak, a company registered in the British Virgin Islands.

Two years before, UK Inland Revenue had asked for information on Citipak's accounts, along with a request for the name and address of the beneficial owner.

Gerry began getting phone calls from confused journos and Michael's London manager, Paul Craig.

Being quite close to Paula and Michael, Gerry was becoming increasingly concerned. She noted Michael's slow deterioration and depression and approached his management, even some of his famous friends, warning them that Paula was keeping him on edge with her stories. The couple's drug use was excessive and escalating. She felt convinced that *someone* in that house was going to die and was genuinely afraid it could be Michael. If only she, or management, or *one* of Michael's friends had called his *family*. If only.

• • •

Michael was not one to fall back on formula. An artist with a passion for his craft, he constantly searched for new sounds. He began writing and recording tracks for a solo album, with Andy Gill producing, in mid-1995. The two often slipped away to Michael's villa to write and record. For Michael it was also a respite from the stress of life in London.

Manchester-born Gill was a founding member and guitarist with the influential post-punk UK band Gang of Four. Gill had produced not only early Gang of Four recordings but the first Red Hot Chili Peppers album, and also worked with The Stranglers.

Michael's friends knew he had a habit of playing a favourite new album over and over. After thrashing Beck's *Loser* for weeks on end, he switched to English band Black Grape's debut album *It's Great When You're Straight . . . Yeah*, co-produced by LA-based musician and producer Danny Saber. Michael fell in love with the sound of the band that had grown out of the ashes of 'Madchester' band Happy Mondays, and blared Black Grape's album from his car's sound system as he drove through the French countryside. U2's Bono and The Edge were neighbours (as was Tina Turner at Eze, on the French Riviera). They later told Danny that they knew when Michael was about to drop in for a visit from the slow fading in of *It's Great When You're Straight . . . Yeah*.

Danny remembered the first time Michael contacted him in 1995.

'I knew he was going to call as he had gotten hold of my manager and had sent a couple of versions of "Get On The Inside", which he had done with Andy, and I liked them,' says Danny. 'INXS were big and Michael was an international rock star, so I guess I was expecting him to be obnoxious or something, you know. But it only took about ten seconds for me to want to work with him. There was something in his voice. He was so quiet and there was something so humble about him when he asked me to join him in London. I mean, I was like, of course man, I mean, you're . . . you're you! I was the one who needed a [career] break but he made it the other way around.

'When I arrived, we had a couple of sessions at Andy [Gill]'s house, sort of vibed it out. Andy was putting on some tracks, all great tracks but it was the sound that Michael brought me in for. He wanted me to sort of make it cooler. Then he and I started writing together, which is only natural.'

On the third night Michael took Danny out for dinner and told him how pleased he was with the progress. 'He was really genuine about it; you could really tell he meant it', Danny said, 'that's how real he was.' Afterwards they went to Browns, a popular London nightclub. 'Mick Jagger and Ronnie Wood came in and sat at our table and I'm, well . . . Michael's introducing me to all of these people, telling them about his solo, and when Mick says he wants to do a solo, he totally put me onto him. It was unbelievable because few are that generous. He really set the table with me working with the Stones; Michael gave me my career.'

Danny is known for his diversity in production as well as for the artists he has worked with, including the Stones, David Bowie, U2, Seal, Marilyn Manson, Busta Rhymes and Madonna. But when Michael asked Danny to join him in the studio, he had only one production credit. Michael clearly heard something he liked in that Black Grape album. He had a vision for his solo work and he saw Danny in that picture.

'As you know, Michael was such a funny guy, such a contradiction if you think about it because on one hand he had this image of a playboy but the reality is, his work ethic was—well, he should have had a hardhat with a mining light on it,' smiled Danny.

John X, the sound mixer on Michael's solo recordings with Danny and Andy, was technically very proficient and experienced. They say that as a seventeen-year-old engineer, he was running the first studio he ever worked at. Having mixed for the who's who of musicians, John was always conscious of the vibe in the studio.

'John, what time do you get up?' Michael said to him one day. 'What's say we get in early and lay down the vocals and they [Andy and Danny] can sort it when they get in later?'

John X recalled how Michael would arrive at Nomis Studios in the morning right after dropping Peaches and Pixie off at school. He would walk in complaining about the media hanging around and how much more difficult his day-to-day life was for that even when performing the most basic parental functions.

'On the other hand, he was totally ready for the day's work,' John said. 'His enthusiasm for the project was obvious. He would walk over to the mike, give a flawless first take and ask if another was needed. This was typical Michael. He never had to force finding his voice, although he also liked to vary his phrasing from take to take. It often only took two takes, and then it would be a matter of personal taste as to which was best, because both of them would be faultless.'

John X assured me that during these sessions he would give it his all, from a whisper to full strength. Michael made the same natural hand gestures in the studio that he would in front of an audience. John said that in his experience, it was extremely rare for a singer to arrive in the morning, let alone with optimum vocal preparedness and ready to roll.

Danny Saber expanded on Michael's out-of-the-ordinariness in this respect. A singer's voice usually sounds a bit cracked, dry, low and smoky when they wake up in the morning. That was the sound that Michael was going for on this album.

'We catered everything to Michael but it wasn't in a superficial sort of patronising way. Not a star trip thing; just trying to help him. It was serious but we didn't take each other seriously. The environment we created together was what he needed at the time and that's what matters. It goes back to supporting your artist,' Danny said.

Now I realised, for Michael, just how much working on his own music in the studio was his safe haven in London. John X described how they put up a chalkboard where Michael could jot down name suggestions for his firstborn baby. Tiger Lily was always there, but he was listing other possible choices too. Hiraani, Harmony, Heavenly and Harleigh were some of the choices.

Danny Saber travelled between LA and London to work with Michael on his solo material for some months at Nomis Studios in Hammersmith, London, over this period. One evening they went to Café Rouge and were not there long before Paula arrived unannounced.

'It was the weirdest thing,' said Danny, 'nobody except Paula knew we were there and she just showed up and started wigging out, started screaming at him in the middle of the place. Just embarrassing him.

Michael's just saying to me, "Sorry mate." He calmed her down and we left soon after. When we walked outside there were cameras everywhere, press everywhere, just waiting.

'You know, he would say he was happy with Paula, but there was always drama—so much drama—and he didn't strike me as the kind of guy who liked drama.'

At the same time my own life was busy. I had met retired Los Angeles businessman Ken Schorr, and two months later he proposed. Michael was thrilled that the grounds of Vieille Ferme des Guerchs would be the setting for the happy occasion of our wedding. As I planned the ceremony there were calls and faxes back and forth between Michael's housekeeper Linda, Michael, Mother and me. Linda was excited for me and happy to have a wedding to organise, albeit a very small private one. She was in a continual flap about preparations because the date we had decided on was Saturday, 13 July—the eve of Bastille Day, France's national day.

While we were in Paris before the wedding, Mother and Ross visited Michael and a very pregnant Paula among the chaos in the London home. Bob had taken his time making the move to Michael's Smith Terrace house and Paula was dangerously close to her due date but insisted on making the move anyway. They were surrounded by packing crates, children, pets and movers.

Michael called me in Paris and explained that, as a surprise, Paula had instructed his gardener Nestor to paint the interior of his villa and he had not yet seen it. When I asked Nestor about it on the way to the villa, he became so distressed he could barely speak; when I walked in it was obvious why. In place of the white walls, crisp white fabrics and gorgeous heavy natural wood beams, there was colour chaos. Paula had chosen several colours and ordered Nestor to paint the 400-year-old beams along with the walls.

Sacrilegious.

She had also sent some of her extra lounge chairs down to the villa, some in need of repair, with fabric thrown over them. I had never seen so many fabrics and patterns and colours in one room before. Every lamp had a scarf draped over it. There was such disharmony that I found it uncomfortable to sit in many of the rooms. I had a fair idea how Michael was going to react too.

Previously Helena had contributed to the villa's tasteful, minimalistic, light and airy decor in keeping with the traditions and spirit of the beautiful old home. A style Michael was familiar and relaxed with.

Before Paula's makeover, the house had been used for fashion shoots and available for commercials and movies. One magazine aerial shot even claimed it was Helena's property! Now, it was deemed unsuitable and eventually taken off the books.

Despite my dismay at the new interior design, I pulled myself together enough to recognise that the weather was brilliant. And Nestor had outdone himself in readying Michael's garden for my wedding. The roses were flourishing and every day I basked in the scent of fresh blooms. The brilliant red Australian bottlebrush was looking healthy too.

Michael called before arriving in Nice and asked for his Aston Martin to be 'summoned'. Like most of Michael's cars, it had actually spent more time in his mechanic's garage (in Nice this time) than his own. Nestor and I drove off to collect it together and I got to drive it back.

What a magnificent piece of machinery! Only 1059 were built. I must admit, that with the French Alps in the distance, it was awesome to navigate those meandering bends, gripping the fine timber wheel as the car hugged each bend. I understood Michael's romantic attachment to it.

After such a high, I was genuinely shocked when Michael arrived the day before my wedding and walked towards us. He was slumped. By this I mean his usual impeccable posture was gone. His shoulders were rounded; he no longer held his head high. His face was pale and puffy, and his hair dyed a harsh, unbecoming black. His shiny curls were all but gone. The chemicals used on his hair had stripped it of its usual lustre and bounce. When I inquired about the new hair colour, he replied that Paula messed with her hair colour all the time and she had fancied this on him.

He said he was on a health kick and refused hard liquor. I don't know how long he had been abstaining but he did not look healthy to me. Looking back, I remember not only his shocking physical appearance, but also his quiet demeanour. He seemed to be preoccupied, but I attributed this to imminent fatherhood. Calls from London with updates on Paula's condition were coming thick and fast. The baby was due in ten days or so. I told him he was going to make a good father and he smiled broadly. But his eyes remained dull. It was like his spirit was broken. I thought of Emily Dickinson's poem 'After great pain, a formal feeling comes'—published in 1890. 'A Quartz contentment, like a stone—/ This is the Hour of Lead—/ Remembered, if outlived,/ As Freezing persons, recollect the Snow—/ First—Chill— then Stupor—then the letting go' . . . of grief, shock or anxiety, perhaps, under sedation.

My room was next to Michael's master suite and we were sharing a bathroom. On the day of the wedding, as he walked out and I entered, I noticed a small pill container on the counter; the label read 'Paula Yates' and 'Prozac'. When he came back into the bathroom he zipped me up with a complimentary wolf whistle, which made me laugh. I asked him what the antidepressants were all about. He replied that it had been a troublesome year; he loathed having to spend so much time in London being harassed by the press and having his life controlled by Geldof's decisions; sometimes he got so low. Consequently, his physician had put him on Prozac. I pointed out Paula's name on the label and he said that she took the same medication. Our conversation was hurried since Father Guerrero was waiting in the garden for the vows.

Of course the ceremony was overwhelming and precious, and I needed to experience it to the full. I did make a mental note though: I ought to speak with Michael at length at some stage. But when? London beckoned, and I myself would shortly be off on a honeymoon in Venice.

Thereafter, in his usual way, Michael avoided the unsettling topics. Depression and Prozac would have to wait. He made it clear he wanted to enjoy his time at the villa.

During the reception on the terrace Michael played some rough versions of tracks he'd been recording for a solo album. The music was a surprise departure from the INXS sound. His voice was better than ever. We were all impressed and asked to hear tracks replayed.

On the three evenings Michael spent at the villa, he took the younger generation of the family—his nephew, Brent, and his friend Dan, and Erin—to a number of all-night clubs. The kids had a wonderful time. As Erin tells it, wherever they went, they were taken directly to a reserved table and drinks arrived on the house. They later visited a cafe and discussed many things, including recreational drugs.

Michael admitted to having tried heroin but assured them that he had quickly stopped when he learned firsthand how destructive and habit-forming it was. He warned them of the dangers of such a drug. He made it clear to them that he indulged in illegal substances only lightly, preferring to occasionally heighten his senses with pot or ecstasy.

After this sage attempt at Drug Safety Instructions for the Younger Generation, the next night he disappeared at some club and reappeared looking rather more ecstatic with various girls in tow. He clearly planned to matchmake them with Brent and Dan. He admitted later that he'd found some ecstasy.

On Michael's last evening in France they were taking a late-night swim when he suddenly insisted on more clubbing; apparently the boys hadn't danced enough with various local and visiting girls. On their return he sped over several roundabouts in the jeep before hanging screaming wheelies around the neighbourhood.

The next day Michael returned to London for the birth of his child. At that address he could not even walk out of his front door without being mobbed and harassed. His French villa, with its large electric gate and driveway to the secluded house, was the only home that could not be invaded by the media.

After his death, I discovered that Michael had not been entirely truthful when talking to Erin and Brent. I can understand why, of course, and appreciate that he did not want to divulge the full extent of his substance abuse to his niece and nephew.

In fact, Michael was hiding mixed drug dependencies from the whole family. A London doctor was supplying both him and Paula with Prozac and Rohypnol, sleeping pills. Of the so-called recreational drugs, by mid-1996 he was very fond of both opium and ecstasy and had been using cocaine for a long time. He also smoked cigarettes and drank heavily at times. I should have remembered that people addicted to substances can be accomplished liars about their level of dependency.

A few days after Michael returned to London, our mother and Ross travelled on to the beautiful city of Genoa in Italy. Checking into their hotel they were handed three messages.

'Michael phoned please call him.'

'Linda phoned please call Michael.'

And 'Michael phoned please, please call.'

Before Mother could dial out, Ross switched on the television, and there on the newscast was a photograph of Michael and Paula. Across the screen it read 'Welcome Heavenly Hiraani Tiger Lily— congratulations Paula Yates and Michael Hutchence'.

When Mother got through to Michael, he was euphoric. 'Tiger', as he called his little daughter, was gorgeous! He went into her vital statistics. He said he was drinking champagne with a few friends. When Mother called back, Michael's London manager, Paul Craig, answered and mentioned that it was lucky that the midwives had been able to release the cord from around Tiger's neck just before the paramedics arrived. No doubt Michael was hesitant in sharing this with our mother: she had been against the home birth. When Michael came on the line he said Tiger was healthy and beautiful and there was no need to worry.

He wanted to get out of London though. The house was surrounded by press. He made plans to meet Mother and Ross at the villa in two weeks. Realising that there were no supplies for Tiger at the villa, they returned early and purchased the finest convertible, laydown stroller-cum-pram, bassinet and infant car seat they could find.

Ross and Nestor each took a car to the Nice airport to meet the charter flight carrying the precious cargo. Besides Paula and Michael, there were the three Geldof girls and their nanny, Anita. When Paula saw the car seat she refused to use it for Tiger. She insisted that she had to hold her. Nestor refused to drive that way, knowing it was dangerous and against the law. Michael insisted but Paula refused to hand him Tiger. There was a stand off and it took much begging for her to give in.

When they arrived at the villa, Paula was disagreeable towards everyone. Perhaps she was tired or showing signs of postpartum depression, but it was a vastly different Paula from the one they had seen just one month previously and certainly nothing like the charmer they had first met a year ago. She barely acknowledged the Rolls-Royce of infant carriages, and minutes after Michael handed Tiger to Mother for her first look at her new granddaughter, Paula snatched her back and headed upstairs to the master bedroom.

Tiger Lily was a sweet, docile little infant, sleeping all day, as did Paula. She told Mother that the child needed to stay with her in the bedroom all day to be fed every 30 minutes. I had not heard of this technique, but Paula held herself out as the authority on motherhood, and she was Tiger Lily's mother. Mother was not going to step over boundaries; it was not for her to say anything. She looked forward to six o'clock each evening when Anita would bring Tiger downstairs. Mother said she did not see Tiger Lily's eyes open for a couple of days as she didn't seem to want to wake up. On a number of occasions Anita had to hold her under lukewarm then cold running water to arouse her. This was unusual, she said, and she seemed concerned. Mother recalled that she never once heard Tiger wake during the night.

During this visit the Geldof girls got up to some mischief. While Michael, Mother, Ross, Linda and Nestor were in Nice, Anita took the afternoon off. The children were left to their own devices and, no doubt feeling a bit left out with their new baby sister taking up their mother's time, desecrated the gardens. It's the only word for it, because Michael returned to find his front lawn covered by a carpet of pink, yellow and red rose petals. Not one rose was spared from the garden. While chopped or half-eaten fruit and vegetables from both the kitchen and the garden, along with cotton buds, floated on top of the pool, the fish in the pond were circling Barbie dolls and baguettes. The pathways were strewn with squashed tomatoes and downed lavender bushes. It was if someone had taken a machete to his garden.

Michael immediately ran upstairs to Paula and there was quite an argument. The children ate in their room with lights out early that night. From then on Linda and Nestor were always nervous when the Geldof girls visited.

After I returned from my European honeymoon, I spoke with Michael, who was naturally joyful and in wonderment over observing childbirth. In subsequent phone conversations I always asked him about the Geldof girls and Anita, and noticed he was cooling on the nanny. I questioned him about it and he reluctantly told me that Paula was concerned that Anita was siding with Bob and that she didn't trust her with Tiger.

MICHAEL

I was shocked: Anita had been with Paula and her girls since Fifi was born and had proven to be extremely reliable. She loved the children. Michael said that she had been making up stories about Paula's mothering skills and it had the potential to cause embarrassment and possibly harm Paula's livelihood as an author of books on parenting.

Some years later, Gerry opened up and told me that she had been with Anita when Tiger had a seizure and she rushed them both to the emergency department. There was no blood test taken and the baby was found to be fine at the ER. When they told Paula about it, she accused them both of making up stories. She admonished them for possibly opening the door for a scandal when she was known for her books on motherhood and child rearing. (In fact, Paula had only written one semi-serious book that gave tips for the first twelve months of life, *The Fun Starts Here: Practical guide to everything you need to know from conception to the first birthday*, in 1990. In my view she couldn't possibly be held up as an expert on childcare.)

This was not the only time that people witnessed Paula behaving with seeming indifference to her children's welfare. Danny Saber told me about an odd incident he witnessed when they were in New York, where Michael was auditioning for a movie role. 'One day Michael's agent Lesley was taking him to Robert De Niro's Tribeca offices in lower Manhattan', said Danny, 'and he had been studying his lines and they're on their way to the meeting to read for the part. And Paula starts pushing the baby in traffic, out in the road, just stressing him out beyond. You know, just outrageous insanity ...'.

Michael really took everything that Paula said at face value. I doubt he had even seen any of Paula's books. She convinced him that Gerry and Anita were overreacting when they took Tiger to hospital. I learned that this was not Tiger's first seizure, but Michael didn't know it. Michael's mistrust of Anita began to take hold that day.

206

17

moving target

ANDREW FARRISS was also living in London by this stage, and in April 1996 he and Michael had co-written enough new material for the band to join them there for rehearsals for their tenth studio album, *Elegantly Wasted*. They prepared to record what would be Michael's final INXS album, in Vancouver, with Bruce Fairbairn, the Canadian producer who had guided mega sellers like Bon Jovi's *Slippery When Wet* and AC/DC's *The Razor's Edge*.

Michael touched down in Sydney in September 1996 to talk about the recording of the forthcoming album, even though it would not be released until March 1997, with the title track preceding it as a single. He made a few appearances and did some media. The band would perform a new track from the album on a live telecast of the ARIAs—the Australian Recording Industry Awards—on 30 September. On his first night in Sydney he invited Michele Bennett and another close friend to dinner with Colin Diamond and his colleague, Australian lawyer Andrew Young, at Neil Perry's famous seafood restaurant Rockpool.

When two-month-old Tiger arrived with her mother, they joined him at the Sir Stamford in Double Bay. Mother and Ross took this opportunity to reconnect and see their granddaughter again, after the awkward situation of the Geldof sisters' destruction party at the villa six weeks before. They booked into a suite one block east, at the Ritz-Carlton.

INXS's publicist Shawn Deacon hosted a party at her home for the band, inviting several industry movers and shakers. As Paula sat on a sofa nursing Tiger, she suddenly announced to Susie and Mother that she and Michael were getting married. It was a secret but the announcement was coming. Mother walked over to Michael, kissed him on the cheek and congratulated him. She pulled back to see a puzzled look on his face but, before he could say anything, Kell appeared and hugged him. When she told him what Paula had said he threw his head back and laughed.

'She's just having you on,' Michael said. 'We're not getting married.'

Four days prior to the ARIAs a bomb dropped. Newspapers from London to Sydney trumpeted about 'Drugs Found In Paula's House'. When Mother and Ross arrived at Michael's suite, they found him half out of his mind with dread. Diamond and Young were there and Paula was announcing to all and sundry that this was a set-up and Bob was going to take Tiger away from them. The two lawyers agreed, naturally. They convinced Michael that even though the premises raided were Paula's, the authorities would think him an unfit parent with this latest development. He was absolutely petrified that he would lose Tiger.

The secondary yet still major concern was that a drug charge would endanger his US working visa, needed for touring the USA of course. INXS did so regularly and extensively. It was a huge market for them.

Diamond insisted that Paula return to London with Young as soon as possible to face the charges, while Michael would return with

Tiger at a later date, having secured her Australian passport. Rhett's partner, Mandy Nolan, was the obvious person to help Michael care for Tiger. Mandy stayed at the hotel with little Tiger and her own daughter, Tiger's cousin Zoe, while Michael performed on the ARIAs.

I was so hurt for Michael. It took unbelievable courage and strength to appear on national television amid scorching headlines. Although he sang with such sadness and anger, his voice and his phrasing on 'Searching', the most soulful of INXS's songs, were superb.

The following day he chartered a flight to take himself, Mandy, the two babies and Diamond to his house on the Gold Coast.

So what is the truth behind the drug bust—which actually wasn't? Well, some years later, Gerry Agar told me the inside story. In July 1998 Mother and I went to London and also spoke to Anita about what happened at this time.

Gerry's daughter was spending the night in Anita's care. According to Anita, during the night the alarm on Michael's Jeep Cherokee went off and began to raise absolute hell out on the sleeping street. Anita began searching Paula's room for operating instructions or car keys.

When Anita frantically moved some magazines aside she came across a manila envelope hand-addressed to one of Michael's pseudonyms, 'Mr Kipper'. The envelope had already been opened, she said, so she dumped the contents out onto the bed. Out came a couple of Smarties tubes containing a brown substance.

Anita claimed that a neighbour then helped her find the 'off' switch for the car alarm and she went back to bed. When she rose in the morning, she found the children in Paula's bedroom, playing with the brown substance from the Smarties tubes. She removed it and called Gerry, who immediately came over. Together they tried to determine what it was. After a call to a friend and another to the drug helpline, they decided that it was most likely opium, although the substance was never tested and the presence of opium never proved.

Disturbingly, the friend Gerry called was the infamous Piers Morgan, then editor of the racy British tabloid the *Daily Mirror*. When Morgan had been editor of Rupert Murdoch's muck-raking *News of the World* (since closed down over the phone-hacking scandal) even *Murdoch* chastised his editor for going 'too far'!

Shortly after Gerry's call to the *Daily Mirror*, Bob arrived to collect Peaches and Pixie for lunch and took Gerry's daughter along too. With the children gone, Anita and Gerry searched the house. They went through Paula's bedroom closet and found Polaroids of Michael and Paula, the kind that people sometimes take of themselves to keep things interesting in the bedroom. It is no crime for two consenting adults to take or keep such photographs—especially when they are hidden away in a closet. They removed them and would hand them over to the police with the Smarties container.

As the children's live-in nanny for fourteen years, Anita was considered part of the family. During that time she had of course come to love Fifi—who was now at boarding school, so not involved in this fiasco— Peaches, Pixie and now Tiger. In that sense, she was most protective of them, so perhaps their safety was foremost in her mind. As a mother, of course I understand too how upset Gerry must have been when she was told her child had been handling suspected drugs.

Two days after discovering the suspected drugs, Gerry said, she called Paula about it, but Paula did not take her call seriously. It seemed to Gerry that something drastic needed to be done. She and Anita decided to approach Bob Geldof, who immediately called his lawyer, who took affidavits from the two women and applied to the court for a hearing date for interim orders to make *him* the primary custodial parent of the Geldof girls.

It was Anita who suggested they go to the media. Of course Piers was already sitting on this bombshell, with hopes it would get bigger— and when it did, his employer, the *Daily Mirror*, would be first in print. Bob agreed with leaking the story, Gerry said, but wanted to be sure the timing was right.

A deal for an exclusive scoop was soon set up with David Montgomery, chief executive editor of the *Daily Mirror*, a friend of Bob's. Montgomery summoned a journalist who wrote most of the 'drug bust' story—*before* Anita laid the Polaroids and Smarties tubes of suspected opium out on the kitchen table and called the bobbies.

The *Daily Mirror* broke the story. The media in both Britain and Australia began a tidal wave of coverage, complete with the customary florid regurgitation of past scandals.

Unfortunately, child welfare is no simple matter, and in the situation of a clearly hostile climate between warring parents, no charges were laid. The 'drug bust' fizzled out. But the damage to reputations had been done.

Unsurprisingly, Paula would now trust neither Gerry nor Anita. She turned for help to another mother at the school her girls attended, Belinda Brewin, girlfriend of Colin Diamond's friend/ associate/colleague Andrew Young.

18

trying to avoid disaster

IN LATE 1996 Michael came to LA to shoot the *Elegantly Wasted* cover with Danish commercial photographer and director Pierre Winther. Winther's work in advertising included a stuntman actually riding a big tiger shark at the Great Barrier Reef. They had met at Helena's apartment in Copenhagen in 1994.

'I felt an immediate connection—Michael and I simply clicked,' Pierre told me. 'We shared a slightly sarcastic sense of humour. We were laughing about the same things. He was just also a very likeable person, very down to earth. Not how you'd expect a rock star to be.

'I had a business card with an image from one of my Diesel campaigns on one side and the shark-riding image from my Levi's campaign on the other,' Pierre continued. 'Michael really liked that they had the look of something out of a movie. So when we got together for the first official meeting in London, he wanted me to come up with a concept for a shoot that would create similarly potent images.'

Michael played him the *Elegantly Wasted* album. The title song grabbed Pierre immediately and he developed a concept featuring fluorescent green and red, showing, as he put it, 'an excessive lifestyle, crashing sports cars, illuminated driveways and a lot of fun within the absurd'. On the day the album was released, fluorescent promotional cars were driven around New York and Paris. In London a lurid vehicle even dangled from a crane over the Thames.

Pierre's work on *Elegantly Wasted* creates a strange reality in a series of staged shots with no beginning or end. Each band member played a role in costume; there were some uniformed officers and Kirk looked like some kind of flash gangster. For Michael—perhaps unsurprisingly, given his love of Tiger Moths—he chose the role of a jet fighter. He was very enthusiastic about all this but stressed to Pierre that he didn't want to be the focus of attention this time. The model seen wearing an INXS T-shirt in most of the shots deliberately dominated the foreground. Michael wanted to be just one of the band members, almost an extra. And that's exactly how the cover and promo images, shot in Los Angeles, San Francisco and a patch of Californian desert outside Edwards Air Force Base, turned out. It was a tight schedule filming all day and often into the night over twelve days. Pierre said it seemed like everybody, including himself, was in character, in a sort of collective trance.

'Back in London, after I presented the material to Michael, he invited me over to the house in Chelsea where he lived with Paula and Tiger Lily at the time,' Pierre said. 'They were both very welcoming and it felt like we'd known each other much longer. Michael often cooked at home. Sooner or later in all conversations the custody fight came up. Paula was more quiet, but Michael talked about it every time I was there. He clearly felt harassed by Bob Geldof and the English press circus. He told me many times that he didn't feel at home in London and this situation didn't make it better. But of course, he couldn't escape.

There was Tiger Lily and he really adored her. I remember how much he loved to cuddle and hug her. He was so happy to be a father.

'One night we went to a concert and Michael and Paula took their little daughter along. I brought her a leather jacket with a tiger on the back that was custom made by a Danish designer friend. Michael loved it.'

When we celebrated Thanksgiving in LA in November that year all our guests entertained us with side-splitting stories. Michael peppered his with a range of convincing accents as usual. He used a very earthy Aussie voice for his story about taking Helena into the outback for a real *Australian* experience and getting seriously bogged when he tried to ford a river in his four-wheel drive. Fortunately, they were rescued by some locals who gave them an earful of colourful language about how they weren't used to seeing a magnificent, rangy model in a hiked-up sundress wading through their creek. Michael said he could have been taken by a crocodile and nobody would have noticed.

Then he recounted a very different story, this time set in downtown London. I guess he and Ian Astbury from the Cult were tying on a good one when Michael mentioned that he had never trashed a hotel room. Well, clearly this situation ought to be addressed. Just to prove they were not fey weaklings who could hurl nothing heavier than a mike stand, they ripped the bathroom door off with their bare hands and hurled it out the window. Luckily, it landed on the roof of the restaurant next door; it would have been terrible indeed if they'd injured somebody below. This vision of what-could-have-been was sobering and they meekly awaited their comeuppance, expecting the coppers to haul them down to the station at the very least. But when no thunderous knock came at the remaining door, they called it a night.

The next morning when Michael went to check out, he was handed a bill, 'of like a thousand pounds for the mini bar'. Before he had time to squint at the detail, the clerk, straight-faced and as bereft of emotion as only the British can be, said—and here Michael affected a very pretentious British accent—'And that'll be £90 for the door, sir. How would you like to pay—cash or American Express?'

After we'd all cracked up and the night was winding down, I asked Michael about his plans for 1997 and the solo album he had shown great enthusiasm for. I was concerned that after the debacle of the Max Q project, this too would be derailed. He assured me that Martha was right alongside him on this one. Although he was resigned to first completing his contractual obligations with INXS promoting *Elegantly Wasted*, together he and Martha would not let anything interfere with their plans. His intense hostility and distrust towards Bob Geldof and abhorrence of the circumstances in London were also on display. Michael made it clear that if it were not for his daughter, he would be living anywhere else but there.

He did return to London though, where he consulted Dr Jonathan Boreham, the general practitioner who had been treating Paula for some time. At this appointment Michael asked for a referral to a psychiatrist. Boreham referred him to Dr Mark Collins, a consultant psychiatrist with the Priory Hospital in Rockhampton, London, with a letter stating Michael had asked to see him in conjunction with Paula over their relationship problems. He said that he'd only been looking after Michael for the past eighteen months, and that when his patient had arrived he was already taking 20 to 40 mgs of Prozac; he wasn't sure why it was prescribed by another doctor. He suggested Michael might want to see Dr Collins solo as well as with Paula. He said Michael was physically well but 'fairly stressed' in his role with Paula's family connections 'and his re-establishment on tour with INXS'. It is telling that Michael felt the need to talk to a psychiatrist, not only about his situation with Paula, but also about going on the road with INXS.

Later, in the course of the investigation following Michael's death, Dr Collins confirmed that he had seen Michael twice during this time, and that he had already been taking Prozac for many months. Paula had accompanied him on his first visit. He noted in his statement that concerns over an ongoing dispute between Paula and her ex-husband regarding finances and childcare were areas of stress for Michael: 'He had concerns about the effect of this on his partner and also concerns over the future direction of his career and how his band INXS would be received on its forthcoming tour'.

As 1996 was coming to a close, Michael arrived on the Gold Coast for Christmas with Paula, Tiger, Peaches and Pixie. Soon after arriving he went into Ross's study and sat down to take a look through the former pilot's flight logbook. It was a thick, handwritten diary of every mission Ross had flown in his illustrious 30-year career in the Royal Australian Air Force. It was full of fascinating information and also had pictures of the various aircraft he had flown. The men in the family especially loved to look through that book and ask Ross questions. This day Ross presented Michael with a bomber jacket he had worn in Korea. Several weeks later, Michael called to tell Ross to be sure to watch an interview he did on television when it came on—he was wearing the jacket.

While Michael was with Ross, Paula and the girls were having tea with our mother. Suddenly Paula leaned in close by Mother's ear.

'Anita's writing a book and there are some really damaging things in there about you,' she whispered, then turned and walked away. With what seemed to be a deep and senseless cruelty, Paula planted a huge anxiety like a thorn under Mother's skin in that moment, knowing very well that she had no means of dealing with it except to fret and worry.

In fact, the nanny was not writing a book at all. This was just another classic example of Paula's 'gaslighting', a common abusive technique.

The term came from a 1930s stage play, *Gas Light*, in which a manipulative husband convinces his wife she is imagining their gas lighting
flicker, when in fact he is making it happen. (In an ironic twist, the
victim in the 1944 movie version is called Paula.) The perpetrator seeks
to undermine their target's confidence and trust in their own percep-
tions in order to gain control. Of course Mother didn't understand this
concept at all at the time. Paula may not have understood the term
herself, but this manipulative, cruel behaviour was something she had
been known to subject carefully chosen victims to.

In an effort to lighten the atmosphere, Mother remarked on
Peaches' beautiful (if rather flimsy) dress, which was falling off her
shoulders. Paula admitted it was actually hers. Alluding to a wedding
ceremony, Pixie announced that they all had special dresses for this
holiday. Mother looked at Paula, who was thoroughly enjoying the
exchange, and decided that she must be delusional; if she knew her
son Michael, he was not about to marry Paula Yates and it seemed
more likely that Nanny Anita would have something to say about
her lifestyle.

• • •

In January 1997, Michael filmed the MTV special *A Rough Guide to
Hong Kong*. He proved a natural current affairs–style host and interviewer, with a strong sensitivity to the political changes coming over
the city of his childhood as it prepared to return to Chinese rule.
Immediately after returning to London it was time to get back on the
touring treadmill, whether he was anxious about it or not.

INXS worked the international media and played some warm-up
gigs, beginning with a private acoustic show at the ABC Studios in
Sydney. Five days later, a VH1 special *INXS Rocks the Rockies* was
recorded live at the Wheeler Opera House in Aspen, Colorado, the

band in red-hot form, fresh after a break. Then they swung back to the continent to tape *TFI Friday* for the UK's Channel 4.

Most of the next month was spent promoting *Elegantly Wasted* in London, Paris, Brussels, Toronto, Chicago and New York, where the band performed two songs on the *Rosie O'Donnell Show*, with Michael in great voice. But when he sat in the guest chair to chat with Rosie, I noticed he wasn't quite his usual, playful self. She soon changed that by asking him about new fatherhood. He told her how amazing nine-month-old Tiger was.

'She's just perfect, I can't believe it. Sleeps all night and just laughs in the day. Giggles and smiles, never cries, you know.'

Then Rosie asked him to share something unusual he had experienced with fans. Michael recalled a girl in Sweden who'd invited him to stand outside a toilet cubicle and listen as she peed. He didn't notice anything except she kept stopping the flow. She was disappointed that he hadn't recognised that she was peeing 'Need You Tonight'. Both Rosie and the audience roared with laughter.

Released in March, *Elegantly Wasted* would turn out to be the final studio album from INXS's long-lasting original line-up.

Michael returned to LA in March and called to wish Rosanna a happy birthday. He invited her to dinner and later played her some of his new solo tracks in his hotel room. He was pleased when she showed enthusiasm for this new departure. He shared how liberating it was to work without having to get a consensus on his ideas. He also shared his concerns about his baby daughter being tied to a city where he didn't feel welcome.

INXS continued the small-scale tour (organised that way because their drawing power was on the wane, unfortunately, but not unpredictably, after the heady successes of *Kick* and *X*). They played in Dallas with Matchbox 20 and Beck, then an appearance on David Letterman's *Late Show* was followed by two more months of gigs in the USA, UK and South Africa. In Germany they appeared at the Rockpalast Festival with Simple Minds, Sheryl Crow and Nenah Cherry. Back in California, they played another excellent show at the gorgeous old Mayan Theater in downtown LA. The following day the kids and I met Michael for brunch, and when I hugged him he winced in pain. He'd fallen and bruised his ribs during a recent video shoot. He held his side, groaning every time he laughed.

The Beatles and the Rolling Stones had been in the news over their publishing catalogues changing hands.

'Yeah, yeah, don't understand that at all,' Michael said. 'I mean, that's all you have for sure, the royalties are everything and they just keep working for you and your family. Long after you're gone, your children and your children's children will benefit.

'Royalties will be my retirement,' he laughed.

As we were leaving he slipped me some copies of the new album. I immediately began playing it in the car. I found myself playing the track 'Just A Man' over and over, several times. So much of it was close to the bone. I called him to thank him for that song. It was brave of him to bare his story and I told him so. By the end of the conversation he was thanking *me*. And weeping. I assumed it was a release to cry. It was hard to say how our parents would take it.

I knew that he was unhappy about living in London, but I had no idea that his substance abuse was escalating or that Paula was keeping him on edge with her mind games. Five days later he was in Europe, back on the merry-go-round.

Mother answered her phone on the evening of 26 June and the minute she heard his voice she knew something was very wrong. Michael was calling from his hotel room in Vienna, Switzerland. He was scheduled to perform at the Libro Music Hall in a few hours. She said for the first time she could 'feel' his depression.

Very hesitantly, he said, 'I . . . don't think I can go on.'

'Michael, darling, you mean you can't go on tonight?' Mother asked. 'What is it, are you ill?'

'I can't take it anymore . . . I don't want to finish this tour. I'm so unhappy.'

'Oh Michael, what can we do?'

'Nobody . . . nobody can do anything. I just can't take the fighting, the lawyers. Every day is some new crisis and I'm away from Tiger and I'm worried about her. She's the only thing that keeps me going but I can't take it anymore.'

'What would happen if you dropped out of the tour?'

'I can't.'

'So try to hold on, finish the tour and think about your baby,' she told him.

'She's my first priority,' he assured her. 'I love Tiger so much it hurts.'

As a mother she wanted to comfort her son immediately, needed to hug him. She said she got the sense that he felt trapped and could not see a solution. He asked if she and Ross would meet him in Los Angeles—he would be there in eleven days. She assured him that she would book the flights immediately. She called me and asked if I could cheer him up.

When we caught up with Michael in LA, he looked happy. We were instantly relieved. His anonymity in Los Angeles felt like freedom, I guess, and he was temporarily released from the Paula versus Bob pressures as well. It was clear his spirits had lifted.

The first night he took Mother and Ross to a private screening of *Face/Off*, the John Travolta and Nicholas Cage movie that featured 'Don't Lose Your Head', a track from *Elegantly Wasted*. Michael's companion for the evening was an attractive girl he introduced as Erin Seem, a journalist for *Rolling Stone* magazine. After the movie they returned to the Mondrian Hotel's popular Sky Bar, owned by Cindy Crawford's husband, Rande Gerber.

While Michael left to track down some food, Mother chatted with Erin, whose cover she was not convinced of.

'Why don't you take notes?' she couldn't resist asking.

'I have a retentive memory,' smiled Erin. Mother rather liked this young woman. We would see a lot of Ms Seem. She accompanied Michael to the San Diego show and the Santa Barbara show and regularly appeared walking out of the elevator with him. Mother rather hoped Erin was more officially 'with' Michael. She was so obviously making him happy.

The eleventh of July was a long day for INXS. They started off with an early afternoon, fan-attended sound check at the Greek Theatre along with a live interview that was broadcast over 'the world famous' KROQ with the immensely popular DJ Richard Blade. Only recently did Blade explain—in his book *World in My Eyes*—that it was Michael who came up with that slogan, when he said it in his first interview on Blade's show. The station liked it so much that they looped it up and kept it. We attended the concert at the Greek, a beautiful, outdoor, city-owned venue in Griffith Park, LA. A lot of long-time fans were there and Michael and the band were fantastic.

From the first note everybody was on their feet. The fan directly in front of me was wearing a very colourful 'rasta cap'. It was by no means the size of Lenny Kravitz's one, which we came across at close range that Christmas six years earlier, but it was nonetheless distracting as it bobbed about. I did not realise Johnny Depp was in disguise under there until he appeared backstage after the show.

Martha Troup kept Michael busy with film-related meetings whenever possible. One morning as she sat in the lobby patiently waiting for her charge she was approached by several industry executives offering their business cards.

'Wow, this is great!' Martha grinned at me. 'I don't even have to walk out of the hotel.'

During this visit Mother and Ross enjoyed catching up with INXS, and spent a lot of time with Michael and his friends, old and new. He seemed happy, proud and loving when introducing them.

I remember thinking how lucky Michael was, with so many people to look after him. Martha would take good care of his career, I mused. He never had to worry about paying the day-to-day bills—his accountant Andrew Paul did that. He owned his properties outright, with not one single mortgage payment to make.

When Tiger Lily arrived with her mother she was a bit under the weather, and although she rallied for a combined birthday party (her first and my Erin's nineteenth) she became worse in the days following, with vomiting and a fever. Michael called our mother about it and she suggested at the very least to send out for Pedialyte, a product that prevents dehydration in children. Paula was yelling in the background that she was the mother and therefore knew what was best. Tiger did get better but I do know she was never seen by a paediatrician on that trip.

Even after Paula arrived, Michael continued to see his new friend Erin Seem. With a buoyant social life of her own, she was determined not to chase him, but Michael often paged her to meet him privately at Johnny Depp's house. I don't think he could have been clearer about his feelings; he loved his baby girl but was never going to marry her mother. He was not going to 'settle down' or be monogamous.

Michael had signed with an agency to represent him in his acting goals and on the day Mother and Ross were leaving, before taking off with Martha for producers' meetings, he went to their room, for breakfast and a talk.

'Ignore the things you read about Paula and me,' he told them. 'We have never discussed marriage, so until you hear it from my lips, don't you believe it!' Michael's refusal to commit to exclusive love seemed by now intrinsic. He suggested they remind Paula about the lunch date they'd made, though, so as not to miss out on seeing their granddaughter Tiger before they went.

Mother and Ross made numerous unreturned calls to Paula's room throughout the day. Then an hour before they had to leave for the airport, disaster struck.

Paula arrived at their door with Tiger, extremely agitated. Mother and Ross had no idea why she had become absolutely furious at *them*, but she certainly was. She then made it clear that she not only would *not* be having lunch with Ross and Mother *that* day, but *never again*: in fact, she had no intention of ever *talking* to them again.

'Michael should have told you this,' Paula snapped, depositing Tiger on their sofa, and left. Mother and Ross looked at each other in shock. What was once a warm relationship had been shattered, and they had no understanding at all as to why. It wasn't hard to imagine Paula might be furious at Michael, but they couldn't comprehend her verbal attack on them. With minutes to spare before the car to take Mother and Ross to the airport was due to arrive, Michael returned to this emotional maelstrom.

And there it was. A very sad, bewildering, scarring ending to a special holiday that had started out with such promise. How were we to know that although we would be *speaking* with him over the next fifteen weeks, this awful day would be the last time Mother and I would ever *see* Michael alive?

The last, bone-crushing hug.

The last infectious smile.

The last wink.

The last wave . . .

The last picture I have in my head of Michael alive.

19

disconnections

WHEN PEACHES AND PIXIE flew in from London in early August 1997, meeting up with Paula, Tiger and Michael, he had ten days, mid-tour, to be a full-on Hollywood dad. Along with thousands of other summer holiday-makers they drove south to Disneyland, 'the happiest place on earth', and on to San Diego Zoo. On the way back to LA they checked into a beach resort to give the children time to play in the warm Pacific to wriggle their toes in the sand. Then it was time for the girls and their mother to head back to England, while Michael went back to work.

INXS resumed their Elegantly Wasted tour at the University of Illinois' traditional Q101's Block Party in Chicago, 22 August 1997, with Violent Femmes, Matchbox 20 and Meredith Brooks. *The Chicago Tribune* responded with an underwhelming review headlined 'Uncertain Futures, Faded Glory'.

'The band's initiative and the showy vigorousness of Michael Hutchence was impressive,' wrote Allison Stewart, 'given the fact that *even rock's better acts* [my italics] tend to put little effort into radio station festivals beyond simply showing up.'

Had Michael read this he might have been unnerved. By now INXS's press was quite sporadic in terms of critical praise. The English had often been savage, while the media in Europe, South America, Canada, South Africa and Asia—all strong markets for INXS that they had toured through, sometimes repeatedly—varied.

Meanwhile, back in Australia they had suffered from the tall poppy, 'off-with-their-heads' syndrome for some time. There was the feeling among some that INXS couldn't wait to abandon their homeland, the first chance they got. There had been discord at management level on *Australian Made*, over the summer dates spanning 1986–87, which reportedly led to a huge blow-up backstage between Chris Murphy and the manager of Mental As Anything, Martin Fabinyi. The wash-up from this was the Mentals did not appear in the resultant movie, which was a pity.

There had been further flak flying over Chris and INXS's handling of The Concert For Life, a fundraising show held in Sydney's Centennial Park in March 1992 for the Victor Chang Cardiac Research Centre and AIDS treatment at St Vincent's Hospital. Also on the bill were Crowded House, Yothu Yindi, Wendy Matthews with Jenny Morris and Kate Ceberano, Jimmy Barnes and Diesel, James Reyne, James Blundell, Ratcat, Def FX and Troy Newman.

The Concert For Life had drawn more than 60,000 paying customers to Centennial Park and grossed nearly $2 million, with just over $600,000 of that going to the charities as profit. Many of the other acts and their managers resented that INXS had hired a 75-piece orchestra to re-create the album versions of both 'Baby Don't Cry' (from their latest album *Welcome To Wherever You Are*) and 'Never Tear Us Apart' (from *Kick*). This cost, together with bigger perks for INXS on the day, in terms of dressing-rooms, limos and so on, caused much heated response. It was alleged that management then forbade INXS from commenting. The band's silence in the face of criticism simply exacerbated the problem. INXS were suspected of spoiled elitism. Failing to deal with reasonable questions over a charity event in an open, down-to-earth way affected their media coverage in their home country, not only at the time but into the future. The massive sum donated should have overshone everything, but given that around twice as much disappeared in costs, despite acts donating their time, it's probably true to say that INXS's reputation at home, in the music business at least, never fully recovered from the controversy.

Anyway, back in North America, the 'caravan' moved on, from one city to another; Michael was swept up in his usual roundabout of interviews and sweat-drenched gigs under a barrage of lights promoting the album.

By now, we—Michael's family—had little knowledge of what was really going on with him. I had my own concerns. By August 1997 it was clear that Ken and I were not suited. Maybe it was bad timing; he had retired quite young and I was still in the midst of my second career running a make-up school and travelling for lectures. We were living separate lives in the same house. He was bored; I was busy. Later in the year he would move out.

And as for Michael, our family just assumed that since he was on tour, surrounded by the band, management and crew, he would be far too consumed with promoting the album to be depressed about life back in London. Paula did not always pass on messages from us and appeared to be vetting which message from which friend might reach Michael too. He was getting more cut off.

In truth he was deeply conflicted, his mind in constant chaos overload with what seemed to be a new crisis unfolding daily at the London home. His heart and sense of loyalty was with 'his girls' back in England, but he just couldn't cope with being alone. Now he also cared, in his typical non-exclusive way, for his new companion, Erin Seem, the tall, attractive young woman accompanying him on the road.

The work ethic of INXS was the toast of many business managers. They had rarely missed a show up to this point. But their scheduled 27 August gig at the Modjeska Theater, Milwaukee, got cancelled. An apologetic press release explained that Michael had sprained his ankle.

The truth was much worse.

Tiger Lily was barely thirteen months old and in Paula's care as INXS toured the USA. One night her mother downed so much alcohol on top of drugs of some kind—pills—that she passed out cold. Luckily, the Geldof sisters were there at the time. Pixie had just turned seven and Peaches was eight. The poor girls thought their mother was dead when they found her unresponsive body on the bathroom floor. Tiger was crawling beside her, crying with distress. Pixie and Peaches ran out into the street and alerted some passers-by who called an ambulance. Despite their primary-school status, they showed bravery.

The paramedics arrived and by the time Michael was informed, Paula had recovered, but he desperately needed to see for himself that Tiger was all right. He took the first flight back to London and did what he could, rejoining the tour in Kansas City soon afterwards.

It is hard to imagine what it took for him to tear himself away from Tiger's side to board that transatlantic flight.

Touring would never, ever again be the same carefree thing it once had been to him.

• • •

In St Louis on the afternoon of 30 August, the tour was shocked by breaking news. Diana, Princess of Wales, had died in a high-speed car crash in the minutes after midnight on 31 August, across the globe in

Paris. The car in which she was a passenger had been fleeing a swarm of paparazzi on motorbikes through a tunnel near the Seine when the driver was blinded by photographers' flashbulbs.

Diana's loss was an overwhelming blow felt around the world. Michael, having played a royal command performance for her, and having met, admired and liked her, felt the sudden death of this shy young woman so close to his own age more keenly than most.

Unbelievably, seatbelts were not being worn—although this was possibly, in part at least, because Diana was twisting right around in the back seat while simultaneously crouching with her head down in a struggle to avoid being photographed.

Absolutely key to the collision was the high-speed chase given by paparazzi hunting in a pack. At that time, this predatory behaviour was evolving and spreading internationally.

Michael loudly condemned the tactics of the media culture so clearly at fault. Of course, he knew what it was like, intimately, to become the prey.

Already traumatised by the deep dysfunction in the heart of his London home, Michael stepped onstage with a heavy heart that night and gave one of the worse performances of his life.

In fact, Michael's appearances on the Elegantly Wasted tour, one which would turn out to be INXS's last with him, were erratic. Some lacked the spirit and wholehearted investment that fans had been guaranteed until then. He was in no shape to be on the road. Even before the run of dates began, it's hard to understand how the band members who had played with him for twenty years could miss this.

When he was assaulted by that taxi driver, shoved backwards, fracturing his skull, Michael lost more than those two key senses of smell and taste. As devastating as that was, his resultant brain injury had also diminished both his positive outlook and his self-control—apparently for good.

With his anxiety and depression now rising, Michael had begun throwing back Prozac and Valium on top of alcohol, cigarettes and sometimes so-called 'recreational' drugs like marijuana, ecstasy and cocaine.

But habits like these are likely to have side effects. Even long after giving up ecstasy use, users have a higher likelihood of anxiety, depression, insomnia and memory loss. The highly addictive stimulant cocaine is certainly a common trap for any rock muso, since other people are likely to offer it regularly in an effort to ingratiate themselves. Side effects of regular use include depression, psychosis and paranoia. Even marijuana is renowned for increasing anxiety and paranoia.

Michael told us he was anxious about his finances. Meanwhile, the constant updates he was receiving from Paula on the Geldof–Yates custody battle and other vexing London problems were eating away at him. He was acutely afraid of losing Tiger. Being apart from his baby on yet another international tour was not only desperately hard, it could also hardly help him look like a caring parent. When she was around he just melted. She was still just a toddler. She needed him, he knew it. And how he needed her! He was racked with anxiety and did not want to choose between being there for his innocent Tiger and touring with INXS. His happiness was slipping away.

In the non-entertainment world, if someone is so ill that their work is being compromised, it's not unusual to suggest they take a break and come back when they're healthy. Other bands have postponed or cancelled tours over health crises. Tours are insured for such emergencies.

'Those were the saddest days of my life with the band,' Tim Farriss admitted later. 'I just didn't want to be there. I drank a lot more than I should have and didn't want to know about anything. What we needed to do was get off tour.'

Michael would have been relieved had they cancelled the tour. His expressed feelings to me were that he didn't want to let the band down.

Martha, who was travelling with the band, wrote a letter to Michael expressing concern for his health. It was found in his belongings when he died. She too had the power to shut the tour down. So why *wasn't* it stopped, at least pending rescheduling? Trapped in the tour's demands, Michael could hardly do much about his deteriorating mental health.

He had recently accepted an unpaid, cameo role in a small indie film, *Limp*, to be directed by Duane Lavold and shot in Canada. Jarringly, his character was a cynical artist and repertoire (A&R) record-company man called Clive, who applauds Kurt Cobain's suicide—after all, it boosted Nirvana's notoriety and sales.

Michael asked his companion Erin to help him rehearse his part.

'It was brilliant on his part,' said Michael/Clive, reading to her from the script. 'Otherwise he would have ended up just another flavour of the month, flavour of the day, whatever.'

In another scene Clive had to scream at a musician: 'Give me one good reason why you shouldn't kill yourself! Alive and healthy with nothing to live for, it's all been done before.'

Although Michael was keyed up over his role in this independent production, in hindsight it really wasn't very healthy material for him to be projecting himself into.

INXS played their last American show—the last live show they'd ever play with Michael—on 27 September in Pittsburgh, Pennsylvania, where they appeared with Savage Garden and 10,000 Maniacs.

They weren't due to start rehearsals for the Australian leg until mid-to-late November. Michael took a break in London before heading to LA to continue work on his solo album with Danny Saber.

As the tour would end in Australia, naturally he wanted to spend the holidays in the sun with his family. We were all going to convene at Main Beach, Queensland, at Mother and Ross's home. Michael was keen to bring his little Tiger to meet up with family and friends.

Paula wanted to arrive early with Tiger, Pixie and Peaches, to join Michael on tour. Martha had negotiated a contract for Paula to do a talk show on Australian radio to begin in January. Perfect for her—she was a natural. She would be able to tape several shows in one day, and still have time for her children. Michael had told Martha that Tiger's mother also needed the financial independence.

They met with Bob Geldof—a rarity—to talk things through. Bob later told me that he was in agreement and did not object to the girls missing school if they could have a tutor. I am not sure if he expressed this during the meeting.

Some days later, Michael told Martha that Bob had gone back on his word: he was *not* allowing his children to visit Australia before their Christmas holidays in December, which seemed ages away. Michael was very upset, lamenting that Paula would have to go back to court to persuade the judge to let her leave with her children. She refused to depart London without Peaches and Pixie.

Michael was frustrated that Geldof seemingly had the power to dictate his private life. On 6 November he flew to New York where he saw Martha Troup and her husband, Bill. Martha later told me that Michael was concerned about his finances and had needed to borrow money while in New York. This was very much unlike him, and hard to fathom.

When one journalist asked about his relationship with Geldof, Michael replied that Bob was not the saint he was portrayed to be, branding him a 'Satan' instead.

'If only you knew the truth. He has completely manipulated everyone, including the press.'

A friend of Bob's was quoted, countering, 'Bob is well known for not talking to the press. He couldn't possibly have manipulated them.' It is well known in media circles that Bob often has 'friends' speak for him as well. It is a very effective manoeuvre from a very media-savvy man.

The sad fact is that Bob actually feels that he did *not* go back on his word. He said that a day or two after his meeting with Michael and Paula, he actually contacted his children's school, and their court-appointed child psychologist, and was advised that it would be detrimental to the children's education to take them out of school early. Peaches and Pixie were only in grades one and three, so you wouldn't expect that to be so crucial.

What Bob told me was that he voiced his fatherly concerns in a meeting with Paula and Andrew Young. He had no objections to his children spending *Christmas* in Australia or missing classes in January. But he would not sanction their missing the last three weeks of schooling before the holidays.

Martha accompanied Michael to Los Angeles, checking into the Bel Age Hotel in West Hollywood, conveniently set behind the notorious, rock-royalty-frequented Viper Room which had been co-founded in 1993 by his friend Johnny Depp. Michael often joked in a self-deprecating way about how actors just wanted to be singers, while singers just wanted to act. He and Johnny exemplified this paradox. Martha stayed a couple of days to accompany him to meetings with movie connections.

Martha told me how she and her star client were driving to a meeting in LA when Michael told her he was calling Geldof, to try to convince him to let Paula and the children come to Australia early. Martha couldn't help but overhear their conversation.

'Bob, you said they could go. Why are you changing your mind now? I sat there with you. You said there was no problem, why are you lying?'

'Michael, sometimes I need to be a daddy and sometimes I need to be a father and taking these children out of school would not be the right thing to do. They need their education.'

'If you are such a daddy,' snapped back Michael, 'why am I supporting your children?'

'We'll have to deal with this in court,' Bob replied. End of phone call.

'Michael hated Geldof and Geldof hated Michael,' sighed Martha.

• • •

Initially Michael neglected to call most of his usual friends in Los Angeles when he arrived. He hung out with acquaintances instead, some of whom were known to be heavy substance abusers.

Nick Conroy, one of his oldest friends, visited Michael in his suite. It was full of people and Nick noted to Michael that they were not actually Michael's friends.

He sensed that Michael was in a place that was hard to reach.

Feeling uncomfortable, Nick decided to leave after a short time, telling Michael to call if he needed him. He even suggested that Michael could stay at his place for a while. Declining his offer Michael hugged Nick. He never called.

Michele Bennett had several calls from Michael while he was in LA. She said he sounded strange, a little out of it, scared, angry. On one call he began laughing for no reason and rambled. There was a knock at his door, and she heard several noisy people enter. He hung up without saying goodbye.

He also phoned his old friend Ollie Olsen, who was in Melbourne. Ollie would later share the concerns he had for Michael around this time, and the way he seemed to easily lose his friends in rooms crammed with strangers.

'There's one of the things in my relationship with Michael that I always found really weird,' said Ollie. 'He'd call and say come up to the Hyatt. And I'd sometimes say to him, "Why don't you come to *my* place and we'll get a pizza?" And he would never do that. He had this thing about you had to go there, but inevitably there'd be all these other people there.

'He didn't like to be alone,' Ollie continued. 'It's like, why don't you just see *me*, rather than all these other people? He's a conundrum to me, and he always has been. I've often thought about him and, you know, felt for him. I've got other friends who knew Michael in different ways, and who expressed fears for him at times, for his state of mind. Especially, you know, in the later stages of INXS.'

Michael only saw Erin Seem once at the Bel Age. She returned some clothes he had left at her apartment and told him to take care of himself. Once again his hotel room was full of people, so a private goodbye was not going to happen. She left in a hurry and he ran after her, following her to the car. He said that it would be all right; he would call her from Australia. She had a feeling they would not see each other again.

Michael badly needed the positive inspiration and relief he got from the creative process by now. So he called his friend and collaborator Danny Saber, to talk about the tracks they'd been working on together. Danny picked him up and they drove the short distance to 1032 N. Sycamore where they spent some time at the Record Plant recording studios. With Danny on guitar and Michael singing, they wrote and recorded 'Baby It's Alright'. (The track would end up on Michael's eponymous, posthumous solo album, featuring a slightly different, likely more polished version of the words claimed in *The Last Rockstar* to be Michael's 'last lyrics', supposedly found in his room at the Ritz-Carlton the day he died. Whether or not they were Michael's last, clearly the lyrics to 'Baby It's Alright' were not written in Sydney.)

He asked Danny to put a band together, for a small-scale tour when he returned to LA in early 1998. He had learned from his Max Q experience that when there were no live gigs to accompany an album and he couldn't promote it, the album too easily failed to sell very many copies. He was making post-recording plans this time.

Danny recognised that Michael was wrestling with some personal problems on the domestic front. Michael told him, as he had so many by now, that he didn't want to finish this INXS tour, yet felt obligated. Danny told Michael he didn't owe anybody anything.

Danny also invited him to the Viper Room for the forthcoming all-star jam. The Viper jams were a regular institution in West Hollywood, and Danny was piecing together a great line-up for this one. His friend Bernard Fowler, backup singer for the Rolling Stones since 1988, was coming and Danny really wanted Michael to come too. He demurred, pointing out he was about to depart for Sydney. Danny persisted and in the end won out, although Michael insisted he would *not* be coaxed into singing.

'Fine, no pressure,' shrugged Danny.

But once the night arrived and Michael saw some of the most talented players in the business up on stage with Danny having a ball, he couldn't resist. He grabbed a mike and sang Bowie's 'Suffragette City' while the crowd shouted their approval.

The INXS email group reported the following information about the evening: 'An hour into Nicklebag's set, INXS' Michael Hutchence came up to sing David Bowie's "Suffragette City" with the group, which also included [guitarist] Stevie Salas ... And for the grand finale, Hutchence, [Counting Crows' Adam] Duritz, [ZZ Top's Billy] Gibbons, [U2/Bowie/Garbage remixer Danny] Saber, and [Ivan] Neville all joined Nicklebag onstage for Rod Stewart's "Maggie May".'

It was 12 November: Michael's final live gig.

Early in the evening of Sunday, 16 November, Michael called me from his room at the Bel Age.

I was sitting in my spa bath, jets streaming hot water, wearing a new pair of Levis. Perfect time for a chat. Michael was intrigued with the 'shrink to body' method and we discussed this for a few minutes. I told him that this was not new; people had been doing it since the 1960s.

He reiterated it was his final tour with INXS. I was not shocked; he'd told me this a number of times in the past, especially at the end of a tour. But this time he said it with great resolve in his voice and I knew he meant it. This tour had been extremely hard on him and he felt that he had fulfilled his obligations to the band.

Once and for all he longed to get on with fresh projects, his own projects, without being made to feel that he was somehow hurting INXS. I was relieved. It seemed that he had known for a long time that he wanted to go out on his own or at least take an extended break, but when it came down to it, he felt responsible for the band. He had given INXS twenty years; like Danny, I didn't think he owed them anything and once again I told him so. I felt that they didn't seem to know him, didn't seem to care what he wanted; certainly they were no longer the close-knit 'band of brothers' that their fans assumed they were. It was a nice act onstage, but they had been leading separate lives for at least ten years.

We talked about Christmas. He was looking forward to having a calm, joyful Christmas holiday with the family minus any dramas. I assured him it would be. He sounded tired.

I didn't want to press him on the particulars of the Geldof girls' arrangements; I sensed he just wanted to talk about his little Tiger, and I indulged him.

His plan was to relocate Paula to Sydney for a while where Tiger would be closer to family, which would allow him to divide his time between Sydney and Los Angeles. He said it was not definite.

'Well, we're working on it,' he said.

He was adamant that he had no plans to return to London, which made me wonder about the Geldof girls, although I sensed he didn't want me to ask the obvious question. I assumed this was a decision for Paula and Bob to make anyway. Perhaps Michael was thinking about lowered expectations. I wanted to soothe and comfort him, rather than dwell on negative fears or imaginings, even if they were predictable.

For all Michael confided in me, sometimes I felt out of my depth. So I listened; I listened and I was there for him. Still, as I tried to help him make sense of the slippery edges of his shifting world, sometimes clear answers seemed to sink away into the darkness, out of reach.

We would never speak again.

20

paradise lost

ON THE EVENING OF SUNDAY, 16 NOVEMBER, Michael boarded a plane at LAX and looped around the globe from the northern hemisphere to the south, crossing the International Date Line. He touched down in Sydney on Tuesday, 18 November. As a footloose Australian, this anomaly was completely familiar to him. He had experienced the losing and gaining of days through jet travel all his life. From Sydney airport he was driven to the expensive eastern harbour-side suburb of Double Bay and checked into Room 524 at the Ritz-Carlton. For his pseudonym, he chose the name of the vast river system crossing south-eastern Australia, Murray River.

Between phone calls to and from various family and friends, he attempted to get over his jetlag before starting rehearsals on Thursday. One of the phone calls he received on Wednesday was from Bruce Butler, who was by then managing Ollie Olsen. There was a discussion about the two Max Q main men getting back together for a rave shortly.

'Michael really was looking for something new and challenging,' Bruce said. 'He didn't want to do the big stadium rock stuff. He'd got to a point in his career where he'd *done* that. You know, he wasn't doing it for money. Max Q—it didn't matter if it made money. He needed to do that *artistically*. And for the fun—I suppose to recapture what he got from those early INXS albums.'

There was something else Michael and Bruce had in common now. They were both fathers of their first child; both toddlers. Bruce's son, Beck, was just a few weeks older than Tiger.

'My last conversation with him was really joyous,' Bruce recalled. 'It was two old mates talking. He was in a very good mood, one of the best I'd heard him in for a couple of years. He was, like me, a proud new father. We discussed our kids and getting together when INXS were in Melbourne so they could meet. Tiger Lily was coming out from England with Paula, you know, for the tour. They were going to all be in Melbourne, and our kids were going to meet for the first time. This was exciting, and he was happy.'

Michael spoke to Ollie on the phone too. 'The last time I spoke to him,' Ollie said, 'he actually talked about doing another Max Q record. He said he really wanted to get together with me, and hang out and have a talk and all that kinda stuff. He said, "Are you up for it?" I said, "Sure."'

When Michael called our mother they spoke of Christmas plans. She suggested it would be a good opportunity to have Tiger christened as we would all be around. He hesitated at first, then changed his mind. She thought he sounded frail, that maybe he could see the mess his life had become. She called Kell and warned him not to push for any definite plans.

On Thursday evening Rhett arrived at the Ritz-Carlton, calling Michael's room from the lounge where he and Mandy and some friends had gathered. After a six-hour rehearsal Michael had succumbed to exhaustion and jetlag and begged off. Regrettably the brothers had a minor argument and Rhett departed for the Gold Coast on Friday morning, after having not seen Michael in almost a year.

Before leaving for rehearsal on Friday, Michael called Michele Bennett and made plans for breakfast the following morning. He said he didn't even know why he was doing the tour. He expressed concern about Paula's custody problems and spoke of his desire to get back to a simpler way of life. He was tired of dealing with all the problems. In Michele's words, 'he was looking for the silver lining'.

He also returned a call left by actress Kym Wilson, a friend he'd missed connecting with the night before. He suggested that they meet in the Ritz-Carlton lounge after his dinner with Kell and Susie.

Rehearsal with the band that afternoon was filmed for publicity purposes; some of it is on YouTube. Michael seems absorbed, a little blue. Sections were used on the television news bulletins that evening to promote the tour. Michael always felt relaxed in front of a camera, but on this day even his endearing playfulness looked a bit contrived. INXS reported later Michael was in great form. I assume they meant his singing, rather than his demeanour, because it was obvious to me that something was weighing on his mind. He had told me over and over that he was tired of singing these songs. And although he is making the best of it, his unstable moods are on show.

The longer version of this final INXS rehearsal runs for over 27 minutes, interrupted between songs as INXS take two newly recruited female backing vocalists, still learning their parts, through some fine-tuning. The reception from the band to Michael's various arrangement inputs ranges from blank to permafrost-cold. He sits facing INXS in his black, short-sleeved body shirt and pants, showing that he's once again in lithe and languid shape. He's smoking a ciga-rette and sipping beer from a glass mug when suddenly he remembers something from that last jam in LA with Danny.

'Oh, guess who I jammed with—*Billy Gibbons!*' Michael enthuses. Gibbons, of course, is the legendary lead singer and guitarist of the mighty ZZ Top. Sharing a stage with him was a real coup. But the news seems to garner no response whatsoever from the band.

Michael ploughs on. 'At the Viper Room, so cool, and I turned around and said, "Billy, you're Billy, right?" He says, "Yeah man, I'm Billy." He played like a mother . . . I couldn't *believe* it!'

More silent treatment from the band. Michael goes on to tell them how Gibbons was just walking past the Viper Room with his guitar when the doorman recognised him and invited him in. INXS seem pointedly bored. Then Jon plays the drum intro to 'The Loved One' and they tip right into it.

Michael looks so sad. He puts his shades on and waits for the next intro. Maybe it is my imagination, but it sounds as though there are tears in his throat. I just want to throw my arms around him.

• • •

That evening Michael was picked up by Kell and Susie, who drove him to one of his favourite restaurants, the Flavour of India, in New South Head Road, Edgecliff.

The restaurant's chef, Hayat Mahamud, told the *Daily Mail* in November 2017 (in a piece remembering twenty years since Michael's passing) that INXS's singer was likely to swing by every couple of months.

They were on a first-name basis and shook hands as the three guests sat to dine at Michael's favourite table seven, under the chandelier. He sat with his back to a bay window, with Kell on his right and Susie opposite.

'Which one should you cook for me—which one is best tonight?' Michael asked Hayat.

'Everything is best,' Hayat smiled.

'Butter chicken is heaven. I love your butter chicken,' Michael told him. He ordered this, the restaurant's speciality, along with mushroom saag aloo and chicken tikka fillets as mains. They ordered drinks and had crab in shredded ginger, chilli and onions, served inside potato skins as an entrée.

Kell remembered Michael as pensive. Quieter than usual at first, but brightening up enough to fall into some of his usual mimicry. Nonetheless, his elder son confessed he felt burdened, elaborating on Paula's custody battle, her expenditures and the overall gloom of life in London. He told Kell that Geldof had agreed to allow his children to depart early for Christmas in Australia and then changed his mind. Sensing that Michael was very anxious, Kell tried to pursue this line of conversation. Michael, as usual, changed the subject, ordering another of his favourite dishes, traditional Indian ice-cream with mango coulis for dessert.

The chef dropped by the table to make sure everything was satisfactory. Michael asked Hayat how his business was going, and his boys.

'They love your songs.'

When Kell dropped Michael back at his hotel around 10.30 p.m., he changed and went downstairs to the bar to wait for Kym Wilson and her boyfriend. Two women walked in and he struck up a conversation, inviting them to join him while he waited for his friends. Victoria Morish later told me she remembers him being 'charming and flirtatious'. She did not detect any sign of him being in a 'dark' mood, and they returned to a function they were attending soon after.

Kym and her boyfriend, solicitor Andrew Rayment, arrived around 11.30 p.m. to find Michael alone at the bar. Kym made the introductions and after ordering drinks Michael suggested they adjourn to his room, as he was waiting on a phone call from London. As they were leaving, he made a joke about escaping without paying the bill. He was quite theatrical about it and appeared in good spirits—especially when the barman came after him and asked him to sign the tab before he could make a getaway. With drink in hand, Murray River laughed and signed away.

• • •

Upstairs, Room 524 soon filled with lively conversation. Michael was glad of Kym and Andrew's company, urging them to raid his mini bar. Over the course of the night, drinks including vodka, beer, champagne and strawberry daiquiris would be consumed.

The couple settled themselves on the period furniture arranged on the room's lush green carpet, exchanging news with Michael as he relaxed on the bed. The Regency-style cream print wallpaper behind him framed the dark tangle of hair he pushed back with an open hand.

There was a film script left open on a chair and Kym soon spotted it. They talked for a while about Michael's role in *Limp* and his hopeful ambitions for new parts.

Now they were in private, Michael could also explain more about the phone call he was waiting on. Paula was seeking the court's permission for Pixie and Peaches to come to Australia with her the following day, he said, and would be calling him with the results. He admitted he was nervous, but hopeful. He was particularly pining for Tiger. He talked about how much he had missed the fast-growing toddler as INXS's Elegantly Wasted world tour had rolled on. He wanted Kym and Andrew to stay and lend their support, particularly if the court outcome was negative.

There was an element to this conflict that Michael may not have divulged that night. In fact, he may not have even been fully cognisant of it himself.

Gerry Agar, who was close to the situation, would later write about the Geldof–Yates stand off in her book. Gerry described Paula's situation, in terms of Pixie and Peaches, as 'already on shaky ground, one procedure away from losing them completely' after the fizzled 'drug bust' of the previous year. Now Paula was fighting hard to take them to Sydney in November, when Michael both expected and desperately wanted to see Tiger.

Bob, for his part, had imagined a family holiday with the Hutchences, but it was starting to look more like a seven- and an eight-year-old replacing 1997's last weeks of school with what could well be the excesses of INXS on the road. Beyond that loomed the not-too-hard-to-imagine possibility that Paula might *keep* Pixie and Peaches, in Australia, indefinitely. According to Gerry:

> Something in her insistence stirred Bob's dormant fears that Paula
> planned to take the girls and not come back for a long while . . .
> But Paula was defiant and seemed to be saying that there was
> nothing Bob could do; the plans were set, the tickets bought, she
> would go regardless. Bob had to act fast. I remember his panic as
> he rushed to implement legal proceedings against her.

Back in Room 524 the night ticked on with no call from Paula. Around 1.30 a.m. Martha phoned from New York. She told Michael that Quentin Tarantino did not want him for the small part he had tried out for, alas, but he had a *better* role for Michael in mind. It was a long phone call and Michael was excited by it, sharing the gist of it with his friends.

'Martha, what time do you think it is in London?' he asked at last.

'About 1.30 p.m.'

'Do you think she's back yet?'

'I don't think so.' Martha noticed his concern, his mood change.

'When are you coming?'

'I'm leaving tomorrow. I'll see you on Sunday night.'

Martha knew her flight was actually booked for the *following* day, but by saying she would be with him sooner, she hoped to make Michael feel more secure. By the time they hung up, it was Friday 8.30 a.m. in New York, as Martha left for work.

Michael turned back to Kym and Andrew to confide about how stressful the whole Geldof–Yates custody battle was. He really loved Paula's children, he told them, and Bob was being so unfair. Knowing that not only was Andrew a solicitor, but his father a barrister, perhaps he was sounding him out. Michael claimed that if the law came down on Bob's side today in London, he was considering cancelling the whole tour.

As the night drew into the small hours, Kym saw how frustrated and anxious Michael became. He didn't seem drunk, though, she would later state. At one point he raised the idea of going out, but Kym shook her head; they were here to wait on Paula's call, after all.

'I know, but sometimes I just want to run away.'

The ordeal wore on. Michael's guests grew weary and as the dark early morning hours of that spring day extended, Kym began to fall asleep.

On the other side of the world in London, it was early Friday evening. Before his friends left, Michael decided to try Paula one more time, but her number was busy.

The phone log from his room shows that he also spoke to his friend Nick Cave, who was touring Australia and had just staged his first show in Melbourne.

Around 4.45 a.m. Michael took pity on the exhausted couple and insisted they go home to bed. They'd helped him get through most of the night. Before leaving, Kym and Andrew noted their mobile numbers in the address book lying on his bed. They'd be close by; he should call if he needed to. Michael lay on his bed, drained but too much on tenterhooks over the pending call from Paula to relax.

'I would love a Valium,' Michael said as they waved him goodnight. But they didn't have any.

Around 5.00 a.m. a guest in the room next to Michael's, Gail Coward, heard a loud male voice having a heated conversation—over the phone, she figured, since she could only hear a single voice. It was Michael, possibly responding to the news from Paula when she finally called. Sydney's 5.00 a.m. daylight saving time was eleven hours ahead of London time.

The hearing had been postponed until 17 December. Paula wrote in her statement that she vented her anger to Michael. Perhaps Paula's own storm of emotions stirred Michael up to defensively yell, thump and swear. When she told him she wouldn't leave England without Pixie and Peaches, he became distraught. In her words 'desperate', as if he couldn't stand a minute more without his baby:

'I don't know how I will live without seeing Tiger. What will happen?'

Why didn't Paula alleviate Michael's anguish then by telling him she'd make that scheduled flight with Tiger? The Geldof girls could have followed in three weeks. How could you hear this pain from someone you love, and not decide right there and then that you and your little girl will be on that flight and in his arms in a heartbeat? After witnessing what the last two years had done to Michael's psyche, knowing the state he was in, it would have been the kindest, most loving thing Paula could have done.

He would call Bob, he told her, and beg him to let the children come.

When Michael phoned Bob, to try to convince him to change his mind, Bob was waiting in his car for his eldest daughter Fifi's school bus. This call lasted just over a minute.

Bob stated Michael's voice was low and a little sleepy and that his manner was sarcastic. There were no witnesses to this call. Unsurprisingly, given this is from his own point of view, Bob comes off as extremely rational; Michael the opposite.

'Bob.'

'Who's that?'

'It's Michael, man. Are you happy?'

'I'm okay. Listen, can you call back in ten minutes, I'm on the other line.'

'Ah man, can you call me?'

'I can't, I don't have your number.'

'Hold on, I'll give it to you.'

'I'm in the car and I don't have a pen.'

(Sigh of exasperation) 'Okay, I'll call back.'

This is exactly as it is written in Bob's statement—even the 'sigh of exasperation'. After a brief call to Paula at 5.31 a.m., Michael called Bob back at 5.38 a.m. Michael begged him to let the children come to Australia, Bob stated later. His voice escalated to a hectoring, abusive and threatening tone, according to Bob.

Bob claimed he had once reported Michael for harassment. In Michael's defence, Paula had fuelled the hostility between the two men, according to Gerry Agar, by claiming Bob was causing trouble when he was not. Bob might have suspected as much. He told me himself that Paula had once fabricated a story about his sister Cleo that caused Bob to cut ties with her, his own sibling, for several years. He later realised what a tragic folly it had been to believe everything that Paula Yates said. It had done so much damage.

247

Bob insists he simply told Michael that he would not allow his children to miss their last three weeks of school, to which, according to Geldof, Michael countered, 'I'm their father, little man, when are you going to realise that?'

If he actually did say that to Bob, as the latter alleges, it was an ugly way to speak to a man whose wife had left him and was now with Michael. I am reminded that the approach of Christmas is a sensitive time for many, especially unhappily divorced families.

But Michael was losing perspective. On top of his acquired brain injury, he had suffered so many exhausting trials, changes, media attacks and financial and relationship concerns. He was under siege from anxiety, that invisible enemy at the gates. His mental health was failing and he was self-medicating, taking too much Prozac, adding the paranoia-inducing cocaine and the reckless edge of drinking to the mix. He was indeed 'desperate'. He was fighting to be with his family the only way he could muster, with sarcasm—the last refuge of the powerless.

Michael had been up all night stressing about custody issues and was convinced at that moment that Bob had more control of his little daughter's future than he did himself. He seemed not to *hear*, Bob claimed, when he tried to explain it was out of his hands. Between expletives, Michael accused Bob of trying to take Tiger away from him, insisting he had *proof* he was seeking custody of her. With what seems like extraordinary patience, Bob offered to sit down with Michael and Andrew Young to go over it and reassure them that he had no interest in taking Tiger.

Their call ended at 5.54 a.m. when Michael slammed the phone down. I shudder when I consider how misjudged his tactics were.

The self-fulfilling prophecy of Bob eventually being awarded guardianship of Tiger, after the self-inflicted deaths of both of her parents, looms over this tragic line of thought.

And much as his fear of losing custody of his daughter was spurred by the manipulations of others, perhaps there was also a real premonition of the future there for Michael.

In her statement, Belinda Brewin, who was with Paula during the phone call to Michael, said that when she (Belinda) took Pixie and Peaches back to Bob's house, before she and Paula left for Michael's funeral in Sydney, Bob asked her, 'Did you know I spoke to Michael?' And she replied, 'Yes, I did.' Belinda then said that Bob asked her if she knew whether he was the last person Michael called. She answered that she didn't know, but she thought so.

'Bob kept asking if they found drugs in the room and I told him I didn't know. Over the time I have known Michael, I saw Bob systematically ruin Michael and Paula's lives,' Belinda wrote. 'Anything they tried to do, Bob would interfere. If they wanted to take the children anywhere Bob would take out an injunction. He was constantly interfering in their lives and the dispute became very public.'

Minutes after calling Geldof, Michael dialled Michele Bennett. He was due to meet her for breakfast in a few hours. She was asleep so he left a brief message on her answering machine. It seems he then undressed and tried to sleep. When Michele rose, she played back a message from what she describes as an inebriated Michael.

'Michele, I need to speak to you.'

Martha spoke to INXS's tour manager John Martin around 7.00 a.m., Sydney time. She let him know that Paula and Tiger would not be joining Michael on tour, and told him to let Michael sleep as he had obviously not gotten much rest. John had breakfast and worked in his room at the Ritz-Carlton.

Michael rang Michele back at 9.30 a.m., sounding wasted, as he did when he had been up all night. He was over-tired and upset, she said, but speaking normally, not angrily.

'You sound drunk.'

'I'm not drunk, just sleepy,' he said. 'I have to see you.'

Nothing alerted her that this call was any different from the dozens of others she'd shared with him over their eighteen-year friendship. As they spoke he became distressed. He'd been to sleep for a little while, he said, but was still tired and didn't know how he was going to get through the band rehearsal scheduled for noon.

He began to weep, saying he couldn't sleep and just needed her. Michele promised she would be there and advised him to skip rehearsal, call someone in the band and explain. He agreed. Then she told him to expect her in around half an hour. He should lie down and try to rest until she arrived.

Michele showered, dressed and flew out of the house, grabbing the book by her bed. She had soothed Michael to sleep many times in the past by reading to him. She thought it wouldn't hurt to try again today. Whatever that book was, she has blocked it out of her mind.

Meanwhile, Michael rang down to the front desk and asked them to pass on a message from him to tour manager John Martin: 'Mr River is not going to rehearsals today.'

There were only two more outgoing calls from Michael's room. The first, at 9.38 a.m. Sydney time, was to Martha's New York office. She had left for the day.

'Marth, Michael here. I fucking had enough.' When Martha retrieved the message by calling her answering machine, as people did in those days, the agitation and anger in his voice shocked her. She returned his call immediately but the phone in his room just rang out. Perhaps that was because he was in the bath.

He left another message on her home answering machine, twelve minutes later, at 9.50 a.m. Sydney time. This time his voice was slow and deep and 'sounded like it was affected by something'.

'Martha, it's Michael . . .'

Perhaps he wanted to tell her to cancel the Australian tour. The one that crazily somehow got called Lose Your Head.

But felt he couldn't.

After retrieving this message remotely too, Martha immediately rang John Martin.

• •

When Michele arrived at the Ritz-Carlton she made her way up to Room 524, knocked loudly and listened. Nothing. She knocked again. Tried the door. She went to the house phone next to the lifts and called Michael's room. Four rings. No answer. Deciding he must have finally fallen into a deep, much-needed sleep, she didn't want to wake him.

Instead she went down to the lobby and composed a note telling him she was worried about him and would stay in the area in case he called. She asked a Ritz-Carlton receptionist to slip it under his door and went out to browse the local shops. Then she sat in a cafe with a newspaper and waited. She really hoped they could have breakfast together, soon, like they'd planned to. She was feeling very concerned and really wanted to see him.

Kell called John Martin around eleven that morning. Had he seen Michael? No, he hadn't. Then John found the message under his door that Michael had dictated to the desk clerk for him, about not going to rehearsal. John called Martha for instructions. She told him to let Michael sleep for an hour or two longer.

At 11.50 a.m. a young hotel maid was doing her rounds when she knocked on the door of Room 524. There was no answer, so she used her master key. Something heavy was obstructing the door. Using all her might, she forced it open and was shocked to find the dead weight of a man's naked body blocking the door.

Michael had slept naked since his teens. From the crumpled bedding it looked like he'd been tossing and turning, trying to sleep at least. He was in a kneeling position, facing the door. He had threaded his black leather belt over the pneumatic door-closing hinge behind and at the top of the door to his suite, and strained his head forward into the loop so hard that the buckle had broken with the weight of his body. Or the buckle might have, using Coroner Derek Hand's term, 'broke[n] away' as the maid forced entry, pushing the body and belt away from the hinge.

The room was chaotic. Two suitcases were open on the floor. Various medications including Michael's Becloforte inhaler for his asthma, Nurofen tablets for pain and two other containers filled with unidentified pills were scattered around. In the bathroom lay an open packet of Prozac capsules and some nicotine patches. The bath was full of water. The management was alerted, then the relevant authorities. Michael was pronounced dead.

21

Paradise Papers

IN AUSTRALIA ON 6 NOVEMBER 2017, the award-winning current affairs television program *Four Corners* aired an episode called 'Inside the Tax Havens of the Rich and Powerful'. Their insightful report showed how many high-earning individuals and companies habitually hid their profits by siphoning them through tax havens, often through a maze of trust companies. Thirteen million files from the records of offshore service providers, the majority from the law firm Appleby, were obtained by German newspaper *Suddeutsche Zeitung*, which investigated them in partnership with ICIJ, the International Consortium of Investigative Journalists, including *Four Corners*.

It must be said that Appleby, based in Bermuda, insist that their business is legitimate. But Appleby themselves were named in the Paradise Papers as having been found wanting in twelve compliance reviews over a decade.

Among the famous names revealed in the Paradise Papers were Queen Elizabeth II and Prince Charles, Paul Hewson (aka Bono), Lord Ashcroft (former treasurer and deputy chairman of the English Conservative party), Shakira, Formula One champion Lewis Hamilton, Donald Trump's Secretary of Commerce Wilbur Ross, Madonna, Justin Timberlake, Nicole Kidman, Keira Knightley, Spain's famous bullfighter El Cordobés, Apple, commodities giant Glencore, Nike— and Michael Hutchence.

Yes, Michael's name was hitting the headlines yet again, this time through the public broadcaster the ABC. 'Appleby insists what they do in the offshore world is legitimate,' the *Four Corners* narrator said in the program's introduction. 'But the Paradise Papers reveal . . . some very dubious deals, including one to exploit the legacy of the Australian rock star Michael Hutchence.'

Six weeks before the ABC's program aired, a *Four Corners* producer had asked me if I would do an interview for the show. They were planning to unleash material about Michael's affairs after his death. One of the entities mentioned was Chardonnay Investments. I was quite familiar with Chardonnay, of course, which housed Michael's royalties income. This was the family trust wherein Michael named all immediate family members as beneficiaries: Kell, Mother, Rhett and me along with 'all issue of the settlor' (Tiger). As far as I know none of us has ever received a penny from it.

But, by this time I had already given several on-camera interviews for Channel Seven's two-episode television documentary about Michael called *The Last Rockstar* (let's call it *TLR* for brevity), due to air just before the *Four Corners* episode.

The producers of *TLR* were concerned. The Channel Seven documentary intended to promote Michael's artistic legacy and new music. This was the appealing element its makers had sold me on, and now I was being told that if I spoke to *Four Corners*, all that would be under threat.

I had even lured the shy, very private Rosanna into giving an on-camera interview for *TLR*. Ro's relationship with Michael was so sacred to her that many of her friends had no clue about it. This was the first time she'd ever spoken about Michael publicly.

I felt so comfortable with the Channel Seven project that I let them use my personal, private family footage for their show. My little films, never aired before, showed Michael as son, brother, uncle and boy-friend, with all his natural, down-to-earth charm there for everyone to see. The scenes were shot at Vieille Ferme des Guerchs, on the Gold Coast, at the supermarket, driving through Grasse and St Tropez in France, cooking prawns on his 'barby' and clowning around just like most families do on holiday.

Yet I felt torn. So many aspects of my late brother's financial affairs still disturbed me.

Four Corners did not divulge what they had when briefing me about their desire to interview me. The term 'Paradise Papers' never came up in our conversations. I couldn't see the supposed conflict. I believed the Channel Seven production was about Michael and his music, while *Four Corners* was investigating the financial side. Of course, what even-tuated was much more 'shifting sands' than that.

I was aware that Diamond had been interviewed for the documentary. However, his involvement had been downplayed to me. Danny Saber also appeared in *TLR*. Neither he nor I was given an advance screening, as some of the media were, even though we were booked on television and radio to promote it. We were told that they were too busy editing to slice out some footage for us. So imagine my surprise when *The Last Rockstar* aired and Diamond was 'the star' of the show with his many minutes' unchallenged interview time, meaning that the producers had interviewed him first and should have appraised me of what he had said so that I might have had a chance to reply. Perhaps they chose not to as they would have then revealed how much time he was to have on camera.

When Michael died, Colin Diamond, who was then a co-executor of his will, not only collected everything (169 items) that had been in his hotel room but also various keepsakes, guitars, musical equipment, photographs, jewellery, videos, artworks, clothing, journals and diaries from Michael's various homes—some of Michael's most private possessions.

Four Corners reported, after *TLR* had aired, that many of Michael's friends and family 'were stunned to see Colin Diamond revealing the star's intimate possessions left in his room the night he died. Even his diary.'

22

the investigators

IT FELL TO INSPECTOR PETER DUCLOS to write a report, a dozen pages for the coroner. He was the lead detective investigating Michael's death. Twenty years later in 2017, still searching, I reached out to him, asking him to recollect in his own words the events of 22 November 1997. And the aftermath. He kindly wrote back.

Although the Ritz-Carlton in Double Bay had called the police late that morning, Duclos reported that there was a simultaneous home invasion involving guns in the same suburb. The immediate threat posed by the arms made that case a higher priority, so he was delayed.

'I attended Michael's room sometime after the initial paramedics and ambulance attended,' he wrote.

We were the first [police] responders; a car crew consisting of
a sergeant, two detectives and myself from Rose Bay local area
command. Double Bay did not have a police station.

MICHAEL

I arrived about 12.50 p.m. Michael was lying on the floor, covered with a bed spread. We established a 'crime scene' immediately. This means we limit who comes into the scene to ensure integrity. There were no signs of a struggle or anything to suggest a suspicious death, i.e. a murder. Even so, I assumed, as I always did, that the death was suspicious until I could, on the evidence, be convinced otherwise. Regardless of who the victim is, I always kept an open mind, and this was no different.

'There were no injuries to Michael that would suggest a struggle or self-defence wounds,' continued Duclos.

There was a small laceration above his left eye, sustained when he lost consciousness and his face hit the door, and burn marks consistent with a cigarette burn on his left hand. Contrary to what has been reported, no hand was broken and there was nothing to suggest a third party was involved at all. A log of all officers attending; our forensic police, the medical team and so forth was commenced and maintained until the following Monday when we released the room back to the hotel.

On leaving the Ritz-Carlton Duclos set out to find a next of kin.

No doubt someone had notified the media, as there was . . . a large contingent outside the Ritz when I left . . . That was not unusual. We never found out who it was. Normal police procedure is to notify the nearest next of kin, and then leave it to them to call all other relatives. However, it was impossible to keep Michael's death silent and within hours it was all over the press.

Just about everybody was in the local public telephone directory back then, including Kell.

'As I was met at the door,' Duclos remembered, 'Kell was just hanging up the telephone from a newspaper asking about Michael.'

I had told Duclos when I contacted him about the way our family had been devastated to not only hear that Michael was suddenly, unbelievably dead, but to find out almost every part of it—true or false—through news reports. Duclos showed real sympathy and sorrow to hear that.

'I'm sorry that happened that way,' he wrote kindly.

He is a good man, retired now. He mentions he worked on a suicide hotline for some years.

I can't help reflecting that Michael's death—any suicide, any sudden, violent death, really—can leave indelible marks, scars, the claw marks of the grim reaper on the sides of many. Not just the survivors who are family and friends, but also the first responders and investigators.

The day that Michael died, it was like a great psychic car accident that crippled and burned. Everything happened so fast. There was no time for the heart to apprehend it. I was returning a missed call to Rhett. His usual, confident rapid-speak was so changed, so strange I couldn't properly hear what he was saying. Have you ever been in such shock and disbelief that a firework goes off in your chest, robbing you of the ability to breathe? Something lodged in my throat—I couldn't speak. I looked around and the world seemed underwater. Clogged ears, slow motion. As I held the phone to my ear, the large CNN screen in my living room flashed a long shot of law enforcement walking around a balcony with the words 'Michael Hutchence, 37, found dead'.

I didn't find out till this book was being written how the media actually found out so quickly that day, and how the news spread like wildfire around the globe so Michael's far-flung family was blindsided. I think I've solved that bitter mystery now.

In 1989 Michael had befriended a sixteen-year-old schoolboy who asked for an autograph outside his then Sydney hotel, the Sebel Townhouse. He indulged Richard Simpkin's desire to take amateur, then gradually more professional-looking photos—selfies or straight portraits. He and INXS let Richard haunt Rhinoceros Studios throughout their recording sessions for *X*. Richard would happily wait for hours for the chance to hang out with Michael in particular. His photographic skills improved and in 2015 he published his book *Michael in Pictures*.

Richard reported the following:

On Saturday the 22nd of November 1997 I went to the Ritz-Carlton hotel in Double Bay to pick Michael up to take him to ABC studios for rehearsals. Michael had told me on the Thursday that he was going to leave between 10.30 a.m. and 11.00 a.m. I got down to the hotel at approximately 9.30 a.m., as I did not want to miss the opportunity of driving [him]. Just after 12.00 p.m. a few security guards walked outside the hotel and waited near the loading dock. A few moments passed and an ambulance arrived and drove into the loading dock. I remember thinking that this was very strange as 3–4 security guards from the hotel escorted the ambulance inside.

Soon after the ambulance arrived, a police vehicle turned up at the hotel. About 45 minutes had passed since the police arrived and I was beginning to become slightly nervous. There was no sign of Michael; instead there were police and ambulance officers. A few minutes passed and I saw a man running towards the hotel with a news camera on his shoulders. The man ran up to me and asked 'what is going on?' I told him that I didn't know and asked him 'why, what *is* going on?' He then told me that he was sitting up the road in his news vehicle and was listening to the police radio, when he heard that 'an Australian international rock star had been found dead in one of the hotel rooms'. He then asked me 'do you know who that could be?' From that moment I knew that it was Michael, however I told him that I didn't know ... The first thing I did was ring my girlfriend at work. When she answered the phone I said to her 'I think Michael is dead.'

As Richard said those words the department store his girlfriend was working in experienced a complete blackout.

Despite all her generosity, all her efforts and the depth of good in her heart, Michele would bear the brunt of the hurricane. But she didn't know it yet. She had been shut out by the cruellest handful of minutes, locked a few centimetres of heavy timber away.

She arrived home after her fruitless attempts to meet and comfort Michael that morning just before noon. Around 1.00 p.m. many things happened in quick succession. She got a phone call from her old friend Jenny Morris with the terrible news. No, Jenny, said Michele; it couldn't be Michael. She'd spoken to him less than three hours before. All the same, Jenny dispatched her husband, Paul, to Michele's apartment to help if need be.

Now Michele desperately tried to call Michael. There was no Murray River registered at the Ritz-Carlton, suddenly. She called the police. They wouldn't say anything. Rhett phoned from Mother's, told her what had happened, but she wouldn't believe it. She had spoken to Michael, she insisted, and, although he was exhausted and upset, she didn't think he was suicidal. Rhett told her to call Kell, who asked her to come to his apartment.

The police were there. They took Michele down to the Rose Bay police station and interrogated her and she realised then they thought she'd been with Michael all night. Was she a *suspect* now? *But he wasn't dead!* Only seeing Michael's body, she said, would convince her he was lost. The police complied.

• • •

On camera Paula said that she had proof that Michael's death was accidental. She was positive that he was involved in kinky sex that went wrong. Autoerotic asphyxiation. It was impossible that Michael would choose to abandon her or Tiger. When pressed as to their sexual practices, she described Michael as a risk-taker who would 'do anything'. Her claims went around the world.

But to Inspector Duclos she never once mentioned autoerotic asphyxiation as a possible cause of death. Her statement, taken four days after the tragedy, goes into Michael's despair at not seeing Tiger before Christmas and the battles with her ex-husband at length.

Kell was incensed that Paula continued to keep this story alive. He wrote to the New South Wales Coroner's office, asking if Paula had made an application to overturn the verdict, or if there was to be an inquest.

Their letter of reply included the following:

I am able to see by the tenor of your three recent letters that you are extremely distressed and apprehensive ... I stress that no application [from Paula Yates to overturn the findings of the state coroner] has been made. You, of course will know if and when that occurs. I would like to reassure you that the State Coronial system in New South Wales has stood the test of time. The investigation of the death of your son was most thorough and the State Coroner was in no doubt as to the manner of his death. Should Ms Yates make an application it will probably be considered either by Mr Hand or myself. Let me assure you that the person who handles the matter will proceed not only according to law but according to the evidence, not according to the profile of either your late son or Ms Yates. The Coroner will, I know act according to his oath of office.

The local Rose Bay detectives painstakingly investigated not only Room 524 but its balcony, the room above Michael's, the gymnasium and the roof. They couldn't find any evidence of forced entry.

'I've never wavered from my opinion regarding Michael's death,' Duclos wrote to me.

I guess all of this is extremely hard for you, especially dealing with all the innuendo surrounding such a sad event. For me, it was a part of what I was paid to do and my sole intention was to present as thorough and truthful investigation as I could. Not only as that was my job, but because the dead can never speak for themselves. I hope I have done justice for Michael in that respect.

• • •

Michael's toxicology report was dated 24 November 1997 and signed by Lyn Hunt from the State Coroner's Court of New South Wales. The report found cocaine, Prozac, Keflex, traces of Valium and codeine and a blood alcohol level of over 0.1 per cent—double the legal drink-driving limit in Australia. Quinine traces in Michael's urine indicated he drank gin and tonic that evening. Reported drinks from Kell's dinner included wine and several beers, before returning to the hotel to drink further. There was a small quantity of diazepam, or Valium, found circulating in his bloodstream—a widely used antidepressant, anti-anxiety sedative. Keflex, one of the strongest antibiotics available to treat bacterial infections anywhere in the body, can be bought over the counter in LA. It was probably taken to treat the deep burns between Michael's fingers.

A 'tiny amount' of codeine was present, suggesting he used codeine as a painkiller some days previously. The chances of adverse drug interactions rise with each extra drug taken, the mixing of Prozac and alcohol unpredictable.

Michael was prescribed Prozac in December 1995, probably took it unprescribed earlier, and had been off and on it since then, dosing himself according to how he felt, rather than his prescription. There is an increased risk of suicide in the early use of the drug. His last script for Prozac was written exactly three weeks before his death.

There was no suicide note, but this is not uncommon in suicides.

Anyone who thinks those hoping for fame 'bring it on themselves' should watch a televised interview with Michael included in the television program *Autopsy: The final hours of Michael Hutchence*. Although he retained his dignity, Michael appeared to be quietly seething with a kind of incredulous, impotent fury as he described 'seeing the photographers, in the distance push Pixie, six years old, over—to make her cry, to take a photograph'.

A headline, 'InXcusable', flashed on screen.

'And then,' Michael continued, 'print a front-page headline: "Life with Paula and Michael for Pixie".'

The Channel Seven Australia production *The Last Rockstar* claimed to have a copy of the last set of lyrics Michael ever wrote, found screwed up and thrown into the wastepaper basket of the Ritz-Carlton's Room 524.

But I know, as many fans of Michael would, and those who profess to be expert in his career most definitely *should*, that the drafted, partly crossed-out lyrics scrawled in Michael's hand on a sheet of paper, supposedly written on his last night on earth, were part of the lyrics to 'Baby It's Alright'. He had already recorded that song with its co-writer Danny Saber prior to coming to Sydney. 'Baby It's Alright' was released in December 1999 on Michael's posthumous, self-titled album. It would appear that the so-called 'last lyrics' were just an old draft that Michael had thrown out. The *Four Corners* program, like *The Last Rockstar*, failed to investigate this anomaly; both programs failed to identify they belonged to a song already recorded and released by the time they went to air.

Danny Saber and Michael had recorded 'Baby It's Alright' and some other last songs of Michael's in Los Angeles before Michael flew to Sydney for the last time. They were rough, but Danny had them; they wrote the songs together before he left.

Michael told Danny he would return after the Australian tour, as he was not going back to London, and asked him to put a band together to try out some stuff in some local clubs when he returned in the new year. He told me he'd be back in California on 5 January 1998.

But deep depression can cause someone like Michael to feel hopeless, and helpless, stranded from the rational thought processes that should have kept him going till Michele reached him that final morning. In my mind I have gone over and over this. I believe that Michael knew that even though Michele would comfort him in the immediate future, he would always be at the whim of others. He would never be in control.

Maybe, confused and deranged by fatigue, alcohol and other drugs, the mood swings, frustration, cognitive impairments and anxiety of even small things brought on by his traumatic brain injury, he simply lost his mind. We will never know exactly how many phone calls he received and what was said in them. But it is obvious that Michael was pushed beyond his limit. He was already a man on a ledge. Many people were aware of this and the police statements confirm it. He had been mixing both prescription and illegal drugs for at least two years and, legal or not, drugs and alcohol distort the mind. His perception of his life and future that morning was contorted beyond his capacity to handle it.

Michael had many people watching out for his needs. A personal manager, an accountant, several lawyers, an investment adviser, a tour manager, a bodyguard, a publicist, a record company, a management company for his acting career, not to mention roadies and assistants. More importantly he had many friends and family who loved him but were unable to get beyond the frenzy in his mind.

Mother and I agreed it was a split-second resolve, made in anger and despair. In his own words, uttered repeatedly in the last five months of his life, he just *couldn't take it anymore.*

There is a powerful moment in the film *The Dark Knight* when the Joker turns to Batman, who has just saved him from plunging to his death.

'Madness is like gravity,' he says. 'All it takes . . . is a little push.'

23

the welcome stranger

TWENTY-FIVE YEARS after that amazing Wembley Stadium performance of 1991, a stranger contacted me.

As I read his words, Tim Stewart opened up a whole new world for me. Two paragraphs told me he truly was who he said he was. The fact is, I was a busy young adult back then. I couldn't remember the names of Michael's friends; to me they were always coming in and out of the house in little packs. But Tim sent photographs and stories that made me know he was the real deal.

It felt as though Michael himself was presenting me with a gift.

Below is his story of a friendship between two ten-year-olds, Michael and Tim, in the late 1960s.

Tim had been searching the web for his childhood friend on and off for three decades. But he had been searching for Michael *Hutchenson*. So of course he kept drawing a blank.

It is such a gift to me and our family, and I hope it will be to you; to get to know another side to the man you might have come to think of as that wild frontman who epitomised excess.

Tim Stewart

I took a break from my work to proceed with what I already assumed would be another fruitless web search. As expected I found nothing, so found myself simply browsing the web for old images of Hong Kong. It was there in the small district of Kowloon Tong where two of my most memorable, life-altering years took place.

I was pleasantly reminiscing though a plethora of familiar old images when . . . WHAM!!! I couldn't speak, couldn't move and couldn't react, everything just shut down! Time stood still as I looked into eyes staring back at me that reached deep into my very soul. There was Michael, so very real I could have reached out and touched him. Shock turned to joyful thoughts of reuniting with my long-lost boyhood friend. I had found Michael.

I anxiously browsed further, hoping to find more information, unaware that the next mouse click would usher me into the darkest place I'd ever been. My dearest friend had passed away nineteen years ago! Not only had he passed, but I was nowhere to be found to intervene on his behalf when his life was tragically stripped from him.

It was August 18, 2016. Until that day, I had no clue that Michael had become a global phenomenon and nor did I care at that moment. All I knew was that my childhood friend was dead. For the remainder of the day I sat in a catatonic state, watching a YouTube video of his performance at Wembley Stadium while clutching a personal photograph of Michael and me arm-in-arm at his tenth birthday party. This was interrupted only by bouts of uncontrolled sobbing.

[Tim spent the next day and night scouring the web for more images and articles on Michael.]

After reading countless opposing stories, spun reports and a plethora of biased press and tabloid rubbish, it became extremely clear that none of the reporters, columnists or so-called journalists had even the slightest clue or any insight whatsoever as to whom they were writing about or attempting to describe. I knew Michael in ways they never could or would. That morning I ceased reading anything further about Michael and tried to simply accept the fact that my friend was dead.

The first reaction I always get from those who know me and have witnessed my grief for Michael's loss is utter confusion. Oddly enough they all begin with the same puzzling question I was forced to ask myself: Why does the loss of a two-year boyhood relationship that existed over four decades ago traumatise my heart and soul as it does? People pass all the time, friends and family die—some more tragically than others. This loss was altogether different . . . so very different.

Why did I experience such very real pain and emptiness for someone I've not seen or heard from in well over 40 years? It certainly wasn't an overzealous fan reaction per Michael's celebrity status, for I only knew him as my schoolmate, soccer mate, teammate and close friend. Maybe it's because as a young American boy in a foreign country, he was my only true childhood friend. Maybe it's because he was my only memorable connection to my unusual past. Maybe it's because he was front and centre of the few happy childhood memories I was able to recall. All of those were probably valid reasons, but my heart tells me it's more than that . . . something so much more.

What I do know, however, is that Michael was without doubt the foremost critical player during two of the most vulnerable years of my life. That unique relationship would help create the very foundation on which my life as a man, husband and father would be built. I of course am in no way inferring that a nine- to ten-year-old Michael executed some brilliant strategy that would one day produce a successful adult.

I am, however, going to introduce you to a young lad extraordinaire that few have ever had the privilege to truly know . . . then I believe you will understand.

One evening I kept replaying 'By My Side' over and over again as I swore I kept seeing something that seemed so familiar but couldn't put my finger on it. Suddenly I saw it again and knew just what it was. I rewound and this time paused the scene, walked up to the screen and looked deep into his eyes. There he was . . . Michael Hutchence from Kowloon Tong, the boy I knew and who knew me so well. Oh how I missed him.

The true character of a person is not what's written or said about the individual—people can write and say what they want regardless of what is true or false. One's true character can only be identified in how one behaves in all given situations and how one treats, and/or reacts towards others. True character can never be evaluated simply on how we behave in public, but on how we behave in private when no one is looking.

And this brings me to Michael.

Our family had moved around a lot and rarely stayed anywhere long enough for me to make friends. My parents were also missionaries, and very strict when it came to our interaction with non-religious individuals or groups. Needless to say, as a result I was severely lacking in social skills and was terrified of anything out of my comfort zone—and making friends was definitely not in that zone! To make life more challenging, I was the only lad in Kowloon, or in HK as far as I was concerned, who suffered with Tourette Syndrome, a disability that few doctors understood anything about at that time. Oh the countless nights I cried myself to sleep after enduring a long day of mumbled insults, mocking stares and [being] shunned as a 'retard' by every child and adult alike. I was nine years old when I found my first friend, his name was Michael Hutchence, and he became my best friend . . . ever!

You see, there's a reason Michael was my best friend . . . He was my only friend . . . There were no others. My Tourette's made me quite noticeable, an embarrassment for those who were around me—but not for Michael. Oddly enough, Michael never even seemed to notice my tics. Although they could be quite severe at times, never did he stare nor even acknowledge my grunts and quirks; it was almost as if he never even noticed them. I wasn't stupid; I knew full well he could see and hear just fine, but unlike everyone else who would quickly leave when I jerked or grunted Michael never did. He always stayed.

Although Michael was always an awesome play mate, looking back I'm astounded at the level of maturity he displayed that far surpassed what one would expect from a thoughtful adult. Michael was very aware and in tune with my physical challenges and emotional insecurities, yet as a nine-year-old boy, he chose where he wanted to be. It just happened to be alongside me; a place where no one else ever wanted to be. He became my sole encouragement when all others bullied me and mocked my quirks, and went out of his way to protect me from dwelling in a very dark place. What child does that, or even knows to do that? For the first time in my life I had a real person, not a make-believe one, who actually cared about me, who genuinely liked me—if he didn't then he would have left long ago like all the others. Never once did Michael distance himself from me. That's not what a best friend does.

I really struggled with the knowledge that Michael committed suicide. It seemed like some pieces of my 'Michael Puzzle' were missing. Something was just horribly wrong with this picture and all that my heart knew to be true! You see, it was my relationship with Michael that kept me, a nine-year-old boy, from actually following through with the plethora of suicide notes intended for my parents. Yes, the INXS celeb superstar 'Mike' took his life, but that was not 'Michael' . . . Not at all as there is absolutely no resemblance between the two! Michael would never have allowed life to be taken; he valued it. I know because he valued mine. I'm confident Michael knew all too well the depth of my insecurities and made it a point for me to clearly comprehend just how valuable my life was to him.

I am alive today with a wife, four children and ten grandchildren, and am living proof as to his regard for the sanctity of life. Fortunately, I believe in a very real life beyond this one of pain and sorrow. I am grateful that he may one day shine love on my grandkids the same way he did on me.

I can distinctly remember trying to determine in my mind whether Michael's outreach of friendship was genuine—or was I simply being pitied? It didn't take very long before I got the answer I was looking for. Having been a kid, especially one with unique challenges, I'm all too familiar with peer pressure and how one is critiqued and judged by the company they keep. Michael had absolutely nothing to gain and everything to lose by openly choosing to identify me as a friend. Michael seemed well-liked by everyone and interacted comfortably with the 'cool kids' at school. How shocked I was when my newly found friend unapologetically, and without a hint of hesitation, asked me in front of everyone (including the cool kids) if I would come to his home for his birthday party. I suddenly felt like the most important kid alive, especially paramount to me . . . This was my very first birthday party!

First I was shocked, then thrilled that my dad let me attend, even if he did insist on being there himself. Michael paid it no mind that my dad stayed for the party; in fact, it all worked out for the better. Michael was the perfect host and impressed my father so much that I was given his official approval to revisit unescorted. I know now, but didn't then, just what it was about Michael that made him so likeable. How did he earn my father's trust from just one birthday party encounter? I couldn't even do that!

And what a birthday party it was. I can't recall exactly how many kids attended, just remember being surprised that it was far fewer than I expected. It wasn't because he lacked friends. When I was asked at school to attend, everyone around me was begging for the same invite—they just never got one. Maybe there were more kids present, but the only ones

I seem to remember being there was possibly a couple other boys from school, a couple of neighbour kids that I hardly knew, Michael's parents, his brother Rhett, their Amah who absolutely petrified me, and of course my father who took some pictures that remain on my desk to this day.

And oh the deeper story those few pictures tell. There is Michael (and everyone else) in their casual shorts and flip-flops alongside me in my best summer clothes, knee-high socks, penny loafers . . . accessorized of course with a Cub Scout neckerchief and slide around my neck and a pen clipped to my collar. Who in their right mind let me out like that!!

No sooner did I walk in with my stylish apparel when a boy asked out loud in a mildly patronising tone, 'What are you wearing?'

Before I even had a chance to evaluate his question and conjure up a defence, Michael replied, 'Whatever he wants.' Topic closed; conversation over! What a great day indeed! This may have been Michael's birthday party celebration, but for me it was my grand opening day of acceptance.

Nothing was the same after Michael's birthday party. Everything seemed to change overnight. Up to this point I hated going to school. Being bullied and teased is something I learned to cope with, or at least I thought I did till I became a teen. Being an ostracised outcast is something altogether very different. Bullying you can brush off and bury away deep inside (not good), but being unaccepted and ignored will drain every ounce of energy out of you and simply wear you out! Those days were over! When I woke up the next day the sky seemed bluer, trees seemed greener, the air felt lighter and more breathable and I couldn't wait to get to school and be with my friend.

I no longer ate my lunch alone or sat by the fence watching others play. Michael and I would wrestle during recess, something I had never done before . . . Well, other than trying to genuinely protect myself from a bully. Great thing about wrestling with Michael was that I was bigger and somewhat stronger so could normally keep him pinned—until one day that is, when he tried something new. While I was holding him down he swung both his legs up from behind me and wrapped his ankles around the front of my neck. With all his strength he thrust his legs back down to the ground with my neck still locked in place. When my head crashed on the floor my eyes began seeing double and I could actually feel my brain wobbling in my skull. My best friend Michael just gave me my first concussion.

I saw Michael looking in my eyes after regaining some of my senses and heard him repeatedly asking 'Are you OK?'

When I was finally able to answer him back I assured him I was fine, but could tell by the look on his face that he didn't believe me. We went back to class and I could see from the corner of my eye that he was constantly looking over at me with genuine concern. I was so afraid to tell him I was really hurt. I was afraid of my father's reaction; I was afraid of jeopardising this relationship and was willing to protect it at any cost. Great thing about being a kid is that you normally bounce back from injuries pretty quickly. Although we still wrestled a lot, Michael never pulled that move on me again! And boy did he make up for it when he scarfed some fake blood tablets from his mother's make-up kit. This took wrestling to a whole different level as now I could pretend getting hurt without actually being injured.

Winter was approaching and along with it came the school dance. When Michael asked what time I was showing up I let him know that I was not allowed to go to dances so not to expect me. I can distinctly remember the puzzled look on his face when he heard my answer. I know he could tell by the look on my face that this was a dead issue.

'Well, I might not be going either,' he said.

I knew he wasn't telling the truth but think it was his way of making light of the situation. I asked him the day after if he went and he shrugged his shoulder and said in a dull kind of way, 'Yes . . . but it was boring.' Although I knew he was lying, I knew why and think that meant more to me than had he been honest.

It's not uncommon for children raised in foreign countries to drift from their original forms of speech and begin adapting the language and accents of those they are constantly around. Problem was, our family had travelled the world since I was two years old so I ended up an orating smorgasbord. Another common challenge for mobile children is identity crisis as they can lose touch with their home base and original foundation.

Children with Tourette's face even greater challenges. They make movements and sounds unfamiliar to all cultures and therefore don't fit in anywhere at any time. Throughout that first year with Michael I felt so welcome and accepted and unfortunately began planting unhealthy roots out of fear, in an attempt to create some kind of identity.

I guess about a year had gone by when while walking around the USRC [United Services Recreation Club] tennis courts one afternoon, Michael caught me off guard.

'I heard you said you were raised on a sheep farm in Australia.'

It felt as if every drop of blood just drained from my body and I was ready to physically collapse. I couldn't speak, not even grunt. My body froze so that not even a tic could hide my shame. My lips began to quiver and tears clouded my vision so that even his face became unrecognisable. We stood there silent for what seemed like days. I would begin to open my mouth but there were no words coming out.

'You're from America, Tim . . . I have a hard time even remembering Australia, and I definitely wouldn't want to live on some sheep farm.'

That was it! He didn't ask why, didn't chastise me or make fun of me. He only turned and kept walking so I did the same and he started talking about something altogether different. What just happened??? I don't know, but as we walked it seemed as if heavy weights starting falling off my shoulders and all the fabricated stories I'd hid behind for much of my short life began to fade from view. We walked down towards the bowling green, then again out of nowhere, as if it was a sudden afterthought, 'Your accent isn't Australian, English or even American . . . It's different . . . kind of like cockney,' said Michael.

'What's cockney?' I asked.

'Like poor English—but I like it, it sounds cool.' Just as before—that was it, end of conversation, and we headed back up to the pool.

Being exposed can without doubt be one of the most humiliating experiences in life. Being exposed yet uncondemned on the other hand can become one of the most freeing experiences in life. Something else happened that day, a pivoting point in my life that is mysteriously unexplainable. From that day on my Tourette's began to slowly but noticeably decrease and for the next couple of years my body began to relax as it had never done before.

Michael and I both loved the water and over the summer of my last year in Hong Kong we spent all the time we could in the USRC Olympic-sized pool. We were both part of the swim team; however, Michael was clearly a real natural and seemed to always be the kid to beat. He was always very competitive once he hit the water, but it was also very important to him that I qualify for every badge possible, be it laps or speed. Badges were our trophies with the goal to have as many of them sewn to our little speedos as possible. One thing was certain, whenever it was my chance to qualify, rest assured that every time I turned for air between strokes there would be Michael's face and voice coaching me to stay focused or at times, yelling at me to speed up! A true ten-year-old champion beyond his years who took your winning just as seriously as he did his own. With the support of my best friend Michael, my speedos were definitely worthy of display.

Because I was unaware of Michael's 'rock star' status until August 2016, the only way I could witness him performing was via old concerts on YouTube. I would read comments like 'He loved his audience' or 'He magically connected with his fans' or 'He had a unique way of drawing you in.'

My only response is, 'You have no clue!'

Michael didn't learn that from performing in bands to enthusiastic fans and screaming girls. Michael was doing that in the late 1960s at the USRC. We were familiar with the 'regular' members and could immediately detect when new VIP businessmen, foreign dignitaries, military offices and their families were visiting. Whenever they arrived, one look from Michael and it was 'Showtime'. The pool had three competition-level diving platforms and we would take full advantage of them all. Before too long Michael would have all the newbies engaged and applauding with every dive we made.

On one such particular day, and after hours of entertaining, Michael noticed that the large group of naval officers being entertained were getting ready to leave for dinner at the club house. Michael wanted to keep the show going so came up with the idea that if we had the food delivered to them poolside, they would stay. Sounded great to me, so for the next couple hours we kept having hot dogs, burgers and beers sent to their poolside tables on our parents' club charge accounts. Unfortunately, we failed to take into consideration that a bill would show up at the end of the month. Strange thing is, months went by and neither of us heard about our costly excursion.

Although we were both avid swimmers, neither of us were great soccer players ... Well, at least I wasn't. Regardless we both played on a competitive summer team and had a lot of fun in the process. Our final game was an elimination competition on top of Victoria Peak. If I recall correctly, there were multiple clubs comprised of multiple teams. Each specific club team kept playing timed games until only one team was left standing. The winning team from each club would then compete with the other club's winning team in the same elimination process. Last team standing was considered the champions. That said, there were a lot of kids and parents there for the entire day! I can't remember just how far our team got, only that we had a chance to at least be included in the 'most amount of games won' category. We were in our final game when our goalie got hurt and the coach sent me in as the replacement. I'd never played goalie before so figured he simply needed as many good players on the field as possible, but I definitely wasn't one of them. As the game went on, every time I gained access to the ball I'd make sure I took my three allotted steps before kicking the ball back down the field. I was so nervous however that every time I did so, like a robot I'd take three precise large steps, then kick.

Towards the last half of the game, when it was time for me to kick again, the crowd of players, parents and spectators alike began shouting out in unison with each individual step I took 'One . . . Two . . . Three . . . KICK.' It didn't take too long before I figured out that they were all making fun of me. I just wanted the game to stop and go home. The game did eventually end. We lost, and as I took the long walk of shame back to the Peak tram I could still hear people snickering and occasionally someone would shout out 'One two three KICK.'

Michael's life lesson to me was all about friendship. You see, as the rest of the players walked back to the tram, they made it a point to keep their distance from me. Michael on the other hand walked the entire way back to the tram by my side. No he didn't say anything profound and no he did not tell me I did a great job, he just walked with me.

It wasn't till we got onto the crowded tram that Michael put his hand on my shoulder and with everyone listening, smiled at me and said unapologetically and proudly, 'You're allowed three steps.'

You could have heard a pin drop! In but a few words that ten-year-old boy shamed everyone on that tram, including all the adults and parents. For the remainder of the ride that tram car stayed completely silent. Yes, the crowd was still in the tram but it's as if I couldn't see a one of them— their faces and voices disappeared out the window into the side of the mountain never to be seen or heard of again.

It wasn't until 2016 when Michael's sister Tina began to explain to me what life was really like for the Hutchence family during those early years that I was able to truly comprehend and appreciate the depth of all he brought to our very unique and special relationship. I never knew that he had his own set of challenges. That he had moved from place to place. That his family structure was dismantling. This I do know, that God is wise, that nothing is by chance, not even the bringing together of two young boys with very real challenges. Why did it all play out like this? I'm really not sure. What does seem clear to me however is that there was a time when a young lad named Tim needed to be loved by someone, who found a lad named Michael who needed someone to love.

* * *

Tim Stewart's Tourette's did not completely subside, of course, but he gained confidence with each passing year. To the amazement of many, he won every college debate he participated in and was awarded one of the highest collegiate expository awards. He even became a featured speaker at state academic conferences across the country and toured as a presenter with the leading tech companies of the world, addressing thousands of people in packed auditoriums. It's amazing what you can do if someone believes in you. If someone stands by you when others don't.

If someone reinforces, 'You're allowed three steps.'

24

one thin page of words

LATE ONE SUMMER EVENING IN MID-2015 I drove to Studio City
Sound, once known as Fidelity Recording. As I made a left off Riverside
Drive onto Whitsett Avenue, bittersweet memories came flooding back.
I was taking the route that Michael would cycle twice a day in his mid-
teens, between 1975 and '76. Each day he'd pass by Fidelity, owned by
Artie Ripp, as he travelled between home and school. In 1976 the all-
female rock band The Runaways recorded their rowdy 'Cherry Bomb'
there, co-written by Joan Jett. Others who recorded at Fidelity included
Michael Jackson, the Ramones and Billy Joel. As I pulled into the parking
lot I wondered what other magic had been brewing inside these walls
while Michael obliviously pedalled by on his ten-speed bike back then.

Michael, boy to man, now lost to us all.

But tonight Danny Saber was in Studio B working with some raw
recordings he had made with Michael at the Record Planet one week
before he took his life.

I was experiencing such a mix of emotions. I tried to keep my hands steady for Danny's sake. He greeted me warmly, ushering me into a control room where I made myself comfortable. He turned the lights way down low so there'd be no distraction and smiled in my direction. I smiled back to show him I was ready. Then he hit play.

The first sound I heard was Michael's deep, deep intake of breath. He sang the first line of the song, then the music flooded in. What stayed with me was the overwhelming combination of euphoria and sadness the music aroused. Music he had written with Danny Saber.

For most of Michael's career his creative experience had been sitting alone with pen and paper. As Mark Opitz said, he wrote poetry—he considered his lyrics to be poetry. When I think about him focusing so hard on finding that last missing word in a song he was working on, I think of Emily Dickinson: 'I know nothing in the world that has as much power as a word. Sometimes I write one, and I look at it, until it begins to shine.'

Whether he was listening to one of Andrew Farriss's compositions or just jotting down things that came to him through the ether, he was usually alone—when I had watched him work, at least. I guessed it would have been liberating for him to write with Danny. Naturally I was curious about the processes they used.

'As far as I remember, music would initiate the process usually,' Danny said. 'I think what was cool, what was good for him with me, was the bouncing off of each other. And I was open to anything. That was consistent, that's what he enjoyed: the openness of it all. Sometimes he would come in with a track or an idea or a concept and say, would it be cool if we did something like this?

'Often he would just start singing one line,' Danny continued. 'He didn't always have it down on paper. Other lines would come to him as we progressed and we would go back and forth. It was the "feel" he was going for . . . Michael was always so passionate about looking for new music.

'It didn't matter that I was interpreting his musical thoughts, and then expanding on them. It doesn't matter if he had the idea or I had the idea . . . It was the two of us together with nothing in between, trying to accomplish something. I think that's what he was looking for outside of the band. It wasn't just about maintaining a career or being famous or making money or selling records, it was that he had a genuine need to do his thing and to expand on it and keep moving forward.

'The thing about Michael that was key to who he was as a person is, he had the need to grow as an artist. Michael, even though he couldn't play an instrument to the level that he could sing or write lyrics, his musical ideas were no less sound.'

He explained that a lot of musicians don't grasp this. 'Just because you don't have the vocabulary on the instruments that they are familiar with, doesn't mean that your ideas are anything less. It's not unique to INXS. It's a funny thing, almost comical, what a cliché it is to me. It's like the singer's getting all the attention, the singer's getting all the glory but then the singer's also got most of the press to run. That situation became frustrating for Michael and you know that's one of the main reasons why there was this underlying negativity.

'Those guys are millionaires, the biggest band in the world for a couple of years. The fact is that they couldn't maintain it. And you know nobody can, really no band out there can.

'It's hard, it's a hard thing to do and I'm actually not knocking those guys at all. Everything that is today, they really had a hand in it, because when you think about it INXS really were the first band in the eighties mixing electronica and keyboards and dance music and rock. They really were an amazing band.

'Michael was driven by what drove him,' Danny continued, 'and, you know, I think the stresses and the pressures of the way the media worked back then, which was quite different, put more pressure on him to sort of define himself as a solo artist.

'You know what *matters* is that Michael had a place where he could work on his ideas and it could just be real. And he could get some enjoyment out of it at that time in his life. A very difficult time. But I don't believe he was leaving INXS. Maybe he would have done a couple of solo albums and returned as their frontman. What I'm saying is, he just needed a break.'

Danny has been very carefully working with the tracks he and Michael had created together before he was left to carry on alone—or abandon the precious work that meant so much to Michael. So much, remember, that in the last week of Michael's life he asked Danny to put together a band to play the music they were writing, recording and producing together live. Michael could have chosen to produce new music with just about anyone, but he chose Danny Saber. And now Danny is working to finish and release the last of Michael's solo recorded output. I hope you, dear readers, will enjoy it.

•   •   •

Michael's legacy is extensive. He touched many other artists throughout his career. He inspired several songs I know of. The first that comes to mind is his former writing partner Andrew Farriss's 'God's Top Ten', from INXS's 2005 *Switch* album, written for Tiger. Apart from her parents, it also references Roquefort-les-Pins and the pictures of the family there.

In 1998 Billy Corgan (Smashing Pumpkins) included a track on his *Adore* album that he wrote in tribute to Michael, a slow, hypno-droning song called 'Shame'. He also collaborated on a more slashing rock track by Berlin's Terri Nunn for her 2002 *Voyeur* album called 'Sacred and Profane'.

'He was a very big inspiration for both Billy and me,' Terri said in an interview. 'The song is about my first experience seeing him because that changed my life. He influenced me probably more than anyone else as a performer. I became twelve years old in five minutes wanting to have sex with him. That's all I wanted! Oh my God. Everybody did! You just wanted him. He was the epitome of rock star.'

REM's Michael Stipe is very tuned in to Michael too. REM's 'Strange Currencies' was inspired by him and INXS. 'He raised the bar for both myself and Bono. The middle eight of that is completely taken from INXS and from Michael. He was such an amazing rock star.'

Duran Duran released the song 'Michael You've Got a Lot To Answer For', a group composition, on their *Medazzaland* album on 14 October 1997, a few weeks before Michael died. The lyrics reflect a great and present concern for Michael's state of mind, referring to getting caught up in somebody else's war. There's faith there that he would come out of it, given time, and a request for him to remember what friends are for and to call if he needed help. Simon Le Bon was a close friend of Michael's, who'd drop by the villa sometimes, perhaps often. Rather than point the finger of blame, this gentle, beautiful composition is full of compassion, extending the hand of friendship and belief.

The 1984 movie *Reckless* starring Aidan Quinn and Daryl Hannah featured three INXS songs on the soundtrack: 'To Look At You', 'Soul Mistake' and 'The One Thing'.

'Do Wot You Do', which made it to the B-side of 'New Sensation', was included on one of the most popular soundtracks for 1980s teenagers, the 1986 movie *Pretty in Pink*, starring Molly Ringwald.

One of Michael's best performances on a movie soundtrack, one far less financially successful than *Pretty in Pink*, was the icily majestic Ollie Olsen composition and production 'Rooms For The Memory'. It was not written for Richard Lowenstein's *Dogs in Space* (1987) but it fits perfectly.

The single 'Good Times' backed with 'Laying Down The Law', recorded by INXS and Jimmy Barnes, reached #2 in Australia, #47 in the

USA and #18 in the UK, and was also used to promote the national series of concerts that took place between Boxing Day 1986 and Australia Day 1987. The tracks starred in the soundtrack to Hollywood 'Brat Pack' film *The Lost Boys* (1987), directed by Joel Schumacher. My former husband Jeffrey Bushelman was the sound editor. (Of course, the term 'lost boys' is another reinforcement for the Peter Pan and Wendy connection for Michael; one I have not shied away from in the title of this book.)

Credits on the cover of the ultimate party track 'Good Times', written by Easybeats Harry Vanda and George Young, read 'Recorded at Rhinoceros Studios, Sydney, October 1986. This single was recorded over 3 days of madness and mayhem. "Turn it up and enjoy." INXS & Jimmy Barnes.'

In 1993 when Michael recorded the early Rolling Stones song 'Under My Thumb' at Metropolis Studios, Melbourne, for inclusion on *Symphonic Music Of The Rolling Stones*, he was very aware of the irony of being compared to his friend Mick Jagger. (He said he thought, 'Why not confront it?') That year INXS also recorded 'Born To Be Wild', written by Mars Bonfire and previously recorded by Steppenwolf, for the Australian film *Reckless Kelly*.

It's Now Or Never: The Tribute To Elvis (1994) features Michael singing 'Baby Let's Play House' with US rock quartet NRBQ (New Rhythm and Blues Quartet) in a live performance. Others featured on this compilation include Tony Bennett, Faith Hill, Tanya Tucker, Michael Bolton, Chris Isaak and Bryan Adams.

Batman Forever, another Joel Schumacher production, features Michael's rendition of Iggy Pop's 'The Passenger' in its original movie soundtrack (1995).

The most popular songs covered by other artists for which Michael wrote the lyrics include 'New Sensation', 'Slide Away', 'Don't Change', 'Never Tear Us Apart', 'Need You Tonight', 'Suicide Blonde', 'Devil Inside' and 'What You Need', covered by (but not limited to) Tina Turner,

Beck, Matchbox Twenty, Bruce Springsteen, Goo Goo Dolls, Sir Tom Jones, Natalie Imbruglia, Paloma Faith, U2, Tina Arena, Ben Harper, Joe Cocker, Bonnie Raitt, Kylie Minogue, Justin Timberlake, Smashing Pumpkins and Prince.

What a line-up! Michael, take a bow.

When INXS's Nile Rogers-produced 'Original Sin' hit the American airwaves it caused a furore. Michael's lyrics 'Black boy, white girl/black girl, white boy' caused bomb threats at radio stations that dared play the song in the south. Astonishingly, years after all that the civil rights movement had achieved, 'Original Sin' was banned on many stations in the USA. That's when Michael gave us the quote that sits at the beginning of this book.

Following up on the controversy 'Original Sin' had generated, a writer from *Stiletto* magazine asked him about racism.

'One day there'll be an end to all of these racist problems,' Michael said, 'because we're still tribes and still separate and we've got millions of years to go but eventually there will only be one race. That's all. Ultimately it won't exist.'

Probably the most famous song written for Michael is 'Stuck In A Moment You Can't Get Out Of', by U2. The song won a Grammy for Best Pop Performance by a Duo or Group with Vocal in 2002 after being included on U2's *All That You Can't Leave Behind* album. Bono's rather angry, frustrated lyrical message is that the moment will pass, along with a recognition that for his friend, he truly was stuck down a rabbit hole that seemed never-ending.

Even so, it was just a moment. And moments pass.

What we hope, with all our hearts, for all would-be suicides, is that they find the strength to hang on until help arrives, even if that help comes from the well of their own inner resolve.

This book is full of writing and poetry. Here's one last hurrah, a beautiful, simple poem written by Jimmy Barnes' wife, Jane, to their old friend.

To Michael
I will light a candle
To show you the way
Just one of many, but it will shine brightly
So you can see
Follow the Love that shines from it
And the Respect that makes it burn
It comes from me

I will light the incense
That will make you calm
And take you messages of Peace
So you will know that no one judges
And that all is well

Go on your way
You Great Explorer
With your gentle, searching Gracious Heart
And take with you your
Courage and passion
Slay those dragons and
Rescue your maiden with Love songs
Like the true Hero that you are

I honour you and am blessed
To have known you
Albeit for such a short time
And I look forward to hearing
Of your tales and adventures
When next we meet, my Friend
Until then I will miss you

With love from my heart,
—Jane Barnes

Michael is missed, yes, greatly, but his music, his poetry, continues to touch so many people around the world—and that is his legacy. Because he loved and respected the written word of the great poets, writers and philosophers that would make him so happy. He is with me throughout my day, and not just in my heart. I am reminded of him when I am in the supermarket, the bank, a department store—how fortunate I am that he is played everywhere I go. He will always be my 'Babe'.

tours and albums

Tours with INXS

1978	West Australian mining towns tour
1981/82	Fear and Loathing Tour
	Campus Tour
	Stay Young Tour
	Tour With No Name
1982	New Zealand Tour—supporting Cold Chisel (first OS tour)
	Una Brilliante Banda De Musica Ameniizara Espectaculo Tour
	(nationwide 78 dates)
1983	North America—supporting Adam Ant (first US tour)
1984	Hot Tunes and Sand Dunes
	The Swing World Tour
1985	The Big Swing
	Kiss The Dirt Tour
	Listen Like Thieves Tour
1986	If You Got It, Shake It! Tour of Europe
	The Tour De Force
	Si Lo Tienes Muevelo Tour
1987	Australian Made Tour
	Australian Kick-Off Tour
	North American Kick-Off Tour

289

1988	European Kick Tour
	North American Kick Tour
	European Summer Kick Tour
	North American Calling All Nations Tour
	Japanese Calling All Nations Tour
	Australia/New Zealand Calling All Nations Tour
1990	Australian Northern Queensland X Warm Up Tour
	European Suicide Blonde Tour
1991	South American X-Factor Tour
	US X-Factor Tour
	Australian X-Factor Tour
	European Summer X-Factor Tour
1993	Australian Get Out Of The House Tour
	US Get Out Of The House Tour
	European Get Out Of The House Tour
	North American Dirty Honeymoon Tour
1994	Australian Dirty Honeymoon Tour
	South American Back To School Tour
	US Dirty Honeymoon Tour
1997	South African Elegantly Wasted Tour
	European Elegantly Wasted Tour
	US Elegantly Wasted Tour

Studio albums

1980	*INXS*
1981	*Underneath The Colours*
1982	*Shabooh Shoobah*
1984	*The Swing*
1985	*Listen Like Thieves*
1987	*Kick*
1990	*X*
1992	*Welcome To Wherever You Are*
1993	*Full Moon, Dirty Hearts*
1997	*Elegantly Wasted*

Live album

| 1991 | *Live Baby Live* |

Album with Max Q

| 1989 | *Max Q* |

Solo (posthumous)

| 1999 | *Michael Hutchence* |
| 2018 | (forthcoming) untitled second solo album co-produced with Danny Saber |

acknowledgements

We would like to extend a very special thanks to those who opened their hearts and shared their memories with myself and Jen Jewel Brown for this book, including Michael himself, my mother, Mark Opitz, Rosanna Crash, Nicole Bartleet, Richard Lowenstein, Michele Bennett, Danny Saber, Ollie Olsen, Bruce Butler, Richard Simpkin, Chris Bailey, Paulie Stewart, Wendy Murphy, Nick Egan, Peter Duclos, Joanne Kelly, Tim Stewart, Gerry Agar, Ricky Watcham, Tina and Gibson Kemp, Terri-ann White, Michael Lynch, Jeff Bushelman, John Thommeny, Gary Lilley, Erin Seem Hamilton, Brent Lewis, Erin Bushelman, Vincent Lamaro, Shanon Clark Steele, Kelly Poulter, Amy Zellmer, Richard Blade and Simon Le Bon. A very special thanks to Michael's good friends Jane and Jimmy Barnes, for extending permission to use Jane's moving tribute poem 'To Michael'.

We wish to express our warmest appreciation to Richard Walsh who commissioned this project and gave us so much inspiration from the start. And to the splendid, hardworking professionals at Allen & Unwin, including editors Jane Palfreyman, Angela Handley and Susan Keogh, and our very knowledgeable agent, Lyn Tranter. You have all been marvellous.

I also wish to thank the wonderful people who have supported us, the fans, friends and those in the entertainment industry with our project and Facebook page, *A Statue for Michael Hutchence*.

And to anyone who ever enjoyed Michael's work. He would appreciate that very much.

about the authors

Like her younger brother Michael, **Tina Hutchence** grew up in Australia and Hong Kong. She followed in the professional footsteps of her mother, Patricia Glassop, forging a career as a make-up artist for film and television before moving into education and the lecture circuit in the USA. She has spent most of her life since then living between California and Australia. In the wake of Michael's shock death, she co-wrote *Just a Man: The real Michael Hutchence* (2000, 2001) with Patricia. Tina became her widowed mother's loving carer before 81-year-old Patricia passed away from ovarian cancer in 2010. She continues to cherish time with her own children, grandchildren and wider family. She also manages and contributes to the website michaelhutchenceinfo.com and is currently involved in a project to honour Michael with a statue in the country of his birth for the benefit of Michael's fans and his memory.

MICHAEL

Jen Jewel Brown was the first Down Under reporter for Australian *Rolling Stone*. She met and interviewed Michael in mid-1980, also dueting with him on his first solo single, 'Speed Kills', from the soundtrack of *Freedom* (1982). When Professional Manager at MCA/Gilbey, Jen helped sign INXS to a worldwide music publishing deal which helped fund their overseas touring. The author, poet and journalist first made contact with Tina when interviewing her for an essay about Max Q for the anthology *Rock Country* (2013). She's an interviewer for the National Film & Sound Archive of Australia and part of the writing Brains Trust for television/live show *RocKwiz*. Jen wrote *Skyhooks Million Dollar Riff* (1975), and more recently about Frank Zappa, an essay for the press kit of the documentary *Eat That Question: Frank Zappa in his own words* (2016) and liner notes for Frank Zappa/Mothers *The Roxy Performances* seven-album box set (2018).

sources

Gerry Agar, *Paula, Michael & Bob: Everything you know is wrong*, Michael O'Mara Books, 2003

Roberta Bayley, 'Beyond the Thunderdome', *Spin*, 3(9), February 1988

Jen Jewel Brown, 'Hot new group is taking the city by storm', *Sunday Telegraph*, 6 July 1980

Richard Guilliatt, 'Chris Murphy and the devil inside INXS', *The Australian*, 1 February 2014

Steve Harris, 'A very awkward interview with the late Michael Hutchence and the ornery Andrew Farriss of INXS', 3 October 1988, <www.youtube.com/watch?v=X4QH5UTQY2g>

Dan Jones and Nathan Hull, michaelhutchence.org, exclusive interview with Andrew Farriss, viewed 16 November 2018 (no interview date given)

Gary Lilley, 'The gift he gave is going to last forever' (part 1), <www.michaelhutchenceinfo.com/the%20gift%20-%20part1.htm>

Kate McClymont, '$20m mystery of the disappearing estate', *The Age*, 20 August 2005

Kate McClymont, 'Brother in court over threatening witness', *Sydney Morning Herald*, 22 October 2004

Elly McDonald, 'INXS', *Roadrunner*, 3(6), July 1980

Richard Simpkin, *Michael in Pictures: A celebration of the life of Michael Hutchence (1960–1997)*, New Holland, 2015

Dave Simpson, 'Michael Hutchence remembered', *The Guardian*, 22 November 2007

South China Morning Post, 'Hutchence's fortune is gone, HK law firm tells late singer's family', 21 August 2005

South China Morning Post, 'Michael Hutchence talks about growing up in Hong Kong, fame and making music in 1994 interview', 23 November 2017

Eric Spitznagel, 'The unlikely story of how INXS came to rule the late '80s with "Kick"', *Billboard*, 19 October 2017

Lyndsey Telford, 'Kylie Minogue "very emotional" over ex-boyfriend Michael Hutchence on BBC's Desert Island Discs', *The Telegraph*, 13 December 2015; repeated in the *Sydney Morning Herald*, 14 December 2015

Tony Wall, 'Mr Diamond and Michael's elusive fortune', *Sunday Star Times*, 4 September 2005

WalesOnline, 'Me and Paula, the true story', 11 April 2006, <www.walesonline.co.uk/news/local-news/paula-true-story-2343455>

Amy Zellmer, 'Life with a traumatic brain injury', *Huffington Post*, 9 February 2015

index

297